The Blue Basin

Andre Paul Goddard

iUniverse, Inc.
Bloomington

The Blue Basin

iUniverse books may be ordered through booksellers or by contacting:

iUniverse
1663 Liberty Drive
Bloomington, IN 47403
www.iuniverse.com
1-800-Authors (1-800-288-4677)

ISBN: 978-1-4759-5108-0 (sc)
ISBN: 978-1-4759-5110-3 (e)
ISBN: 978-1-4759-5109-7 (dj)

Library of Congress Control Number: 2012917622

Printed in the United States of America

iUniverse rev. date: 10/03/2012

Introduction

I FIRST CAME TO know the artist Elwood Lucien through a letter he had written to me without knowing who I was or whether or not I could be of any use to him. At the time I was Editor in Chief at The Daily Gleaner.

The point of the letter seemed innocuous at first and I was tempted to dismiss it. However it struck a chord with me – my inner self, my youth – or was it perhaps that I had nothing political to write about that day. And then again, how was I to know that the writer would eventually become *the* Elwood Lucien – the great Obzocky!

His subsequent correspondence which came periodically and without any encouragement from me struck me as someone reaching out to communicate in their loneliness that they were indeed here and alive. I suppose I was at first impressed by his somewhat prim and stilted writing style and then by the frank and unabashed tone of his messages, but I kept it all though paid it little heed, till that fateful day when all seemed to come together in one tragic rush.

His diary filled in the gaps leading up to that moment, as did unsubstantiated accounts from some of the people in his life – all telling a tale that eventually, through the greatness of the person and that negative counterpoint that rounds off a person's being, became a story too of my own life; one snatched from the brink of futility and despair.

For this, I shall be ever grateful to him.

I have taken some licence in the telling of this story but it is, essentially if regretfully, true.

Warren Toth.

Part I

CHAPTER -1- the fight

IT WAS NOT THE first time Bossy had seen such a play unfold and, as he proudly admitted to the reporter, he was not totally unprepared for it.

"It was like a dance at de same club; de same band, de same music, an' wit de same people. Like yer go in, yer have a lil booze, yer stan at de side an yer look on. An den yer see de girl, yer ax she to dance, she boy-frien' doh like dat an' tell yer so wit a cut eye. Buh she full a tan-ta-na[1] and de nex ting, she smilin' at yer. An' de nex ting, yer dancin' wid she boy-frien' outside in de parkin' lot."

Still, for all his knowledge and preparation, Bossy was as shocked by the volatility of the cause as by the ensuing action itself, as well as the strength and ferocity of the tall, skinny young man with the unruly hair and protruding ears who, until that moment, Bossy had pegged as the classic victim.

Things had been quiet in the early morning hours with just a few of the regulars coming into the deli

1 Adventure and excitement

for coffee or orange juice and a few of their usuals – donuts, muffins, egg sandwiches with ham or salami – and some of the unusuals, often reheated leftovers from the previous evening, but mostly Bossy's morning specials – buljohl with zaboca, shark and bake; even a choka and smoke-herring for Kingsley, the night watchman. His usual! At any rate there were never more than three sets of customers at a time and the waitresses, Emelda and Oprah, had taken turns with far more talk than service. And then the young man had entered around nine. Just when things should be slowing down.

Emelda had served him – the supposed victim. He had ordered a curry chicken hot-plate with some dhal and, after she had served it to him, remained to fuss a little more; straightening his cutlery, filling his glass and asking questions that at one time caused the young man to smile. The smile, bare though it was, was an expression that radically softened the sharp lines of the young man's long, angular face and relaxed the otherwise penetrating glare of dark, gloomy, almost foreboding eyes; characteristics that seemed to have no negative effect on Emelda for she was still talking to him when Tony and Jackson opened the door to the eatery.

Bossy had been alerted to their arrival by the heavy revving of Tony's 750cc Kawasaki, his pride, joy and principal means of strutting, and he, Bossy, was still talking to Oprah when the two – Tony and company – strode across the floor and sat in their accustomed seats by the front window where they could view the traffic. In particular the female traffic.

At the counter, despite all the sauce talk with Oprah complete with her giggly smile and ever batting lashes, Bossy's eyes never once left the duo. Even when he lifted his chin in a pointing motion, alerting Oprah to the new customers, he tried to read Tony's mood, hoping Emelda would break off talking to the unsuspecting young man. She did not and thus enforced Bossy's uneasiness, for Oprah would be no substitute for the other wide-hipped waitress who always served Tony with a little more than breakfast fare.

Bossy got the answer to Tony's mood when the hefty *saga boy* called out to Emelda; his voice loud and impatient. Thankfully, she responded to his call promptly and with hardly an apology to the young man. But as she approached Tony, Bossy could hear her excusing her tardiness by explaining who the customer with the large ears was. Tony was obviously unimpressed, sucking his teeth and scowling at her words. Still, although he seemed incredulous if somewhat overshadowed by Emelda's fawning respect for the young man, there was little doubt that his interest was piqued for he could hardly keep his eyes on his own business, and after he had ordered his *shark and bake* he rose and headed across the room to the gawky figure with the quiet disposition.

There was little talk; most of it anyway out of earshot though Bossy figured the young man was too busy with his breakfast to be drawn into an argument. But then Tony suddenly rubbed the young man's head and, as if not enough, did something to his ears.

The blow to Tony's somewhat excessive belly came almost reflexively and sent him sprawling back into the tables by the counter. The young man was up, his face a mask of rage as he moved toward Tony. He swung twice missing with one and catching Tony on the shoulder with the other. Then he connected with an uppercut that drove the heavier man backward once again before he tripped over a chair. Despite his size, Tony was on his feet quickly and grasping the heavy, tubular chrome chair as though it were made of Balsa, threw it at his assailant. The tall young man dodged it easily and as Tony ploughed in, as though seeking more to wrestle or man-handle his opponent, he was suddenly on his back again, placed there by a right hand which even Bossy did not see till after it had been thrown. It was then that Bossy reached for the phone.

He didn't hurry the call and by the tone of his words seemed to be enjoying the scrap as well as the actions of the other onlookers, although he might have been a little concerned for the furniture.

Over at Tony's original table, Oprah had been screaming and continued to do so as Emelda grasped Jackson's arm preventing him from rising though Tony's buddy seemed hesitant to enter the fray perhaps because of the rage on the tall man's face or his prohibitive height or his somewhat lethal fists. Or it could have been Emelda's constant words of recognition as to who the young man was, or perhaps the very word, *Obzocky*, holding a certain caution in its application. But then she suddenly let Jackson go. He stood up but did not otherwise move.

The brawl had ended; not a knockout but indeed a clear-cut decision with Tony leaning bloodied and unsteady against the counter and the young man standing over him, unsure or perhaps unwilling to pursue the incident further. Exhaustion! Or perhaps it was the police whistle outside, blowing in short bursts, its volume increasing in urgency as it approached the front door.

And then the door opened, the crowd parted and the uniform entered, and only then did the young man finally drop his hands allowing Bossy to take a deep breath and let it out slowly as Jackson muttered to no one in particular:

"Well, dah's de en a dat!"

CHAPTER -2- Arrest in Carapichaima

EDITORIAL ON RASH OF Bicycle thefts
BY WARREN TOTH

Bicycles! There's a lot to be said for them! In fact, of this little unassuming opus in engineering, it was once expressed in awe and exclamation that such a simple piece of work has within its composition, a nobility of reasoning, an infinity of facilities. In form and moving is it so express and admirable! In action, how like an angel! In construction how like a god! The beauty and freedom of elementary travel! The paragon of simple mechanics!

Of course we of the horsepower set tend to take this, as all other modes of travel, a trifle lightly, but to some of our street brothers this quintessence of bipedal exercise is not only conveyance, it is friend and brother with a purpose and personality all its own. In present day lingo, this bottom line is but a single word; one that best capsulates the above trifled with, Shakespearean tidbit. The word is: cool.

Not only is the bike itself cool, it makes you look cool. In fact, at least to this individual, the very personification of cool is clasped fingers behind the neck while coasting on his baked-on orange enamel twelve speed Empire down Fordham drive. You could almost hear the sighs of awe and envy from the group of do-nothings at the corner of Fordham and Avenue road. Or the whistles from the girls on the steps at number 223 Avenue as you turned the corner and coasted past them. That's when your bike becomes your truly good buddy; by not hitting a stone or a crack, or riding against the curb and sending you sprawling in sublime indignity.

For only the second time that morning, Elwood Lucien smiled.

The newspaper clipping that had caused this smile had fallen out of his wallet. He had picked it up while still very much in that state of unbridled almost uncontrolled anger when a man feels wronged yet is forced to meekly accept whatever justice and fairness is handed him. But Elwood never just accepted anything; least of all justice. He preferred to mete it out himself. Still, even he might have realized that this was no time to be meting out anything. So he submitted; to the curious eyes and the unasked questions although he was hardly able to control his trembling hand, barely managing to cram the tightly folded snippet back into the wallet without betraying that anger.

But the editorial had taken away much of his anger and with nothing more to feed it than the benign attention of curious onlookers, Elwood settled in to wait.

He had already sketched the little sandwich shop tucked into its allotted space along the boardwalk on the outskirts of the town of Carapichaima and reviewed the interior outline of the deli with its Lautrec-like figures – the owner/chef, the two waitresses, and those others who had dropped in for a meal and were now long gone – all positioned in the order of conversation and relaxation, quite unlike the strewn-about furniture he had left behind in the shop. Now as he sat on his motorbike surrounded by the two lower ranked policemen while waiting for the third – a somewhat officious sergeant – to get back to him, he once again removed the article from his wallet. Crooking one long leg over the saddle, he opened the well creased paper, carefully this time, and re-read it to the end.

Trigger, Champion, Silver; cowboy horses that took their heroes across the plains of the wide west! That's what a bike is too....

Memories flooded back – though not entirely prompted by the clipping. But as he once again folded the slip of paper and carefully returned it to his wallet he entered into that world of memories as though he had actually opened a door and shut it behind him.

A carry-over from his lonely youth, this habit of reflecting on the past had been to Elwood a kind of retreat – a place, as well as a position – through which he found resolution from within his loneliness. In earlier days these reflections had been more immediate, hourly or daily in their lapses, but so easily recalled or addressed that he had little trouble capturing them either in his diary or on his sketchpad. Soon he could merely glance at a person and from his fingers would flow an animated likeness that often baffled the subject. Even his caricatures, derogatory though they always were, were sketched with such attention to detail that the subject seemed always honoured by the insult. It seemed too that the only way Elwood could effectively insult his subjects, was to ignore them.

These days, however, though he ignored many, he never wanted for attention. And it was perhaps because of this that he seldom sketched or painted faces anymore. Nor did he encourage those reflections on his troubled youth though now the images came randomly and uninvited.

Often triggered by some association with the past they dwelt in regurgitated scenes, some pleasant, some sad, but most exercises in poignancy and self analysis to the point of regret. And yet no amount of time could diminish their haunting reality. Or their immediacy Faces that he could picture right down to the minutest freckle told stories and conjured up scenes in which they would act out that special moment in their lives; lives of which he had been a part. This indeed was the terrible irony of his own singular life: a past that seemed far more real than that present which his paintings now attempted to capture as the unfolding seconds of his immediate future. But past, present or future, those reflections were as gateways to those moments whether wonderful or base; events he once climbed or descended like rungs on the ladder of his life.

This editorial in the Daily Gleaner for instance.

It must have put a smile on everyone's face that morning all those years ago. And yet behind the smiles Elwood saw and shared with the Editor so many of the points in the item: the friendship, the capacity to use and the intimate knowledge of the device. And of course, the loss of said device - his bicycle – for the article meant even more to Elwood. More than the humour, the analogy, the clever ramblings or the detraction from the more serious crimes of the time. He had initiated it; his first traumatic loss; his first retaliation with a pen.

He remembered his rage that morning almost fifteen years ago when he stood looking at the empty spot where his bike had been and realized in a kind of slow-motion, delayed acceptance that it had been stolen. It was the first time he knew he could kill someone; not only kill, but tear asunder, rip apart, ground into the dirt. In fact he had destroyed that faceless swine so many times in his mind he had almost believed he had done so in fact. But he had neither the 'scum-sucking pig' in his hands nor a knife to *slice the flesh off his bones.* He had only a pen. It was not enough; but it would have to do.

He had written to the Daily Gleaner lambasting the police, all the stations of Law, all the avenues of Justice and anyone even remotely connected to the criminal world, for not understanding that there are some things that are indeed sacrosanct and that defiling such should be considered an act against Society's most important thread - Trust. These were not his actual words however. His actual words were more terse, pointed and, many, four-lettered. Simply put, he had claimed that there were certain sins that are beyond forgiveness; certain crimes for which no punishment is too severe. Stealing, for instance, even in the broad sense of the word and under certain circumstances, might be considered acceptable; even forgivable – dire need or abject necessity where food or clothing or any of the elements of basic survival are at stake. But stealing a fellow's bike, under any circumstances, should never be tolerated, and would never be forgiven. It was akin to horse theft in the cowboy days of his movie-going youth. A crime punishable by hanging.

The empathetic editor's reply suggesting a kinship of sorts had done much to ease Elwood's mood at the time and though Elwood could not visualize any newspaperman, even a young one, riding down a street, *clasped fingers behind the neck,* he felt as close to him that day as to anyone he had ever known.

Of course Elwood knew there must have been a certain license in the newspaper statement – no two individuals could so equally share such a fanatic objective. At least not the way Elwood did. For more than just fixing bicycles, Elwood knew everything there was to know about them.

He knew the makes and types, from fragile racers to rugged mountain bikes, their good and bad points relative to their performance and use, and the prohibitive prices that put a great number of them out of his reach. He knew their emblems and their baked-on colours from stony grey to sunset orange and all the in-between hues that flanked the rainbow spectrum. He knew the weights of the different bikes and the metal alloys used to make them light enough or tough enough for their designated functions. He knew the cycle clubs and the bike gangs, from the saga-boys[2] who had the prettiest bikes and the latest gear and were always dressed in the coolest fashions, to the individuals who excelled in the sport of cycling – those Olympic hopefuls whose fanaticism and dedication equalled his own.

However in his case it was all academic; he neither aspired to glory nor relished talking about it. Knowledge alone was enough.

Besides, all that was in the past.

Or was it!

---

2 show-offs

CHAPTER -3- The bike

WOODY'S BICYCLE WAS NOT merely a thing; it was an extension of himself. Those who knew Woody in those days knew also his bike; its colour, make and the unusually long saddle-pole, a clear indication that he was close by.

It began on his thirteenth birthday; a friendship born of necessity and meagre means that soon became the signet of his youth, for into this tapestry, where friends and adventures crowded those days, the bike too was woven.

On that day Elwood had handed over thirty five dollars to a kid he had never seen before. He had felt like a criminal, he confided to Adrian. Thirty five dollars for the four-hundred dollar treasure; a Raleigh, Cobalt green and chrome though no less a mix of colour than a presentation which immediately appealed to Elwood. But there was even more to it than its aesthetics. Though second-hand it was prime; that is to say, it suited Elwood to a T. As if by some strange coincidence its first ownership seemed misguided, that previous owner shorter in stature than Woody, but richer, and, like all the rich kids he knew, possessed expensive acquisition tastes and a lack of regard for anything remaining in their possession for more than a year.

Elwood remembered the tiny scrape no one other than the kid (and of course he himself) could see, where the kid must have brushed against something hard and unforgiving, ending perhaps his dream of eternal perfection. Perhaps too the twisted handle-bars and the flat tire giving it that hang-dog look, an indication that it had not been used for some time, had something to do with the lower asking price. As well as the 'give-away' price, which more than met Elwood's limited funds and, in spite of its twenty-four inch wheels and slightly off-kilter appearance, nothing could sully that name or the prestige dealt through clever advertising of such a renowned product. Half an hour after the purchase, as he stood a pace back, sweaty, dirty and reeking of motor-oil but with a smile of ultimate satisfaction, (or as his mother put it: *grinning like an imbecile*) the bike could have been resold as new. But reselling never entered his mind. He was in love for the first time; his own first love. A first love that would last forever.

Or so he believed.

When the little ten-speed itself was stolen three weeks after that sixteenth birthday, Elwood moaned and fumed all week.

The trauma was so much akin to a dream state that long after the loss, he had the feeling that if he went to the back yard and looked hard enough, he would see where he had... misplaced the bike.

As the tragedy became known among the friends, Simple Potter (his name was actually Simon) had offered Elwood his own bike; though his motives were less than honourable. Simple planned on telling his mother his bike was stolen so he could get a new one - no questions asked. But Elwood would have to hide the bike, or repaint it, concealing it as a thief from the rest of the Simple household.

Elwood had refused. But his reasons were far more complicated involving honour and possession and affinity. However, it came down to one thing: it would have been a betrayal of his old machine. They had been buddies, spending three plus years together, and if one could capsulate one's life in all its fullness into such a frame of completeness, this was his. In its memory and with its absence as a constant reminder, the years before took on even greater importance. Still, with all his success as almost a direct result of the tragedy, he wondered if given the choice would he have opted for the change or elected to keep the status quo. Or was he destined to play this present role in spite of whatever might have happened in his past.

But fated or ill fated, whenever he looked back at the events that moulded his life, the bike, it seemed, was always there.

Like the Basin.

And Adrian.

Funny! The things that mould a man from what he once was to what he finally is; the little things, the silly things, the downright stupid things. And then there are the important things. Not necessarily the good things or even the honourable things, but those things that Fate has decided would be rather curious ingredients to add to the mix. And what about those things that are so despicable that the final man dares not look upon them too closely! They matter too, don't they?

Oh God!

CHAPTER -4- Mrs Metcalf

"THAT'S REALLY GOOD."

The voice had come suddenly from deep inside the quiet and Woody jerked around almost as if he had been caught stealing or perhaps about to steal something of great value.

He had been so focused on his work he had lost all sense of time or place. He remembered once looking at where Adrian had left off; his incomplete painting, the 'Basin', struggling to find a perspective that would depict that sense of completeness all the boys knew yet none could adequately express. Woody felt he could express it; competently. He had opened his box of poster paints - an almost unconscious move - and found himself copying Adrian's general outline. But as he looked back startled at Adrian's words and more so at the evolved difference between their two works, he could only smile.

"Yours ain't bad!" he attempted patronizingly.

"Nah! It's too damn heavy, too complex, too cluttered," Adrian Metcalf scowled. "Cheeze, I like yours though. How do you get it to...?" Adrian put his arm forward, his fingers reaching. "...like you could step into it. Like I could poke my finger... Ahhhh," he screamed in desperation. "Movement! That's what I'm trying to do. He looked again at his work. "It's too flat."

"Oh! You're too critical. Yours is rich. Richer than mine anyway."

"That's oils." Adrian dismissed him. "That's colour talking. That's Madder and cadmium milled with linseed and safflower and all kinds of shit six-hundred years of evolution took to produce the highest concentrations of pigment just so you could say: 'oh, that's great!' But that's not what I'm talking about. You see, colour is one thing. You could throw it at a canvas, put a frame on it and offer it for sale. And of course some idiot'll buy it... What am I talking about! That's what I do, don't I," he grinned wearily. "But that's not what you do. Even with that pasty shit. Why don't you try oils instead of that wussy stuff?"

"I do have oils. At home I paint in oils. But they're expensive. I can't just throw it away like you. That's why I use these poster paints. Besides, I buy my oils from Nubie's. It's real cheap – though not as cheap as posters.

"You kidding me! Nubie's! He makes his own stuff. You should be using Michael Harding or the higher end Windsor-Newtons."

"Naa! I could buy a whole box of colours for one of your whites," Woody countered, picking up the large unopened tube of titanium white.

"Take it. It's yours."

"Yea! How's one tube gonna help."

"Take the whole set then. I don't feel like painting any more."

Elwood felt guilty. Adrian was like that when he was frustrated. He pouted. For him it was all or nothing. Typical rich boy with too much other stuff like money for lessons and heaps of knowledge for bragging when all he wanted was talent. The same with running or jumping. Whenever Elwood beat him in a foot race, which he did often, or occasionally at long jump, Adrian would so take it to heart that he often could not bring himself to talk to Woody. In Art his attitude was only slightly better. Here Adrian could at least employ a type of teacher/pupil relationship which would mean some of the credit would belong to him.

"I ain't taking your stuff. It's late anyway." Elwood started putting away his paints. But Adrian took the painting, still water-logged and limp in the pad and held it up with two fingers.

"Hey Mom," he yelled out the opened door. "Get in here."

He'd done that before. It always frightened Elwood. He was going to show his mom something he valued, but this time it would be Elwood's watercolour. Elwood accelerated his packing speed; but he wasn't fast enough.

"Let me see," Mrs. Metcalf asked flowing into the room. It was not a request to be taken lightly. Refusal would have been met with the sounding brass and crashing cymbals of silence - her eyes narrowing. They'd all seen it when she used it on Joe or Pete. Deadly!

Mrs. Metcalf was an imposing figure; a moderately tall, very stately, very handsome woman whose bearing adequately reflected her connections with the art industry as well as certain political aspects of the community. Quoted often by at least one organ of the media, the Daily Gleaner, she had been on several government commissions, presently chaired the Junior Chamber and was often called in by the ministry of culture for advice on advertising and marketing. These were the facts of her station that carried great severity and a significance not easily dismissed. She owned an art gallery in a prestigious part of the city and had exhibited Adrian's works from time to time. None had sold; unless her own purchase for encouragement sake could be considered a sale. But that encouragement's true value lay in far more than just buying her son's early attempts. She shared his art with him. If not for her manner, her warmth and easy dialogue, she could just as easily have been feared by Adrian's friends. Not by Elwood. He had other concerns; private ones that caused him to be afraid. For himself. And from within.

She was, from the very first day of their very first encounter, in his little eyes and his little heart, the most beautiful woman on the face of the earth. (By the time he officially reached puberty, he had a box-full of sketches of her – all carefully hidden away in his bedroom.) For this reason alone he always hung back, clinging to the background least she talk to him and he unwittingly betray the crush on her. It may even be due to her that he developed a practiced reticence that was considered even by the other boys unusually cold and distant, unmoved in all but anger, and unfazed by even the most startling revelations. Yet all this was housed in a shyness fanatically secured for that reason alone - to hide his face from the dictates of his heart. Any such display would not be taken kindly by the others. Boys (in spite of what girls say,) notice each other. Theirs is a wordless communication, but one filled with truths. Denials are more protestations to be regarded with suspicion, even as humorous (at times cruel) in the face of truth. Crushes were accepted of course. However there were certain taboos; tacitly, mothers in general, but Mrs. Metcalf in particular.

As she entered the room she was already in the process of slipping off her high-styled Lipow sunglasses in an anticipation that would not even consider the barest possibility of hesitation on Elwood's part and far less an outright refusal.

"He's going to take my stuff," Adrian announced, "...brushes and all. What do you think?"

She did not reply quickly. Holding the glasses from her face and up close as though pointing to some part of the work Elwood could not see, she hummed and made little clicking noises with her even, white teeth.

"Yessss," she wheezed out as more expelling breath than answering. "Elwood, you create a shadow with the same stroke! Why do you not use two strokes and blend the dark with the light?"

"I don't know."

"Oh Elwood, surely you must know," she almost admonished, pointing at him with the glasses. "Did you learn that in class?"

"No!"

"Woody doesn't take art," Adrian interrupted. He often talked for Elwood. "He takes Latin."

"Latin!" Mrs. Metcalf raised an eyebrow. "You must be good at it then."

"No! I'm pretty bad," Elwood said shyly.

"Woody's going to be a priest," Adrian informed her. "Father Hawkins is always talking to him about it."

"A priest! Does your mother know?"

"No! And it's not priesthood, it's archaeology."

"Archaeology!" both mother and son exclaimed.

"You never told me that?" Adrian accused.

"Well I'm still lousy at Latin, so..."

"But if your Latin is bad," Mrs. Metcalf, puzzled, "what... how does that affect you? Your desire to be an archaeologist I mean."

"I have to give it up."

"Then take art. Let your mother speak to the dean? He'll change subjects."

"She doesn't know I still paint. Only sketch. I told her I stopped painting. I... don't want her to know I paint." It was a plea from his soul but he feared Mrs. Metcalf paid it not the slightest attention. She hummed and made more clicking noises, and then turning away, abruptly stomped out of the room.

Elwood was convinced she hated him; his ineptness and his vacillation on a subject so close to her heart. He quickly gathered up his paints and the two brushes and dumped them into the little box. He could not retrieve the painting Mrs. Metcalf had handed back to Adrian because it was still wet and would smear or even tear if not handled properly.

"So, how come you never told me?" Adrian asked.

"I don't know."

"But you couldn't lie to mom, right?"

Elwood started to leave.

"Now don't get all huffy on me, Woody Lucien," Adrian admonished. "Mom's right. Take art. I know what I'm telling you. And all this stuff's still good," he pointed to his array of art supplies. "Mom's going to buy me a whole set anyway. You know how I like new stuff. I'm going to England, you know."

That stopped Elwood. He turned and came slowly back into the room.

"Next September," Adrian said without emotion. "University."

"So, how come you never said anything?"

"Nah! Din't think I was going to bother going. Then... Just don't let anyone change your mind for you, okay. Especially no girl." He fell silent then lifted Elwood's still damp work and looked at it again. "You're lucky as hell, you know," he said wistfully. "I'm the best in my class and I ain't half as good as this. Lucky as hell."

Lucky!

Less than a week later, Woody's bike was stolen.

CHAPTER -5- Sketches

AS ELWOOD SAT ON the motorbike listening to the prompts of the policeman and replying as best he could in spite of the absent distractions of his memories, he wondered where it was all leading to. What hand, what muse, what fate had selected for him this journey with no end in sight, only a present that seemed as meaningless as the idiotic questions he fielded as a punishment for being well known!

Finally, he could restrain himself no more. He withdrew a pad from the saddlebag and began, surreptitiously at first then reflexively and without restraint, to sketch his surroundings. It was as natural for him as tapping a finger against a cheek or brushing a strand of hair from the eyes. In his case the tic required some preparation. Pad and pencil, or crayon with slate. He never traveled far without some form of artist's accoutrements. He had moreover taken to carrying a small case of oils, some knives and an assortment of brushes and a pad of canvas paper; all fitted nicely into a nine by twelve folder. The result was often messy, but forgiven if the work remained in its place of creation. At other times, weather permitting, he brought out his entire ensemble and threw himself whole-heartedly into the work.

Elwood never considered it toil. However when he did think of it he figured all he really had to do was sit, poised in front of the easel then at the dictate of some inner voice he would almost reflexively pick up the appropriate tool – pencil, charcoal, brush, knife – and the art would simply flow out of his fingertips. And though at times it seemed as if his very blood covered the canvas, there was very little work involved and all was just a dream-state where he just watched as the whole thing unfolded.

That's why he liked sound – not noise, at least not those disagreeable noises like idle chatter or grinding machines that might tend to interrupt a perfectly composed concept. He liked birds' song and waves lapping; even the drone of distant traffic. But nothing distinctive that would take him from the unfolding theme once determined and set upon. *Such concepts, in unit form or aggregate,* he once explained in a letter to Mrs. Metcalf, *are often triggered by mood which in turn gives personality to the work. Yet, it is not mood alone that determines the outcome, for whether it is a single tone or some harmonious assembly that demands his attention it is the subject itself more than his personal mood that determines the choice.*

As did that street in that town on that day.

All the business and industry of the entire suburban patch of that part of the little borough on the eastern seaboard seemed housed in that one-block stretch of road that pulsed with activity. Vehicular traffic merged with all other modes of travel – carts, small and large, pulled by goats and donkeys, bicycles of every make and function, and, dodging and darting among them, pedestrians, with utter disdain and at times, animosity, toward all.

The street, by definition, gave some order to the process though the pavement itself, cracked and patched unevenly, seemed fully representative of the indiscriminate planning that governed it. Separated by only a few feet of rocky soil, every inch of which was lost to the hardy Nut grass, the buildings themselves bordered on a state of dilapidation giving each that sense of off-kilter abstraction that artists seemed drawn to. The deli itself, where Elwood waited outside impatiently with the two policemen, sat next to a garage where the smell of oil and gas merged with eggs, onions and curry as well as other spices like Shado-Bene and Spanish Thyme that seemed to burst forth when introduced to hot ghee. On the other side of the deli stood a laundry run by a Chinese family. Its offering of calciferous steam and detergent waged another battle with other odours, in particular those emitted from a row of Indian vendors occupying the street directly in front with little carts of phoulorie and doubles, sugar-cakes, soused mangoes and Kaiser Balls. A Bata shoe store followed next and was in turn followed by a fish market then a long fence behind which stood a large house. Once a proud mansion overlooking a wide estate and now converted to a bed and breakfast sleep-over, it also provided lunch and dinner to the few of wealth who could afford it.

On the opposite corner, a two-storied building offered rest under the guise of a hotel, though as it housed also a rum shop and oyster bar which Elwood knew quite well, it actually afforded very little sleep before three in the morning.

He had nevertheless stayed there the night before, parking his beloved model 351 Indian Blackhawk Chief in the garage which at least offered security for the duration. He had paid Araz, the owner, an acceptable fee for its protection. Araz had oiled, gassed and cleaned it up so that it shone at the ready when Elwood took delivery. In the face of such excellent service he had moreover been reconsidering an earlier decision not to return to the town when his meal had been interrupted. Now as he examined the building exteriors, their flaked paint and loose boards, the not quite horizontal eaves and not quite vertical walls, he changed his mind again. After all, not only was it quaint. It now had personality. And history.

The sergeant finally emerged from the deli. He was stout, heavy jowled and unsmiling under the growing heat. His manner somewhat brusque and intending, he strode toward Elwood and removed a small, black jacketed pad from his upper left pocket.

"Ah take his statement already," the friendly policeman offered. The sergeant ignored him.

"Tony say you hit him first an' he have to go to the hospital. He want to press charges."

"That's a lie..." Elwood began.

The sergeant held up his hand, an official gesture that needed no translation. He would brook no discussion. "Ah don' want to argue here. Come dong to the station and we'll settle everyting dere."

"I'm not going to any station..." Elwood protested turning away sharply.

"Officer! Arrest this man."

"Sir, he not..."

"Officer. Do not argue with me."

"Buh sir..."

The sergeant looked sharply at him.

"That's all right," Elwood sighed, breaking in and holding up his palms. "I'll come along. May I ride my bike over?"

The sergeant frowned. He doubted whether anyone else could ride the machine without putting the town's financial position in jeopardy for this one looked to him as ready at the slightest invitation to sue them all for any injury to his machine, but this did not so concern him as perhaps the fear of losing his authority with indecision. He therefore agreed to the request without so much as acknowledging that the question had been asked. "Follow us," he barked. At which he turned and entered the squad car.

The constable hurried to his bicycle and made the short distance to the jail well before Elwood arrived at the parking lot.

It was clear from the start that, although allowing Elwood to bring his bags into the lock-up, the sergeant was on unsteady ground when he ordered the desk-sergeant to put the prisoner in a holding cell. His words were unsure, and even his manner had changed. He gave Elwood the impression that he needed to be alone with his own superior before any further action could be taken.

But by that time Elwood had cooled, being without any real urgency or inconvenience, he had begun to accept the possibility of turning it into something positive, or in any event making the best of it. With this in mind he no sooner heard the black iron door clang behind him than he was busy into his bags. Withdrawing his charcoals and pad he immediately set about creating the front office with the holding cell in the background. Although this was not the correct layout, he paid it no mind, for his intention had been to imprison the rather unjust sergeant within its borders.

The cell itself was cool, its heavy brick walls obviously responsible for a most effective insulation. The sense of comfort however seemed incongruous to the feeling of helplessness that assailed him. Strange and unsettling it carried as well an excitement he found unusual and alien. Yet it seemed also strangely familiar.

Since he had never before seen the inside of an actual jail he put it down to the lasting effect of Hollywood's fare of gangster movies as well as the many times he, along with some of his more persistently rambunctious friends, had been threatened with this kind of incarceration all those many times throughout his youth. Of course not without reason.

His sketching grew slower, more absent; what others might term 'doodling' as though his mind and fingers belonged to two completely different entities. He was remembering. Years passed, traversing familiar ground and episodes from when they were very young, their first meetings and the circumstances of those introductions, to the present; that strangeness that comes with growing up.

He now saw their faces, the faces of his youth as clearly as if he could simply reach out and pat one on the back or start an argument. He could just as easily have been rolling a dice, pitching a marble or kicking a football and he did not have to look up to see who he was playing with or their reactions to what he had accomplished with his turn.

Looking up would only confirm what he knew in infinite detail.

CHAPTER -6- The gang

THE METCALF'S LARGE GREY house on the cul-de-sac straddling the dry river was regarded by every member of the gang as base camp for every activity involving the boys and their friends.

Adrian Metcalf, the avowed leader, ('Mom's pet') was three years older than any of the group.

He was an athlete of some note, had a kind heart and a pleasant disposition and, as well as being brilliant, articulate, and head of the school's debating society, was an honour student. He painted too, and with a skill that fascinated the others - especially Elwood. It was therefore a foregone conclusion among the friends that Adrian would someday be a great artist.

Their father, Mr. Jonas R. Metcalf, lived in Canada. He was there on the Ambassador's personal staff - in those days a most prestigious position (second only to the Ambassador himself) - and though everyone else suspected he had split with their mother, the boys always talked of him as though he were on a short trip from which he would soon return. (By the time they accepted that he would not return, they were all safely into adulthood.) Still, no one could doubt that he had adequately provided for his family - they ate when they were hungry, had a dishwasher and a car, grapes at Christmas, new clothes on birthdays, ham sandwiches anytime and of course the large, impressive house on the corner standing in full testament to the father's sense of order and duty. And that left the boys to do pretty much as they felt. With mother's approval, of course.

Joe and Pete were exact opposite personalities to their older brother. In common they had neither aims nor dreams, were devoid of curiosity, resisted knowledge, construction and impetus, and consequentially did absolutely nothing to enhance their lives. Joe was slight and somewhat weasel-like, seeking to impress by means of outlandish measures and often crude methods. Pete, the youngest, taller and heavier than his older brother, seldom did what he promised and often threatened as perhaps the embodiment of the saying about the bark and the bite.

Elwood too was their polar opposite, but in a different, more social and temperamental way; not only poor, alone and unique, but with a volatile temper, and although he might readily accept the other attributes as irrefutable, he often defended his temper.

Once, when he was teased constantly by another boy he did not respond, though the slur *'Obzocky'* must have particularly galled him. He had not minded the earlier nickname 'Floppy' as it related to his ears (at least it replaced the flicking) but this new name was too close to home to ignore. Yet he did ignore it... till he was actually hit on the head by a tuft of grass and his temper exploded. He chased the offender and in a raging temper, pushed his face into the effluent of a stand-pipe till Adrian dragged him off the wailing boy. (The other members of the gang had been too surprised at 'Floppy' to take a hand. But after that, they left him alone.) The nickname, 'Floppy' also died that day. Soon after however, the moniker, Obzocky, was born; a name used playfully and humorously by those of his inner circle, and at times even affectionately by Adrian.

Adrian's bedroom was more a studio; a corner room with large windows on both sides and a skylight overlooking all. Adrian's bed, a double, the only indication that it was indeed a bedroom, was tucked into one corner and, at least when the boys were there, piled high with cushions and pillows on which any two at a time could lounge.

Although at seventeen Adrian was still considered one of the group, his duties were as much the first born son and surrogate father as the big brother. As well he was a senior at college which status provided him with greater opportunities of meeting the fairer sex. The girl, who in memory became the catalyst that changed the simplicity and innocence of their lives, had been the direct result of one of the must-attend dances put on by well meaning administrators of both schools. Their objective was to gently introduce each side to that eventual after school reality: the opposite sex. However, though well meaning, the aim would be hopeful at best, and in almost ninety percent of cases, a little too late. The girls' objective was singular: to secure a boyfriend. The boys' objective was singular as well, yet not so innocent. And far more primal. Both Adrian and the girl met their objectives.

It was a pivotal experience in all their lives, providing discussions and confessions for both parties. Elwood, (by then three inches taller than Adrian) was the only member of the group in whom Adrian confided on serious matters, although in this case much of what he had to say confused and at times embarrassed the younger neophyte who at least possessed the very adult ability to mask his feelings with inscrutability. Yet it seemed with that confession and the subsequent questions and puzzling answers there was forged a bond that had a profound effect on both their lives. For the rest of their lives. Not so with the girl whose importance lasted no longer than the duration. It was told that after the eventual break-up with Adrian she cried for a whole day. But Adrian's own sadness (with not a little anger and some impatience) took a strange turn. The very next Saturday he back-packed his charcoals and sketch-pad up to the Basin and added a new dimension to their weekends.

Adrian had, at that time, grown tired of painting still lifes. He had moreover begun to question his talent in oils and to lean toward simple charcoal sketches and line drawings. They were, he protested to his mother, easier and more satisfying and, he feared, more within his scope. She would have none of it. Though she encouraged his sketching, she insisted he use them as basis for the grander oil colours. He had talked so much of the Basin and the forest above that she nagged him to do some of those landscapes. He agreed to try. The new project could very well satisfy them both.

In those days no one knew that Elwood also painted for although he shared in the knowledge of art, it was attributed to the fact that Elwood read voraciously and made a study of everything that crossed his path. In truth, though, he had been painting since he was three years old when some relative long forgotten had given him a box of water colours by mistake – it turned out to be more expensive than the box of crayons originally intended. But whether through chance, innate skill or the physical meddling of some impish muse, his first works – labelled freestyle, for ignorance sake – did indeed possess a certain balance and perspective not associated with three-year-olds. It was therefore, Art, if 'cute', and if only he could do it again... Which he did and which his mother promptly showed off and gave away to whomever she deemed deserving.

Soon, relatives and friends were bringing doilies, ceramic coasters and cups, and every manner of materials that compliment water colours. Till he was seven, every subsequent gift to and from him had to include articles of art.

But at the age of nine he suddenly stopped.

Though he continued to paint he refused to give away what he painted causing his mother the loss of many friends and the annoyance of certain relatives. Elwood did not mind any of this; not even the abrupt termination of gifts that followed his rash act. He had indeed received so many in those formative years that he still had paints from his very first set. Of course whenever he ran short in any colour he would add or replenish as he saw fit. It was cheaper that way.

That Sunday (the day after the big break-up with the girl) Elwood had brought his own little box of poster paints down to Adrian's room where the boys often gathered. Elwood never understood why he chose that day to reveal his artistry and for a time thought that he needed to impress Adrian, but no matter his skill in the medium, it was still water colours and in spite of the fact that it was still art, albeit another form, Adrian could not stand water colours and throughout the morning commented derisively on Woody's large hands holding the small brushes as something more of humour than dedication. Elwood, as usual, ignored his taunt.

Usually Adrian sketched or painted with Elwood looking over his shoulder while they all (painters included) played Monopoly or cards and carried on rambling conversations, the subjects often changing with each new sentence. As well, they listened to loud music, anything from rock and roll to Sibelius depending on Adrian's mood, drank small green bottles of coke classic and ate the little snacks provided by Mrs. Metcalf. On that day however, Adrian too morose, the subject matter too elusive, the art too frustrating and the other boys too not interested in silence, Adrian and Elwood were alone so that no one really witnessed the pivotal moment when Adrian handed over the tools of a trade to his best friend. Or when Elwood Lucien accepted from his only true friend that which he did not know would turn out to be his life's work. Or when, for the first time Elwood, more at Adrian's persistence and to punish him for bringing his mother into their holy sanctum, signed that limp sheet of watercoloured art, a medium he would never use again, with the name, *Obzocky.*

It would be many years before the name Elwood Lucien would appear on that other famous painting of the Blue Basin which still hangs in state on the foyer wall of the Art Museum, greeting all visitors with an aloof simplicity that quite dominates all the other pieces of art within the building.

CHAPTER -7- The Basin

THE THING ABOUT A bike is that it not only shortens time; it provides distance. Where before the group had only one very limited objective every Saturday morning, with their new bikes they now had increased room for choice, time and, of course, distance.

They still started early and still had bananas before entering the Savannah, but often they were already at the bottom of the St. James hill before the sun crested the eastern ridge. But the sky would be light before Diego Martin and bright by Petit Valley though the road would still be clear of traffic along the gently sloping, easy-to-ride route and, enjoying a steady conversation - often taking over the entire road in a V-formation as geese heading south for winter - they would arrive at the top without ever taking a deep breath or pausing to rest at the end. From the ridge, it was a long, bumpy coast all the way down to the other side to the Blue Basin where, it was generally held, Saturday would officially begin.

The 'Blue Basin' is tucked away deep within the southern slopes of Trinidad's northern range, that line of mountains long regarded as the island's main stronghold against the furies of the Atlantic ocean. High above the basin the forest looms as a protective awning, dense and foreboding. Even on the most brilliant of days, indirect sunlight is insufficient to light or warm it fully since direct light is permitted only briefly during the two hour span before and after noon.

The Basin itself is a wide pool - a large basin if you will - into which a high, thin cascade of cold water leaps from rocks some fifty feet above, splays through black, igneous clefts, worn smooth by centuries of erosion but coated somewhat by a light mossy glaze, and plunges into the blue shimmering mystery beneath. The pool is deep; so deep in fact that immediately below the falls, no one ever touched bottom - that is, those who tried. Geologists have speculated that the rock had split many thousands of years ago through some form of upheaval and at the point of separation where a spring fed stream had been severed, the crevasse had filled to its present capacity, overflowing to a pretty brook which gathering smaller tributaries, in turn filled little pools along the many miles that eventually would lead down through the valley finally emptying into the Gulf of Paria to the west of the island.

Arriving at the Basin, the boys would chain the bikes together and climb up the rocky western wall. This was the easiest route to the plateau above. It is a steep climb for about ten feet, though the face provides secure footing and exposed roots for handles. At its top is a path that ascends further. At a more gentle slope, it continues to the area above the Basin and onwards along a high rill that feeds it. The boys would walk along the bank for almost two miles through a grandeur of tall trees and wild flowers that none knew existed till Adrian painted it and his mother, upon seeing it, promised him a career that would take him away to England and to parts of Europe no one else ever dreamed were real or even if accepting such a fantastic reality would never consider themselves fortunate enough to ever visit such places - the places of history books and legends.

But it was not the pleasant walk nor the conversation that caused them to travel up the mountain, stumbling over moss-covered rocks and fallen trunks of trees so entangled and covered with vines and overgrowth, so filled with animal and insect life it could be and would have been considered dangerous - if their parents ever knew. It was instead to reach the very summit of that hill, from which view the distant northern seaboard stretched in blue infinity. But this was a scene ignored by the young explorers. Their greater concern was the grove of fruit trees positioned in a little dell, steps away from a precipitous descent to certain death.

Immediately upon their arrival, they would begin to pick the fruit; especially mangoes (Teen, Vere and Calabash filled the grove). Also growing in profusion were tangerines, balata and chennet; of course not all in season at the same time. But of those available in abundance only the best would be taken. Seldom would they touch fruit lying on the ground (except the hard shelled balata) unless it was deemed to have recently fallen. And they could tell, of course. They had become experts.

There was always some concern about snakes. They had found several - some quite venomous - but they always walked with sticks and often boasted they knew how to handle snakes. Not to their mothers of course.

Soon after arriving and having their fill of fruit, everyone would whip out their onion bags and start filling them to the top. At one time they had used sugar bags but these proved too large, and greed made them too heavy. Now they used the smaller, lighter onion bags. These were of a light, petroleum-based material that would not stand up to heavy use, but were just strong enough for carrying fruit back home.

They all had their own preferences where fruit was concerned. Elwood for instance loved the Teen and Vere mangoes, but, when in season, balata was his favourite. These small fruit, the size of large marbles, were sumptuously sweet, but if not perfectly ripe - their hard shell tinged yellow and brown - they left a strange tongue-tying after-taste that was less than pleasing. The tree from which they fell was tall; its trunk wide and bare from root to canopy which made it quite inaccessible. However when in full season one did not need to climb the tree. Its hazelnut-sized treats fell in such great number they carpeted the ground so that they had to be approached carefully, the reapers gleaning from the outer rim and working toward the trunk. Often all the bags were filled before the base of the stem was reached.

Pete loved tangerines. Three such trees, no higher than fifteen feet occupied an area to one side of the grove and even without fruit were always full-leafed and pretty in a quaint, friendly sort of way in spite of the deterring thorns along its branches. Occasionally all three trees would be in full flower at the same time, presenting three almost perfect balls of white which would stand out against the green grasses flowing up the side of the hill. Green fruit was not touched. But ripe! Ripe; it didn't matter what else were in season, Pete ignored them all for tangerines. Everyone made fun of him but he didn't mind. There was nothing so wonderful in his mind as walking around the tree within easy reach of the full, ripe, reddish orange fruit, picking them, peeling them and pigging out on them.

Joe liked them too - of course not like Pete - but then he liked everything Pete liked just as he did everything Adrian said. Well, almost everything.

A true follower who desperately wanted to do more than follow, Joe, by no means the youngest, was the smallest of the group. Though lacking in many of the skills others found easy, he always tried to out-do the others, attempt at least what others thought stupid, or be first to do it. He once tried to determine the depth of the Basin; an attempt that left the group unable to breath for what seemed an eternity, and one that made Adrian so mad, Elwood though he would beat his brother to a pulp.

Joe had taken an onion bag over to the falls then filling it with stones, had plunged head first into the pool holding on to the bag. Immediately before, all dares and challenges had turned to pleas. Adrian had screamed threats and Simple looked like he was going to cry. But Joe had ignored them. Grinning with a new found insanity, he dove and disappeared into the gently troubled, cold, blue water. Adrian attempted to follow but he was at the other end of the pool. No one spoke. The time dragged. Then Joe broke the surface. Pete announced it had been only fifteen seconds. It was not the point. Adrian looked with killing eyes at him and Pete knew the next thing would be his killing right hand. But Adrian was saving it all for Joe. Adrian yelled into his ear till Joe cried. Then Adrian slapped him about the head all the way home.

Following the incident the group always moved directly to the fruit grove without the traditional first dip in the pool. Nothing else changed. When the picking was done, often before Noon, toting their bags, conversation and energy spent, they returned along the path to the Basin where they would then take a dip in the cold water. Refreshed, they could then ride home at their leisure, take in a midday matinee, play soccer, fly kites, joust, romp, see a four-o'clock movie (an option if there was no midday matinee), go to a game or just hang out at the Metcalf's where they would eat ham sandwiches and drink lemonade.

(Later, Joe, who never let a subject die naturally and not at least without joking about it, explained to Elwood that he didn't mean to dive himself, but his finger got caught in the webbing of the bag. Next time, he grinned at Elwood, he would try it with kite string.)

There was no next time. Unable to determine how far Joe would go, Elwood told Adrian about the plan even suggesting they make an experiment of it. However far from the desired result, Adrian had slapped Joe about the head again and told Elwood if anyone ever did anything so stupid again, he would not go the Basin again. Everyone knew Adrian did not threaten idly, and once promising, he would keep it no matter if he thought better of it afterwards. Joe said he would never forgive Elwood for blabbing on him. But in time that too would become a joke.

CHAPTER -8- Obzocky

IT SEEMED PEOPLE IN general did not think much of Elwood Lucien in those days. Of course they regarded the artist with some awe – those who knew art – but awe is not a particularly loving quality. His inner friends looked upon him with a modicum of hate tinged with respect. But that was in the nature of friends and perfectly excusable, for friends seldom see worth in each other. But when word got back to him from without that immediate circle, there was definitely some rancour to it. Except with Adrian, of course. But when Elwood could think enough, reason enough and so seek to understand why others did not like him (as he often did – he analyzed everything), he often thought it was the fact of his mixed race. Not that he entirely disagreed with the principal of the thing. To him there was something so indefinite and lukewarm about the mongrel that the most one could expect from it was an ambivalent toleration of not more than one of its characteristics. For despite the stories of true love conquering all, not once did any of those romantic authors mention the tribulations of the offspring of that love.

Elwood's father was tall, lank and black and his mother a homely little English lady of almost blue blood – if there was any blood to speak of. He loved his mother of course, but in his world of colour he would have preferred to be any of the primary colours that defined race. Some of his friends were indeed Black – Indian and Negro – and he even had a yellow friend for a time, though yellow here was not so much a colour but a hue. Like pink. But though some of his closest friends were Portuguese white – that is to say a sickly pale about the lower belly – he could never fully associate with them either, except Adrian to whom colour did not matter whether in race or class... or art for that matter. But surely colour – or the lack thereof – could not account for this feeling of separation he had endured his entire life.

At times Elwood felt it might be that exasperating inability to compete in any of the standard team sports that set him apart. He was klutzy in basketball despite his height, inept at football despite his speed, and could neither bowl nor bat in the game of cricket. And yet in certain areas of individual proficiency he could outdo others with an ease they often viewed as arrogance.

There was too his general attitude to be considered – humble and almost fawning to some, proud and aloof to others. He could not see it of course, being a young boy with a certain definite personality that had more honesty than politics to it. But if it had been any of these, surely he might have been permitted to outgrow them as children are left to outgrow infancy according to the dictates of society.

But then there might have been the other thing; a topic not easily discussed by boys of that tender age. Looks! Or in his case, the lack of it. His nickname summed it up: Obzocky; an intrinsically West Indian word that meant awkward, unattractive, out of place, lopsided or misshapen. Or all of the above.

Even before his teens Elwood had been tall; a somewhat gawky kid with hypnotic eyes and large floppy ears that everyone liked to flick. His aunt – Aunt Tina – his mother's widowed sister, would sometimes cover them with both hands and press them against his head while offering some comment on their ability to 'stick out' no matter what. Such action did seem friendly to the very young child and he actually enjoyed the familiarity in those early days. But this was about all he enjoyed about Aunt Tina. What he particularly disliked about her was not so easily addressed. For one, he was directed to call her *Tanté* in the French Creole tongue; a directive against which he balked as a child, thinking Tanté was her first name, and which he forwent entirely in his latter youth – despite her constant reminders.

But at least she never flicked his ears. Everyone else seemed unable to resist it. He, on the other hand, had a very short temper and seemed unable to resist punching the flickers. Jail had been threatened quite frequently though mostly by parents and teachers of those who had flicked and been summarily dealt a responding blow. But although with time the concept of jail would lose some of the impact of a threat, in reality neither was it a threat to many of the offenders and he would therefore be no stranger to some hard knocks himself. It also meant that pugilism - in his case the giving and taking of diverse beatings - would dog his life's footsteps, and most decisions would be arrived at through the medium of the closed fist.

By the time he was seventeen, having sprung several inches taller and with heavier, bonier knuckles and an unforgiving temper, he gave more than he got and very few within his circle of acquaintances flicked his ears anymore. However it seemed Elwood no longer waited for his ears to be flicked and if he did not like someone outside the circle, he did not wait for them to make a wrong move, a wrong joke or even a wrong look. He made the first move himself.

When, for instance, Elwood thought Bruce Fennel was going to say or do something, he did something first. He beat up Bruce to the point at which the police had to be called. But Elwood held to his story of imminent danger and he was released. And then there was little 'Porky' Leighton. He might have been joking when he grabbed Elwood's kite by the race-track, but Elwood pushed his face into the deep sand and probably would have choked Porky if Adrian had not pulled him off.

In Adrian's eyes, Elwood could do no wrong, but on that day even Adrian had refrained from congratulating him on a 'good fight'. And yet perhaps it was something in his look, a shame perhaps, that made Elwood think before lashing out the next time someone crossed his path – at least when Adrian was around.

It was as well on that very day that Elwood realized there must have been something special about him that caused Adrian and the others of the inner circle to forgive him and continue to include him in their ventures. There could only be two possibilities, but they might have been enough. One: he knew bikes. The other: he knew art. But in both, discipline, assiduous to the point of being rather quirky, was the governing factor. So, Elwood would have to remain quirky or give up those other important qualities. It was perhaps to this end therefore that he faced up to those less important qualities and the address they encouraged by boldly signing those first serious oil works, the bike in particular, under the name, Obzocky. It was only later and as a defence against two many questions, making the name more important than the painting, that he began to sign his own name to his art.

It was another one of those steps in life that sets one apart from those around him. Apart and alone!

It was not what Elwood had wished.

CHAPTER -9-
Transition to art

HOME, WAS THE LAST house on Growers drive. It was small; only two bedrooms - both small - as well as a tiny kitchen and a long living room. In one corner of the living room there was a table with four chairs which could conceivably be regarded as a dining area and since the little table in the kitchen was always piled high with tinned food, bags of grain and disused utensils, the only remaining place where food could be served was this little area. When Elwood's mother was well enough - an infrequent state - she would share a small meal there with him.

Ms. Joan Mathias (she never married Elwood's father) was once a mousy little Englishwoman; a teacher who dreamed of her son as a great author and could hardly hide her disappointment when her dream was dashed. As though reflecting that disappointment, she became a pathetic, haggard, prematurely grey haired creature who it seemed delighted in her woeful appearance. She spent most of the day in bed, arising only for visits to the privy or perhaps to change a book. She read constantly, mostly romance, and in the early days often insisted that Elwood do the same. He of course did. In this cause he also wrote little notes to her, leaving them on her table late at night or if he had to go out very early the next day. But what began as an obedient little boy's desire to please his mom, continued into his adolescence and early adulthood as a habit; one that served two very good purposes. One, to carry on conversations he often had with himself, and the other to provide an alternate for her complaints so that they would at least have something else to discuss.

When he first learned to write in the long, cursive style that was more art than communication, he began the first of many diaries. It was a progressive step initiated by the note-writing. These diaries were not those expensive books that force an entry every day, but one in the form of a scrapbook without set dates but which Elwood would date upon making an entry. This too his mother read, though often without waiting for his approval or knowledge. However even as he suspected it, he did not mind. It was written in a certain narrative style, not first person, perhaps with her in mind, disclosing in the bold hand of omniscience his thoughts as well as their relative aspects to his life. However, as age increasingly demanded a certain privacy, he began keeping two diaries - one for her, one for himself. When he was nineteen, her diary ended abruptly.

"A girlfriend," she guessed incorrectly looking up from her book as she posed for him on that auspicious day.

Although he loved discussions with her, he seldom answered her probing and did not then, though she could tell there was something amiss with his life. As he continued sketching her he smiled. He had opened the window for light and his smile was clearly visible. It annoyed her; but in that way of subdued acceptance he found particularly quaint among her wealth of expressions. He would have liked to see her smile. It was the one expression he truly enjoyed and when younger he often went through great pains to elicit one. Not naturally funny he relied on wit and certain subjects which she herself found amusing. The antics of his friends, Joe, Spat, Frank or Simple for instance. Not Pete; there was a certain cruelty there. And definitely not Adrian; Adrian was art.

"Aren't you finished yet?" she asked obviously wanting to get back to her book or at least have him address her query.

"Go ahead," he mumbled impatiently. "Do what you have to do. I'm almost done."

He was becoming annoyed himself. She had forgotten that it was she who had asked him to come into the room. She had something to tell him. He had brought his pad fearing the tedium of the long explanations of her trials. But her news took only ten seconds (Aunt Tina was coming over for tea). His condition took longer. It was now almost an hour since he began sketching her. It had progressed from "hold it there for a second" before she could utter her pressing tidbit, through "turn a little to the left", to "will you stop fidgeting". He knew well that if he didn't hurry, tempers on both sides would flare and Aunt Tina would think the mood was directed at her.

But hurrying was not foremost in Elwood's mind.

He would have liked to try painting directly to a simple outline. But that would mean bringing his oils into her room as he once did with his water-colours. Now she adamantly refused. As with his first few attempts, she complained the smell would linger forever. In any case he had gotten into the habit of sketching fully then making an outline from the sketch. The earlier attempts at direct image to canvas using his bike as the model had been successful because the subject lacked impatience. With it, light and posture were manageable. He often thought that as comparative subjects, his mother presented the very antithesis of his bike's qualities. Nor were these qualities confined to art.

Throughout her days with him it was he who served and mothered. He did the cooking and most of the cleaning (she at times only tidied her own room) and though she often lamented that fact, she made no real effort to change it. In the midst of her many apologies for their state, usually uttered with great sighing and resignation, she often quoted from books or from sayings from her own mother (an indentured Creole servant whose family came from the country and were therefore steeped in folk-lore). Far from expressions of intelligence however, these quotations had one purpose only - to reinforce her part in life's great drama. She could be regarded, without much argument, as being the personification of a fatalist. The script of her life already written, there seemed, in her mind at least, a great tragedy unfolding; with her life, with her luck, with her due. And though she griped often, it was against the incidences and the mechanics of day to day living, not the role to which she had been pre-ordained. Her common-law husband's departure when Elwood was eight was the point at which she resigned to the life she now led. Nor did she complain or rail against it, but rather accepted it as a child did status or condition.

Elwood accepted too his life and the role handed him. But his acceptance extended to those daily setbacks his mother would have considered tragic. His volatile temper (latently discovered) extended ironically to those daily setbacks, but more to the immediacy of circumstances where reaction was hinged upon the lack of time to think. At any other time, given to thought instead of reaction, he handled setbacks with an unusual aplomb. More, he never complained, forgave easily (given enough time) and would often listen to his mother's lamentations not quite understanding why a person complained who had food on the table and a place to sleep.

His mother's allowance (from a trust fund set up by her father) had been diminishing as the cost of living grew, but still it was more than enough to live on. In this above all else the difference between his mother and himself was most evident. With her the cup was always half empty; with him there was always something for which he would be grateful. For instance although he could never replace his bike, he nevertheless saw its compensations.

He was asked more frequently now to accompany Adrian and his mother on 'Art trips'. These were outings in her little green Renault to places she considered worthy of reproduction: stately buildings, quaint hovels, trees that caught her eye, flowers in bloom, vendors, lovers, children at play.

He ran too. Wherever the others rode their bikes he ran alongside or short cut through areas through which bicycles could not negotiate or were not allowed. By the end of age seventeen though, he had grown strong and fleet, running no longer with gangly strides as he jogged with his friends, but graceful and sure-footed. He made it a challenge and the discipline paid off. In corner to corner races he always won, always crowed and always pretended he was not out of breath. Confidence in himself grew. He had already begun to believe that he was the 'handsome young man' Mrs. Metcalf always said he was and had begun to take note of the girls that hung around his slightly older friends. Still, Elwood would always look back on that time with great confusion unsure of the role he should play, with girls, with his friends and, above all, with his art.

"Go to Europe," Mrs. Metcalf had suggested sternly on more than one occasion, usually upon learning that another of the Gallery's less talented, more wealthy students had left or was leaving on such a venture.

The words however, would echo throughout his life as a reminder of what could have been. There were times when he regretted she had lost her force of command where a suggestion of that nature would soon have him packing. But suddenly he was nineteen and there is an element in the twentieth year of a boy's life that rails against logic, structure or predilection toward any singular passion. What she ordered therefore sounded to him more like a desperate plea to stay as one would in a fit of anger refuse food though hungry or a lift in the face of a long walk. Nineteen year old boys must see what is hidden, must touch what is forbidden, and must hear only what they choose to hear. Yet although nineteen reflected his entire life, seventeen was where it all began.

CHAPTER -10-
Elwood retreats

WHEN MRS. METCALF STOMPED out of Adrian's room those many years ago it was not through impatience with Elwood but a desire on her part to interfere for art's sake.

Interfering was Mrs. Metcalf's life. She could allow no situation to remain at its status quo for very long. Only two years before, she had succeeded in creating, with little help, a national gallery; turning the previous little one-room shack the previous government had conceded, into an extravagant architectural display. However though her natural business acumen would not allow it to come into direct conflict with her own little shop, with the opening of the Government's purse strings, she extended her cause to a fully funded art school and studio and could now invite famous artists from America and Europe to give lectures and critique the works of its students. Adrian was one of the first wave of these students.

On that very day, the day of the stomping out, Elwood became the youngest ever enrolled at the National Academy of Art. Later, simultaneous with his first sale, he was automatically registered with the Belmont Art Society and the San Fernando Society for the Arts both of which duly charged him for membership although he never once attended any of their meetings. (Eventually, he would be contacted by both clubs to 'pay back to society the benefits bestowed upon him by their association'. As far as he could tell, the only benefits they could claim were two pathetically produced newsletters twice a year. They asked him to conduct two seminars a year. Each. He laughed in their faces. Twice.)

His environment nevertheless changed and, with it, his life.

Adrian's gifts and his personal interest in the budding oil painter had put his own career into perspective and given him a greater sense of oneness with his art. The discovery - Elwood - under their very noses all those earlier years had made him evaluate his own worth and to a degree this worth gave him the perspective to value what even Elwood still took for granted. With only his mother to fully appreciate his find however, Adrian's boasts and prophecies only embarrassed Elwood who nevertheless eventually had to allow that he was indeed good - at least in art.

In other areas of development however Elwood seemed sadly lacking. In social skills, whether interaction with girls or the basic exchange of ideas among his peers, his solution to failure was to withdraw. Fortunately, however, he could withdraw in only one direction: art.

Few students - few people for that matter – find recourse in their greatest talents and in Elwood's case the discovery began at a very early age. This was of course neither immediately fruitful nor pleasurable for Elwood's retreat into his art had come about as a result of rejection. Not all jokes about him were brought to his attention but that was little consolation for a bright and very sensitive young boy. Moreover the knowledge did not come about abruptly but in that slow process of social anathema that leads from denial to acceptance. Along the way it breeds various emotions; crutches, upon which the wounded heart leans, eventually becoming the weapons of defence and attack, thrust and parry, that result in bitterness and hatred. And it would have been so for Elwood - he had no doubt - if not for Adrian who became much more than a gateway to fulfillment but the means whereby society itself opened the door – if ever so slightly.

Also fortunately for Elwood, although he could not afford to continue going to school, a somewhat precocious student skipping a grade to be in the same class as Joe, Spat and Frank, he had at least completed High school. Now through Adrian's mother, who had insisted and proven she could sell his early oils even as he continued to hone his art, he had bettered the small pension his mother received and now, instead of being supplied by Adrian's mom, could at least buy his own art supplies. Also in a state of acquired manliness, he regularly bought flowers for his own mother and on occasion even shared a bottle of wine with her. All these too he accepted without comment, neither on his good fortune, nor on his mother's incessant moaning. The one thing he did think about with regret was his bicycle. Yet when the day came for him to put it away, he found it already gone. It was puzzling at first, then suddenly clear.

As his art, his life was unfolding as it should. And then, just as he had come to accept that his life had leapt the hedge that had surrounded his youth, suddenly, it took a sharp turn.

CHAPTER -11 - Las Cuevas; painting Mrs Metcalf

"HAPPY BIRTHDAY, WOOD! WHADJYA doin'?"

This was standard for an opening greeting on the telephone; short and to the point. It was obviously Adrian.

"Whada you doing?" was Woody's standard reply. He did not acknowledge the birthday greeting; it would be too much conversation. Besides he already knew that Adrian knew everybody's birthday and didn't want to know how he knew his, though he could guess it had to do with all those forms he had to fill out to join the Art Society. And though Woody didn't much care that Adrian knew that he was now seventeen, it mattered that Mrs Metcalf also knew.

"Mom's taking me over to Las Cuevas... you ever been there?"

"No! The beach?"

"No, the library... of course the beach. Listen, bring your stuff. You know what I mean: not that wussy shit. Get me? And don't forget your suit.

Mom's doing sandwiches, just like a picnic. She wants to know what you like. I told her: anything, everything." He laughed.

"That's all?"

"Yea. And do some talking, will ya. I don't want to be carrying on a conversation with myself. You know you and mom!"

"Okay. Be there in ten."

Adrian had neglected to mention that Joe and Pete would not be along. Nor did he mention that his mother had been taking him all over the island ever since his Senior Cambridge exam when he had to submit a painting. He had chosen a sugar cane scene in Caroni. Elwood had never seen it; perhaps why Adrian often stressed that it was his best work. However as he unslung his back-pack and gave it to Adrian the news of Joe and Pete's absence gave Elwood even more pleasure than the mysterious work. Adrian fit the pack carefully alongside his own bag and paints.

"I've still got the original sketch," Adrian boasted, still talking of his 'Sugar cane man' even as he mentioned Joe and Pete. "When we get back I'll show you."

The route to Las Cuevas is a winding two-lane road over the Northern Range often with sheer rock-face on one side and a precipitous decent on the other. Awe and terror stalks each mile of travel around hairpin turns and paths through cleft rock.

Throughout the entire course on one side of the road tall trees reach up from below, as carpets of ferns and creeping plants swarm up the face on the other side. Great rocks too either hung above or lay spent after a great, tumbling fall had driven them into the ground or where they were bulldozed to one side of the road. Some were obviously recently fallen, their sharp crystalline edges still untouched by the elements. Others, especially those among the ferns were softened and shaded by various mosses and given a certain inclusive dimension within the earth's structure.

Through it all Adrian talked. In spite of the plea to Elwood he still had to take charge of the conversation. Mrs. Metcalf of course drove; a white knuckling experience she easily transferred to Elwood who rode in front with her. Adrian had insisted on it, but spent the trip leaning over the front seat talking incessantly, pausing only to smile as Elwood hammered on imaginary brakes when Mrs. Metcalf was a little late with her foot. Elwood would look around sharply and Adrian would give him a little wink. Then Adrian would continue without missing a word of whatever line had been interrupted.

Yet for every word he swore mentally at his friend, Elwood was in the same word thankful for what he had seen. And when they had descended to the coast and rode along the safer though not less spectacular view of the ocean, he made a mental note to revisit the mountain road one day in the future, if only to check on what his closed eyes had missed.

Las Cuevas is a long, thin beach. On one end is the village and parking lot. On the other there is a face of shear rock bringing the beach to an abrupt end. In the middle a wide but very shallow brook almost divides the strip of sand. This brook runs parallel to the shoreline for quite a distance then connects to the sea by cutting a swathe through the ridge of sand bordering it. It was to this area that Mrs. Metcalf headed the car by means of a long twin-tracked path that led almost to the crashing surf. This track would not accommodate more than one car at a time and Elwood wondered at every turn what would happen if another car from the opposite direction had chosen to use the road at the same time.

But the final unveiling was spectacular.

As the car stopped both boys bounded out. Elwood paused to take off his shoes and pants – he had his trunks underneath. Adrian had already done so but waited for Elwood then together they ran to the water's edge.

"I can't believe it," Elwood gushed. "Look at that expanse."

"You should see Mayaro! For miles and miles. And, at low tide, the beach is as wide as... as a soccer field."

"You go to Mayaro?"

"Sure! We used to go pretty often. There's a great little village there."

"What about this village here?"

"Nah. This is tiny. Just a few shacks."

They had been walking and now Elwood looked back toward the car.

"Shouldn't we go back and help with the stuff?"

"Nah! Mom can handle it. I just want to show you the river... over there," he panted as he began to run toward it.

The river seemed little more than a trickle by river standards though where it grew shallow those parts managed to appear as wide as Adrian's classification. Elwood didn't find anything particularly spectacular about it but shared in Adrian's enthusiasm even as he hoped they would soon turn back. Eventually they did of course, but it happened just as the end of the beach came in sight. This was where Elwood found his own fascination. Detail! The shapes and colours of the rocks and the mounds of white sand into which long, graceful reeds seemed stuck, waving and twisting in the breeze as they sought to free themselves from their very roots.

"Race you back," Adrian yelled already ten feet ahead.

Elwood almost did not hear him. He savoured his fare and making a mental note to return took off after Adrian. He overtook him halfway to the car, Adrian laughing and collapsing in exhaustion. Elwood ran on, waving as he did, intending to teach the teacher a lesson.

The figure emerging from the surf though slowed his steps. He looked toward the car. There was no one else around. He would have run past her had his mind not solved the mystery of her disappearance.

And then the figure removed her bathing cap and Elwood came to an abrupt halt.

Mrs. Metcalf was a full woman. Not the matron whose authority and quick words demanded respect, but that species directly opposite yet complimentary to everything Elwood regarded as male in himself. Her long auburn hair, shaken out of the confinement of the cap, now touched her shoulders as a stroke of vermilion on alabaster. His eyes, shocked came to rest on her form and in disbelief traveled from sculptured head to finely curved ankle.

"What?" Mrs. Metcalf asked commanding his eyes back to her look of bemusement.

His mouth flew open but no sound would come. The sun itself did not match the heat that singed his cheeks from within. Still he tried words; they failed him. He could only stare.

"Elwood," she admonished with a wide smile. "You're staring at me." And as if to emphasize it she stepped toward him and cuffed him lightly on the arm. "Are you going to take a dip?"

"Yes,' he managed even softer than his softest reply. "Ah... yes," he added for emphasis grateful that at least now he could speak.

"Mom! You look great," Adrian yelled from still too great a distance away.

Elwood fled into the waves. He wanted to swim to Venezuela. However realizing such an attempt would only compound the incident he turned and swam parallel to the beach heading toward the village. Adrian yelled at him but he could not make out why he was yelling. Shark? It was a possibility. He turned and clove the water toward shore. Stumbling ashore he heard Adrian again, this time laughing.

"Where were you going?"

Fighting to catch his breath Elwood nevertheless realized how far he had gone. The car and Mrs. Metcalf were about a hundred yards away. He could not see her expression. He did not want to see her expression.

"Did you yell 'shark'?"

"No! Why the hell would I yell 'shark'? Is that what you thought?" He laughed, almost screaming and whooping. "Turkey! That what you thought? I was telling you to wait. Shark! You must have shit yourself."

If only, Elwood thought. "Let's walk anyway," he suggested.

"No, let's eat first."

"You just ate."

"That was eight o'clock."

"It's only ten."

"Son of a bitch, are you hungry or not?"

"Not!"

"Well I am. So let's go eat."

He walked off, now no longer smiling and obviously piqued. Realizing there was no way to avoid another confrontation and hoping and praying Mrs. Metcalf was not insulted, he followed.

Mrs. Metcalf had put on a robe and tucked her hair into a towel. She was kneeling on a beach blanket and setting sandwiches on plates when the two boys approached.

"Adrian get the pop," she ordered not looking up. "Would you like to sit, Elwood," she asked, still not looking up.

"No! I'll just stand over by the car. I... I'd like to look at the ocean."

She stood up and handed him the plate. "Don't be silly," she whispered.

He dared look at her. She was smiling.

"Don't be. Tell me...," she wandered back to the blanket, "how would you paint that?" she waved her hand at the ocean."

"I wouldn't."

"Why?"

"Here," Adrian handed him an orange drink. "Yea! Why wouldn't you. You should see his clouds, mom. Always dark and brooding, like a storm was coming up. He doesn't like to talk about it."

"Why," she repeated now sitting and taking a bite of a sandwich. "Why wouldn't you paint that?"

"Well," he and Adrian knelt at the same time and took bites at the same time, "there's too much. It gets lost in its own... bigness. You know what I mean. Specifics. I would prefer to loose it in background."

"Eh?" Adrian made a face.

"Oh, I know what Elwood means. With a log or a tree, or even a rock in the foreground as the principal subject."

"Yes... If I take that log, for instance," he pointed to a gnarled, twisted branch sticking out of the sand,

"and if I could place it on that ridge... in the middle of the reeds, I would paint them close-up and have the ocean in the back."

"What about Mom!"

"What do you mean," Mrs. Metcalf asked sharply.

"Paint Mom in the foreground. You look really great Mom. Not in the robe of course. Sit over here." He got up and tugged at her arm.

"Adrian, don't be silly."

"Come on. I'm not going to paint you. Woody is."

"Adrian, you're going to embarrass Woody."

"Oh, give me a break. Embarrass Wood? Ever see Woody embarrassed? If you were standing naked..."

"ADRIAN! Adrian you've gone too far.'

"Oh, Mom. We're talking art here aren't we? Woody, correct me, when last did you get embarrassed? Remember Julie? There was this beautiful black girl with big..." he indicated breasts, "...y'know, and all the guys were, y'know, moved. Even Mr. Lawrence... though he pretended to be angry." He snickered and both Elwood and Mrs. Metcalf stifled their smiles. "But Wood never even flinched. Walked right over to her and lifted her arm and set her hand to look like she was talking. Told her to keep it like that. I think she was embarrassed. And she was a pro."

"Adrian!"

"Well... Wasn't she?" He looked at Elwood. "And then all the fags made out like Woody was one of them; said he was latent or some shit like that.

Like what's his face – Michelangelo. Told me I was gay too. That Artemis Brown! So smug. Woody, you remember, I kneed him in the crotch."

Woody shrugged, glancing over at Mrs. Metcalf and thankful for the sun and the orange pop.

"Mom! Sit over here," Adrian urged now pulling her arm with greater urging. "Woody, do I have to get your stuff too?"

Elwood rose and ambled over to the opened trunk. Still taking nibbles from his sandwich he removed his pad and coals and slowly returned to the blanket. Adrian had succeeded in getting his mother to remove the robe.

"You're not gonna make her look like your mom, are you. I don't mean that like it sounds. Just that you made her look so... mournful. Right Mom?"

"That's Elwood's business, son. If he could make me look that good, it would be an honour."

Elwood's face was stinging by now. It was lucky that he was not required to speak.

"Where are you going?" she asked Adrian as he moved toward the car.

"Get my own paints. Don't worry; I'm not going to compete with Woody. Last time I did he pissed me off."

"Where are you going then," Woody found the words though was hardly able to keep the panic from his voice.

Adrian moved toward the village kicking up the sand as he walked. "To find something I can paint.

Don't wait for me. Maybe I'll paint the empty parking lot."

Mrs. Metcalf took her last piece of sandwich then slapped the crumbs from her hands.

"You don't have to, you know," she said noticing Elwood's reluctance to draw nearer and preparing to belie her own nonchalance.

"Woody, I said you don't have to paint me," she continued a little impatiently. "But if you are going to sketch me, then you'll need to come closer. You get up and I'll sit on the blanket."

Woody stood up but before he could turn away Mrs. Metcalf had glanced down, clearly viewing the source of his discomfort.

"Well," she said as she met his eyes once again, "at least you're no Michelangelo." The words were hardly out of her mouth when she seemed to regret it. But the bulge in his trunks had caught her by surprise and not having been paid such a compliment from any man of any age for too many years the inadvertent words were out before she could stop herself. For a moment she hoped he would not understand or misunderstand - but he did neither.

"I'm sorry; that was tactless of me," she offered.

He said nothing.

"These things happen," she tried. "There's really no need to be embarrassed..."

Woody flopped on the sand, opened his pad and took a swig of the drink.

"Woody! Are you going to talk to me?"

He nodded.

"I mean use words."

"Sorry!"

"Sorry is not my idea of conversation."

"Sorr... Okay. But... I am sorry."

"Don't be. I haven't been this flattered in... it seems like a thousand years. You made me feel good. So don't be sorry for it. Promise?"

"Promise."

But his face was still flushed. It did not escape her and she smiled throughout the sitting. He captured the smile although there was something else not quite there of the expression itself. This he developed in the privacy of his studio. The smile remained of course, but now the something else became something far away as a truth about oneself one would rather not acknowledge. He had inadvertently darkened the smile giving it that sense of inner loneliness he knew resided in almost all of his paintings. Upon her cheek just below the eyes he lay a shadow that perfected it so that it seemed her life was now imploded into that expression which now became as a dream, distant and longing and as yet unfulfilled. Her form too was not so much flattering as revealed. Its youth was explored and brazenly faced as though it would be confined forever to the seclusion of the covered easel. Grace hung from her very fingertips. Movement caressed her shoulders, breasts and hips, extending down through and under the blanket covering the lower legs to the one foot wedged into the sand.

Months later when he showed her the painting he had created from the sketch she had originally thought would be the finished product, she blushed like a schoolgirl.

He would have liked to capture that blush.

CHAPTER -12 - the emerging artist

EVEN BEYOND SATURDAYS THERE was plenty and not all necessity.

Adrian had gone to England but in the summer months before his departure he had tutored Elwood in the various methods of oil painting as well as Colour Theory, Design and Composition. Throughout, he painted producing large though very one-dimensional replicas of the Basin and the fruit-grove above. Elwood too had sketched and painted the rocks and rill and the forest through which it meandered showing these only to Adrian whose wistful appreciation offered more sadness than joy. Adrian himself had said nothing at first. Then one day, almost a year after Adrian's departure, Mrs. Metcalf had suddenly demanded Elwood show her the paintings. There was no doubt in Elwood's mind that Adrian had blabbed. But at least it was a good blab. Three weeks later, all the paintings, but for the few personal favourites he kept back, had been sold and suddenly Elwood found himself famous.

He also found himself alone.

That last year, a little before his nineteenth birthday, Elwood went to the Basin for the last time. Joe and Pete, Spat Lester, Simple and occasionally Frank Biggs - now with their new set of friends - had stopped going long before.

But on that day when he arrived at the Basin where the track forked, he came to that point and suddenly, instead of the left track to the fruit trees, took the right that led to a steep embankment. It was this sudden rise that had caused them to avoid the right track in the past. But now it seemed as though Elwood had arrived at a fork in his life and symbolically albeit physically, needed to demonstrate a new direction.

As he clambered up the rocky terrain he found the track continued as somehow a route occasionally used by people in the area. Never in all their visits to the Basin had they encountered anyone from the land above the Basin although there was clear evidence of occupation: the tracks, for one, and then branch cuttings at the thickest spots. Elwood had no desire to meet anyone but still his curiosity commanded him further and when he finally reached the summit a grand scene was displayed before him.

A grove of yellow Poui Trees crowned the hill. They were in full bloom; a state immediately preceding the rainy season. The setting was of itself splendid and awesome forcing Elwood to catch his breath in wonder, but when he stepped forward, further insinuating himself into their midst and feeling himself bathed in their bright aura, he saw beyond their glow the north coast of the island. It was a scene he would never forget: yellow, against the many hues of blue - the sky crisp, the ocean shimmering, the coastline ringed with white foam and the forest of trees below as a border separating fantasy from reality.

That whole day Elwood sat and marvelled, helpless to capture by any means this continually unfolding majesty that moved without changing. He thought of Van Gogh in his sea of sunflowers and, feeling a kinship with the master, wondered that he too might once have been so assailed by beauty. He drank it in as though he had been among the fruit trees eating his fill then, gorged, needing to sit so that he might digest it all. He made up his mind then that he would not return to the Basin nor would he tell anyone of this find. It would be his and his alone. Forever.

CHAPTER -13-
Elwood's early art

WHEN HE WAS FORCED to tell Mrs. Metcalf that he no longer hung out with her sons, she asked about his art. He tried to shrug it off but she went to his home and inspected what he had been doing. She had tea with his mother and a glass of sherry with him and when she saw his world in the art he produced, she was astounded at the evolution of his skill. The subjects were particularly localized; his back yard suffused with trees that were never there, fallen mangoes among the grass, sticks and stones, and his bike.

There were several of these: the bike itself as an almost three-dimensional image; the bike upside down being repaired by himself – an unflattering self portrait; the bike leaning against a lamppost; and his greatest – The Bike and the Basin – with the waterfall serving only as a somewhat apologetic backdrop for his travel companion.

There were others too that Elwood tended to dismiss for one obscure reason or another: his mother's forlorn face and form, impressions of his friends and a girl he had seen once, as well as various line drawings and sketches of his house - bedrooms, his bed, a couch - and one in exaggerated perspective from across the street. As well, Mrs Metcalf saw again the portrait of herself; the very one she had demanded he keep which at the time of his offer sounded much like a refusal. But seeing it again only confirmed her belief that his depth had not been fully explored.

"In all of them there's an excitement, those subjects that you find compelling, personal. There's introspection in them. The 'lizard'", she explained with a pointed little finger at its gaping mouth, "seems in the act of something, threatening, defensive... oh it's there all right."

"I know," he agreed, endorsing her excitement. "I came upon it by chance."

"Her face," she showed him another painting – his mother's, "that too."

"Yes! It caught me too. Even though I'd been seeing it for twenty years. I couldn't leave it as a simple form. I had to make her do something, be something, sad, anguished. Is that bad?"

"No! Not at all. Art is a living thing. If you have to be excited in it, that's to your credit. It only means you must never cease to search for that excitement. You should never have to settle for the dull, just because you can paint it. If you have to go out and find that excitement, do it. And whether it is in movement or colour, form or the very essence of challenge, do it. Don't ask if you should or shouldn't. Do it."

Yes, he thought, there was indeed excitement. Even in her blush. Did she see it there too?

She noted his landscapes; but noted too there was nothing of the Basin. She asked him why, but he did not reply. She demanded he have an exhibition. He turned his face to the window.

"But you won't refuse me," Mrs. Metcalf warned still looking through his stack of finished canvasses. "You are an artist and I know you artists. You need a kick in the pants to get you started. You think you're not good," she wagged her finger at him. "Ahhh! Look at this," she pointed at one, "this log has personality. Life. Even the patch of blue sky through the trees is alive... you don't settle for just blue, do you? You have to do something with it. Elwood that's what artists do: exploit their best talents. Study your subjects, their basis, their provenance, just like the European masters studied anatomy and applied it to portrait painting. I love your other works, but you have a real natural knack for landscapes. And yet you seem ashamed of them. Why? Because they're too easy? Is that what you think? Because you love doing them they must be bad? It's not for you to say. You need validation? Sell... Then go to Europe. See what the other fellows are struggling through. It will give you all the perspective you need. Go! I promise you'll thank me."

It was at that point that the yellow canvas caught her eye. She withdrew it from the stack and placed it on the easel. It was obviously unfinished and she never asked him about his unfinished work, but there was a strange completion to this one. It seemed that he had somehow used yellow on yellow in some futile effort at creating detail without changing the colour. She looked at him as though wordlessly asking for an answer. But he turned his face away again as though hiding something far too painful to address.

She turned and left the room.

CHAPTER -14 - The Exhibition

THE EXHIBITION WAS A resounding success.

Not only were all the paintings he submitted sold but also certain other works he had included as his earlier attempts which Mrs. Metcalf promised would appeal to that other class of patrons – the speculators. Better than her word, they did sell and he did thank her. But not by going to Europe. Ironically the thanks came even before the sale as he transferred many of his landscape sketches to canvas; the ones he had 'merely scribbled off to pass time'. The exercise and renewed dedication brought with it though an impatience for greater scope and dissatisfaction with his limited area and the all too familiar trough from which he dipped his colours. Las Cuevas too had left an impression that would not be easily silenced and he now determined to capture the sea in all its moods and conditions whether it crashed on rock or surged up a sloping beach. But that would have to wait until he got better. Or at least acquired the confidence others felt in his work.

The exhibit itself was an education in pricing. His first sale was an early still-life - a tangerine in a sea of balatas. When Mrs. Metcalf had priced it at eighty dollars, Elwood had almost sniggered in disbelief. Not in a million years, he thought. Was she going to buy it herself like she did Adrian's stuff? What was she thinking? The paints and canvas cost less than ten dollars. And it only took a day. Who's going to pay eighty dollars for a few hours' work? And such a little piece!

But eighty was only the suggested price. The selling price would be determined by bids. It was not the usual way to determine worth but Mrs. Metcalf had used it before and explained to Elwood that she was too close to him to be objective. The only other way was to bring in an appraiser - a costly enterprise. Through bids he would be valued by art lovers who would put their money on the line.

Mrs. Augusta De Lion stood her ground and insisted that she have the Tangerine. Mrs. Metcalf agreed. It sold for two hundred and thirty dollars. Mrs. De Lion walked away delighted with the 'steal'. The rest of the paintings were just as easily 'stolen'. Mrs. Metcalf had waved her commission, but warned Elwood that next time, it would be business.

When that time came however, Mrs. Metcalf hardly fit the profile of a business-woman; flitting about as a fussy hen over her eggs. The eggs in this case were the paintings of Elwood's second exhibition;

the ones he had kept back, not wanting to part with them. No other show would ever haunt and grieve him, nor satisfy him quite so much as this one. She had convinced him, after some heated discussion, to sell all the paintings and had succeeded to a great degree allowing him to keep only a few that were too personal to relinquish. Yet she could see his distress whenever someone leaned too close to one of the prizes he would rather have not sold.

During their discussions on what he should offer up for sale, she found his reluctance greatest with three subjects - his bike, his mother and the one of herself. This last had also caused her some consternation. Originally she had allowed it as a flattering attempt to apologize for his staring. Instead it turned out to be a too sensitive, too skilful expression of his soul, one she could hardly dare to let sit in her living room inviting the all too intrusive questions she knew must come. She had eventually allowed him to keep the one of his mother, offering to display it only as a testament to his art. However she argued long about his bike and adamantly protested his retaining her portrait. When however she succeeded in the latter, he gave in on all the others. Pique, she thought. He then confirmed it by lapsing into a silence through which she tried unsuccessfully to reach him. With threats and admonitions she berated his 'silliness' and accused him of not being adult enough. Still, she noted his suffering.

"It is what an artist has to do," she finally comforted as one of the 'bikes' was sold. Another was quickly taken. The third, his favourite, went much later to a young girl whose father (he explained) had promised her something from the city. Mrs. Metcalf had pointed out the girl, a hauntingly beautiful child ravaged by an illness from which she had only recently recovered and now begun the long road to recovery. Mrs Metcalf beseeched Elwood to look at the child's dark eyes hoping he might see in them the same hopelessness he had found in his mother's face. But even as she relayed the conversation with the girl's father, meant to appease the artist, it did not. He sulked, mumbling it would serve her right if his wonderful 'bike' ended up in an attic somewhere next to dolls and little tin tea-sets. Yet when Mrs. Metcalf's portrait sold he refused all communication; not even wanting to hear the price. She had squeezed his arm then.

"It's special to me too!" she whispered.

"Sell the other one too," he indicated the portrait of his mother, "I don't care," he said, his jaw set and his lips pursed.

"No!" she refused. "I want to keep it." But far from placating a piqued child she found in that casual statement of hers a desire to have something of his that was more the soul of an emerging artist. There was some doubt, though. Did he need that same confirmation she had given her vulnerable son. No! She did not see it. But was she herself too close? Had she lost some of that perspective that kept him at arms length, which distance had given her a greater overall picture of his worth?

In the corner of the great room she caught the family that had purchased his 'bike' and thought to bring them over to Elwood. Even if he would not go to them, he would not rudely ignore an introduction. Hurrying over, dodging smiles and offered handshakes as obvious attempts to stall her, she approached the large table on which the painting lay, ready to be boxed and wrapped.

"How do you do," she offered her hand to the rather portly gentleman whose smile was incessant and whose arm never left the shoulder of the thin, emaciated child whose gaunt, haunting eyes failed at a smile of her own.

"Oh, hello... hee, hee," the man said taking her hand with his other hand; the same which only seconds before was gently stroking the top of the girl's head.

"I congratulate you on an excellent choice," Mrs. Metcalf continued. "I must tell you that Elwood is very proud of that painting."

"Oh... hee, hee... it is a wonderful painting. My daughter was immediately captured by it. I must say... hee, hee... that the price too..." he patted the girl's shoulders with both hands as she looked up at him.

"I am curious, though," Mrs. Metcalf looked at the girl, "what there is about the painting itself that you like? I don't mean to put you on a spot, but I myself feel something about it that is so personal..."

"Yes," the girl agreed. "You noticed it too? I told Da. It is so unlike other art pieces... not his, but other artists' works that they may be good, technically, but I feel he painted this one just for me."

"Oh! Have you seen many other works of art?"

"Yes... hee, hee," her father interrupted with some pride, "she has been studying in London for over two years now."

"At prep school?"

"No!" he girl said weakly, "Oxford. I had to return home."

"She came down with a case of Rheumatic fever and when it was cured I brought her home. She is recovering very nicely."

"Yes! Da is a doctor and they told him in London that it would be better if I came home to a friendlier climate and of course took it easy. I will go back one day when I am well enough."

"Soon," the doctor patted her shoulders. "Very soon. Now that you have your painting..." he looked up at Mrs. Metcalf. "She promised me she would get better quickly if I bought it for her... hee, hee."

The girl smiled shyly and Mrs. Metcalf thought it was a smile, amid pain, joy and even some regret: a look, she was sure, that Elwood would have loved to capture. She looked around to call him.

But he was gone.

CHAPTER -15 -
success and fame

FOR A LITTLE WHILE Elwood was lionized in the press. The Daily Gleaner called him, the Renoir of Growers Drive. Higher society discovered him too. Even Potter's parents sought his company – much to Simple's chagrin. After all, whose friend was he anyway? Then Aunt Tina suddenly became proud of all her relatives. She invited them to live with her in her large, empty house which she probably had hopes of filling with his works.

His mother did not want to go. She enjoyed complaining too much and her sister would not allow it; she herself having, she felt, more to complain about. But Elwood insisted, though to his aunt's disappointment he resolved to stay in the old house himself. He explained that he needed the room and the privacy, though he did not say it quite that way. However when his mother was gone to live with Aunt Tina, he converted her bedroom to a sitting room and atelier and stopped cleaning up. He had the living room repainted a bright bone white and hung lace curtains and bought expensive furniture. He had planned it so that he could throw parties and bring girls home – enough of them now boldly accosted him. But it was not to be. His first party failed within minutes of his first guests' arrival. The fault he eventually determined was all his. Too much expectation, too much analysis, too much reflection. And too much guilt. Without benefit of experience, not knowing where to draw the line, he chose his guests badly and let them have their way. Before midnight the house was in shambles and the police put an end to it. Elwood was devastated, but his conclusion was simple enough. He had to get away.

But he did not go to Europe. Instead, with the money from the show, he bought another bike – this time a motor bike – with big saddlebags and a backpack for his paints and the thing that first caught his attention – handlebars like a black-waxed Dali moustache. Then he retreated into himself and traveled all over the island searching for that special excitement he and Mrs. Metcalf had talked about. And one day after he had bared his own soul in seascapes and landscapes, brilliantly coloured birds and exotic fruit, dried twigs and wet rocks, he admitted to himself, that he was indeed an artist; adult and independent needing neither friendship nor continuity, for only in this state of aloneness could he share his loneliness with the world. And when one day in one of those rare moments when he bared his heart to his mother revealing that he was indeed lonely she had replied: "Everybody's lonely.

"If you are alive, you are alone. When you stop being lonely..." she added in her usual woe-begotten and childlike perspicacity, "it is time to die."

CHAPTER -16 - goodbye to European art

THE TRANSITION ACROSS THOSE lines of friendship from youth to the early stages of adulthood was not as Elwood had feared - abrupt and painful, and in the hands of strangers. The pain, as he had been aware of it, came before and served only to push him gently into that subsequent stage. The move had brought about a most welcome ease. Too, it was his choice. And although he had not consciously considered it as such, it nevertheless materialized as one orchestrated by his determination. Still, as it turned out, even this was no more than a transition.

It had begun quite succinctly at the weekly gathering of artists in a program agreed upon by members of the Belmont Art Society; the Artistes de Jour, as Elwood once referred to them, a quite pretentious group of unsuccessful 'Bohemians' to whom the act was enough for the art it promised. It was not so for Elwood. Whereas they expressed great fuss and rejoicing when any one of their works was sold no matter the intent of the purchaser or its penurious worth or even the weeks it had been exhibited, he on the other hand was concerned if any one of his paintings was left without a bid after a single show. His association with them was therefore even less than rewarding when he discovered it was on his successes that the group had attained, and continued to attain, dignity, respect, credibility, and of course its degree of notoriety. Moreover as a member of the group he was expected to offer advice, criticism and tuition in the methodology and philosophy of art, areas of which he knew little and for which he had no interest whatsoever.

The one great advantage to the association was the monthly acquisition of excellent copies of the masters; in particular the Impressionist and Post-Impressionist Masterpieces. Elwood poured over them all – La classe de danse by Degas, La serveuse de bocks by Manet, Les joueurs de cartes by Cézanne and even lesser known artists like Caillebotte (Voiliers à Argenteuil) and Sisley (L'inondation à Port-Marly). But rotund women a la Rubens, languid fields as per Cézanne or Monet and cubic images as Picasso might depict, did not appeal to him, at least not in the same fawning way they were received by his fellow artists. And however he delighted in certain pieces by Renoir – he called them rich, bold and detailed – he scandalized the entire art class by calling Gaugen's work whimsical and childish, and although he did concede Gaugen's colours were indeed honest and unafraid, he protested even the slightest comparison with Van Gogh whom he regarded as the point at which art had attained its zenith.

He confessed once to Mrs Metcalf that he found it difficult to breathe when looking at even the printed pages of the artist's works, even at his earliest pieces, those unheard of and unheralded samples of his greatness. Indeed he was caught many times so engrossed in works like 'Two Crabs' and 'Vase with Twelve Sunflowers' that discussions of his sanity had lost some of their levity. One elderly curator came upon him looking at a postcard of the 'Portrait of the Postman Joseph Roulin' and reported with deep concern that he seemed to be communicating with it, willing the thick bearded image with his piercing eyes and wounded lips to speak. Still, in spite of this dotage upon his hero Elwood had no desire to visit Vincent's old haunts. He was reluctant too to copy any of the masters, to even dabble in pastiche. And where on occasion he might examine brush or knife strokes so as to explore the mindset of the artist, he would imitate no one, either in style or assemblage of colours.

However his challenge went even further, questioning why any artist would paint Florence when he had at his fingertips the grandeur of Manzanilla, Caroni and Asa Wright, the ramshackle of Caranage and Laventille, or the bustling life of St. James and Independence Square. "You want to be inspired," he sneered at the society members, "then go to Yara and Matelot, the Spring bridge and the Mermaid pools, visit the Avocat waterfall and the Marianne river; don't just sit here and say 'Florence' like if you go there you suddenly become a great artist." This however was neither heeded nor approved but rather was met with turned noses and superior smiles.

Moreover, once the sheen of aloofness was stripped from him through familiarity rather than earned equality, some members of the group began to regard him as they viewed all artists, as homo-sexist objects; if not already initiated, awaiting enlightenment from no less a source as themselves. Their arguments were standard: to be a true artist, you must be gay; you need dimension, a dimension found only in bi-lateral society; homosexuality is the only bi-sexual outlet for art... etc. But he slipped past their invitations, individual and social, till the day at the studio when he opened the door to a room dense with the aroma of the celebrated weed and the lecherous smiles and decadent gaiety of a scene that seemed reminiscent of a 'Danse Macabre' by Henri de Toulouse Lautrec. Elwood turned and left, not bothering to close the door. He never returned.

Things went downhill rapidly after that although the end of the association, when it inevitably came, was indeed abrupt and, for the community of artists, painful. When they realized that the anti-social, enigma who possessed a talent unlike anything the world had seen in quite a few years, though both anachronistic and incongruous to their mode of society, attempts were made to pacify and placate, not understanding that making peace had nothing to do with his decision. As he explained to Mrs Metcalf, 'it had nothing to do with being gay or not, smoking pot or not. It was all about art.' It was then that he completely turned his face to the vast expanse of the North Post and Macqueripe, the colour strewn displays of warmth and energy at Mayaro, the rage of the north-eastern sea coast, of Balandra and Salybea, and when at Nariva he successfully captured a Scarlet Ibis perched on a black rock against a brooding sky and a dark sea, there was no turning back to anything European.

CHAPTER -17 - Woody meet Lombardi

THE AMERICAN ENTREPRENEUR, PETER Lombardi, had brought his second wife, Angela and their young daughter (by his first wife) to Tobago – Trinidad's sister island – some years before and though the child had shown more interest in the sea-shells of Castries than the cannons of Fort George, this second trip she wanted to see more than just Tobago. She wanted to see boys. She was now sixteen and petulant. She was now, too, not only Daddy's only child, but Daddy's very spoilt little girl.

The marriage to this second woman had been unsteady from the very beginning. Angela Lombardi (nee Porter) was a social climber who had, it was reported, climbed high enough. A tailored blonde with a handsome though hawkish face (dipping nose with stern, piercing eyes) and a slavishly tended, exquisitely sculptured body, she had measured him passion for passion, she boasted, and dutifully tutored his child in all the social graces and, it was further reported, in all its cruelties. However, head to head conflicts with little Judy Lombardi had proven too much for the equally headstrong Angela and there was not enough love in all Manhattan to sustain such an alliance. When therefore Peter wrote to Susan Metcalf and announced he was returning to the island for another visit, one long overdue, she was excited at the prospect.

But it was to be all business.

She had tried that first time to entice such a Relationship from him, one that could benefit them both; she obviously from the distribution supplied by his chain of Art shops in Manhattan, Chicago and Toronto, and he by the unique Island art at her command. Angela had balked. Peter had been somewhat instrumental in the cultivation of this negative attitude through his and Judy's constant attention to the Metcalf family as a whole (sans Adrian who was now in Nice) and his little, weak flirtatious remarks to Susan herself. In spite of Susan's demonstrable lack of interest and the insincerity of his own remarks, Angela was not humoured. At the time she not only had Peter's ear, but had other parts of his body well tuned to her needs - and commands. Her wish, once delivered, was carried out.

But she had over-stretched herself. Had she followed the scandal sheets in any of the two American cities, she might have heeded the caution that the sun was setting on her marriage. Several of Mrs. Metcalf's New York friends had warned of

Angela's claws, but not of her exposed throat. And it was now ironic in hindsight that the lessons she taught Judy had indeed returned with an almost vicious lack of remorse to dissever that tailored, blonde head from the rich Lombardi body.

It was daughter Judy who now had a firm grip on the weak but quite handsome, middle aged millionaire and though he now sought that business relationship owed in no small part to the new, young light on the horizon, she now sought the unique island party atmosphere she could not exploit on her first visit. Of course she also wanted to meet Elwood though she could hardly remember what he looked like. But it was really Simon she liked - Simple - and Spats. And the others.

"Of course Peter and Joe," her father quickly included. "How are they doing?" he asked Mrs. Metcalf.

Peter Lombardi had aged considerably since their last meeting. Then, overshadowed by the presence of his father and elderly uncle, both of whom had benefitted from his financial wisdom, he nevertheless showed his youth in the energy and excitement in his many successful ventures. Now, even surrounded by men of business in their fifties and early sixties, bankers, brokers and members of the arts like himself, he seemed well within their age bracket.

Mrs. Metcalf, on the other hand, seemed to have grown younger, a fact he was quick to point out as they settled in for dinner at Le Bergerac.

The table upon which they would all feast was long and wide and perfectly capable of accommodating them all without sacrificing the intimacy usually denied on long, thin tables. However, Lombardi and Mrs. Metcalf at one end of the table had found two subjects that provided another form of intimacy that was separate from the discussions on business shared by the other guests. The problem, however, was that the subjects were out of kilter, lacking the harmony of discourse as with one end and one means to that end. For while Lombardi chose to discuss Mrs. Metcalf, Mrs. Metcalf could only talk about her great Find. Undaunted, Lombardi persisted.

He was convinced she was using Woody to hide a far more profitable truth. It had caused him some reticence earlier, not wanting to offend her in any way, but eventually he came right out with it. But she would not waver and getting quickly to the point she denied having a beau in a closet somewhere. Pointing out, for his ulterior benefit as well, that she was still married in name at least he seemed content and pleased that she was at least, therefore, accessible. The game, therefore, was on.

"Boys!" she replied to his inquiry as though the simple word would strike a chord in his memory.

"Ah..." it did, "getting into mischief. Isn't youth wonderful? But I can't get over the way you look. Is it some special elixir you have discovered... perhaps I should change my business and we could go into this new venture together. Tell me it's some Island concoction we could bottle and flog. We could take the world by storm."

"No, no... It's just the island perhaps, spring perhaps, Carnival in the air maybe..."

"Ah... I have heard rumours... They make me quite jealous you know, that Frenchman... a terrible painter! Oh, did I strike a chord," he laughed.

"Not at all. This is the island. They invented gossip here," she smiled but was notably subdued. "Of course it was a big moment when he was here, we fussed over him... He is quite well known in Europe, you know."

"Oh, yes, yes... Louie... I have some of his work... quite mediocre. Do you still have connections there?"

"Oh no, that was a long time ago... and only talk."

She knew there would also be talk after this visit but this one at least would be a timely distraction, one she could well afford.

The waitresses came and took their orders. Lombardi's guests chatted and flirted with them and there was great merriment on that side of the table. They chatted with Mrs. Metcalf and raised their eyes at her guest. It was quite casual, perhaps too casual, not the way in Manhattan or in Europe but Lombardi was not as put off as Angela had been on their first visit. This time too he did try the flagrantly Creole dishes they suggested, the pelau with jerk chicken and plantain, and sipped strange concoctions with rum and coconut water as the main ingredients.

"I'll be flying tonight," he quipped. "It's a good thing Judy stayed at your place. She would have wanted to try this. It is illegal here, isn't it...? I mean for sixteen year olds."

"Absolutely. Though not very difficult to get. But I'm sure she would not like rum. I don't. Except in a Planter's punch. But even then, it's not good to make a habit of it; no matter your age."

"I'm headed back to whiskey after this one, don't worry. Now tell me about the young man. I'm listening now. He that good? Really?"

She met his eyes confidently. "Better. A little strange you'll find, but even at his age, I'll match him against the best. Have you seen any of his pieces?"

"Not yet. But tell me, if he's that good, why isn't he over in Paris or Europe where the big markets are?"

"He likes it here. I've been trying to get him away since he left high school, offered to pay his way myself, but he'll have nothing to do with Europe."

"Scared. What'm I talking...? Shit, I'd be scared. How old is he?"

"Just turned twenty!"

"Fuck... I mean, shit! Well you know what I mean. Twenty! Has he been laid yet?"

She blushed furiously. Even her eyes seemed to redden.

"Oh, I'm sorry. I am a crude sonofabitch, aren't I? I mean, does he have a girlfriend who's keeping him back."

"I don't think so. I'm sure he doesn't."

"What's he look like, then? One ear missing?"

She smiled. "No! Nothing like that. I'm not going to tell you any more. I want to see your face when you meet him."

"That ugly, eh?" he winced.

She gave him one of her enigmatic smiles and sipped her own concoction.

Mrs Metcalf caught herself pacing the house like a distraught hen deprived of her eggs. Both the cause and the result annoyed her. As did the unflattering description of herself.

Elwood should have been over at the house early. He had certainly promised he would be. However he still had not appeared by the time Mrs Metcalf and Lombardi with his entourage returned to the house. As well, Mrs Metcalf had had to put up with the inane chatter, antics and puerile games of her younger guests.

Judy, who had seemed unconcerned with Elwood's tardiness, soon displayed a control over the young men. She had Joe and Pete eating out of her hands long before their parents left for dinner; rubbing Joe's goatee and telling him how dashing it looked and oooing at how tall and masculine Pete was she coerced them to get all their friends and throw a pizza party. (She settled for roti and chicken wings though one nibble of a hot roti barred it forever from her taste buds.) She particularly wanted to see if Simon had changed from the shy little cherub she remembered. He had. The thin, elongated version was quite pleasing to her. Not, as Pete imagined in conference with Simple, that it would be as pleasing to Simple's girlfriend - who was of course not invited.

Spat fell in love of course. They once said that he fell in love every second Sunday, but not on every second Sunday did he explain at length to any girl why no one called him by his real name - Algernon, or how the name 'Spat' (not spats as she had earlier assumed) originated.

"Oooo... gross," Judy responded to the telling. Not the desired effect; but still, it was off his chest (as was the disease that caused it.)

Frank Biggs was there too, in the background as usual but at least true to <u>his</u> girl.

The sound of a motor bike caused Mrs Metcalf to jump with relief though it failed to stir the senior Lombardi from his reverie. He seemed mesmerized by the paintings Mrs. Metcalf had placed on the wall in the living room - a show place for special guests, she explained. Much of what she said, including her explanations, he did not quite hear. And as he continued to stare, examining sections of the art with a single-lens device, the smile on her face widened.

"That's gotta be Woody," Joe shouted from the kitchen where he had gone to replenish drinks. "Is the door open, Mom?"

"Yes," she replied.

The door in question was the side door leading from the driveway. Elwood would have parked his bike behind her car and was walking into the little open foyer, a side entrance to the living room. His footsteps sounded - boots; he would forget.

"Hi!" he said, opening the door without knocking and striding in. "Sorry I'm late. You have pizza?" he asked Mrs. Metcalf.

"Hi Woody," Joe yelled from the opening to the kitchen, "ya hungry? We still got a bunch of wings... there's roti if you want one," he added, teasing.

"Hi Woody," Mrs. Metcalf greeted.

As Lombardi turned to greet him, Woody hung his head, almost ignoring the presence and the outstretched hand. This new gesture had begun to puzzle Mrs. Metcalf. Where once she had thought it shy, she now began to see an arrogance, an impatience begin to build. "This is Mr. Peter Lombardi."

"Good lord... this is Woody?" Lombardi exclaimed in disbelief.

"Yes," Mrs. Metcalf grinned. "See! Both ears!"

"Hi," Woody said softly, taking Lombardi's hand gently but meeting his eyes with a daring that convinced his benefactor of her well warranted fear. But it was, in terms of time, little more than a glance, and turning to Mrs. Metcalf he smiled.

"I got held up. I couldn't bring it over. It's wet and I thought I would have to hurry, which I did, so I couldn't' use just loose paper and I didn't have a bag. I need some of those fold outs. The card-board. Just in case. I could keep them home. Could you..."

She nodded just as Lombardi glanced over at her and saw something she did not intend him to see.

"Doesn't he talk a lot," she covered. "Woody, Mr. Lombardi is here just to see you."

"Oh..."

"Oh, no. Not only you," Lombardi protested. "But, I'm glad I came. This is a thrill," he said, not yet conscious that he had not released Woody's hand. "I can't get over that painting. And you. You'd be a God in New York. The fucking fags'll love you. You know what I mean. Come back with me, will you. Let me take you back. Come on, my dear (turning to Susan Metcalf) bring him over with you. The whole show."

"In the first place," Woody said coolly as he stopped Lombardi's pumping hand and removed his, "I don't want to be any God."

"It's all right, Woody," she assured him, "he means it as a compliment."

"Do you?"

"'Course I do, my boy! Woody, you've got talent. Who is this?" he indicated the final painting.

"His mother. He won't sell it. It's not his best - it's one of the really early ones. But have you seen such emotion, such passion in sadness."

"Yes, yes. I... You have that element of sadness, of darkness in all of your works, don't you? This above all. Vincent... self portrait. Doesn't it remind you...?"

"Don't..." Woody winced. He sighed and looked at Mrs. Metcalf. "I must be hungry. I'm a son of a bitch when I'm hungry. If I don't eat I'll be soon calling him all kinds of names. So I'm gonna grab a roti and something to drink. All right?"

She nodded as he strode across to the kitchen. As the loud greetings erupted from the kitchen and carried on to the family room where the others had assembled, Mrs. Metcalf glanced at Lombardi who was now engrossed in the painting as though seeing it for the first time.

"God! He paints like an old man; with a full, spent life of tragedy and a depth of soul I've not seen anywhere. Shit! The more I look, the more I see. I mean, does he know...? Truly, know? And that face; its haunting depth. Compelling. God! When he looked at me I felt like Montezuma had glanced at me. Ugly? God! No! But to call him handsome would be like calling the faces of Easter Island, pretty." He glanced at her and asked with just the hint of a smile:

"Is that only pride in your eyes, my dear Mrs. Metcalf?"

CHAPTER -18 - avoiding Cola; the repair shop

THE INCIDENT WITH COLA came fresh to mind every time Elwood saw the nasty gash on the battery cover of his motorbike. He knew it would give him no rest until it was repaired.

The *Trainers* had become quite a nuisance over the past few years. Like hunters waiting for the ducks to go south the gang of bikers had lain in wait for Elwood's own annual migration to the North Eastern tides of summer. Cola, in particular had taken a personal affront to Elwood's infringement on their territory. Tessa of course had something to do with it and for her part Elwood was a little more than unreasonably annoyed. Still he could not blame the girl for the boy's being a boy. He would have loved to put it completely out of his mind... but for the gash.

The thing was he could not. And that was because of Logan's obeah.

It had been raining off and on for two days and Elwood had been sure he was over the worst of it when he took a long skid and damaged his radiator against a curb. He had slipped a few times but that was just getting to know the rebuilt, re-powered motorbike which was not even a month into its rebirth. The power was certainly there; but along with that kind of power came the fear of it. In first he could almost do a 'wheelie' if he twisted the accelerator/handle-grip too fast. He never did of course; that would be showing off. Otis Maan, the then lone rider (avowed chief) of the Jaggernauts (the correct, incorrect spelling) who often passed him on the Churchill/Roosevelt before they actually met, warned him that showing off was okay for dirt bikes but not for the cruisers. That could get him into a lot of trouble.

"You ever do a wheelie?" he had asked Otis the first time they talked during the coincidence of that first meeting. Otis' bike, the one being serviced (he had two) was a Kawasaki, but the type that can be used off-road as well.

The meeting happened at Logan's garage, a large, cluttered building with wide opened front doors as wide as the wall itself. It was the favoured hang-out of many of the serious North Country bikers, and although its excessive notoriety might have caused Elwood to avoid it, Logan's own fame as a mechanic made the visit a must-go-see. The Indian Chief's former owner, the teacher, admitted he was the best. Meeting Otis there confirmed it.

Otis, as Elwood soon discovered, always laughed at his own jokes, and often even in the absence of a joke. He was earnest in his speech and it was this earnestness more than any joke he might attempt that brought smiles to his listeners' lips. In answering the question about 'wheelies', Elwood at first wondered if he intended answering, but he was patient.

Otis had laughed in his 'don't tell anybody about this' way and was moreover well into the story before Elwood got the point. After a preamble about several girls he had met and the different conditions in which he had met them as well as the unmistakable signs of infatuation, he settled down to the question on the table.

"The firs' day I ride out of Cycle Worl(d) feelin' I have the worl(d) by she tail, I go up to Waller field because I want to see what she could do. Y'know - how fas'. An' also they have the dirt trails there. I eh want nobody to see me fall on meh ass," more laughter, "but I want to see how she handle too. That was jus' before the 'Gymkhana', you know, the big dirt-bike meet in Santa Cruz. Well, you know the bend when you turn into the long stretch? Jus a little before that is a dirt road. I was goin' to pass but I see this car that was giving me some grief back in San Juan. The chick was eyeing me, man. I tell you, if Mister Ugliness wasn't there she and me... Anyway the car turn in to the road. I decide to follow an' see. They stop below a wide willow and I slow down. But the young fella get out and I could see he real jealous an' want to fight. Then the woman get out. An' she

pretty, man. You know when a pretty woman look at you and you feel like superman? To tell you the truth, I wasn't even thinking when I gun the gas and pull back on the handle." He laughed hysterically this time but demonstrated wildly with flailing hands the effect the acceleration had produced. "I din only bus meh ass, but make a ass of mehself in de bargain. Den ah pick meh ass off the dirt road while the two of them laugh they freaking head of and I jus get on the bike, start it up, and ride back to the main road."

That disclosure alone was responsible for both initiating and cementing the strange, distant friendship between them. If not for Otis' unfamiliar surname, Elwood would not have given it a second thought. But it remained fixed in his mind for only those two reasons; the name and the story. Logan's friendship was the same – but different.

Logan repaired the bikes well within earshot of his clients and often while playing All Fours with a group of them gathered around a small table inside the shop. He was a quiet man who at times shockingly divested this trait by loudly uttering comments or laughing uncontrollably. He had listened to Otis in silence while attending to both bikes; draining Otis' gear-case oil and installing a new rad on Elwood's motorcycle.

Known as Mister Logan or simply 'Mister' by the schoolchildren constantly passing through or on the street outside the hillside workshop, or Logie, Gee-gee and several other pseudonyms closely linked to the surname which now stood in place of all his birth names whatever they be, Logan (the one most respectful name in Elwood's eyes) was a powerfully built, squat man of medium height who further accentuated his squatness in the manner of his walking; wide, skating strides, his back hunched and his head always down. When he sat he used a small wooden stool with legs as sturdy as his own and a canvas covered seat that probably had been changed many times and was then also in need of some repair. Around him tools lay in long, flat boxes, one and a half to two feet in length and each according to some order only Logan could explicate. He nevertheless returned each tool to its own box when he returned them at all and this was never while the tool was in use. Upon completion of that job, or the function of that tool, he would then assemble them all and place each in its respected container as diligently as one might deal cards to players in a game of All Fours.

"So how come you din kick he ass," Logan wanted to know. He asked the question without so much as glancing up from the tool-box.

"No man!" Otis replied quickly. "I was out on parole. They would lose meh ass in jail if I even smell him. Wasn't him I wanted to smell anyway. An' she had a nice laugh. That does always get me."

Elwood remembered he looked around at that very point of the conversation and all elements of time and place seemed to fall into an unreachable reality.

It was the one scene Elwood truly wanted to paint yet dared not. In the first place – the one that really decided it - he had nothing with which he could even draw an outline. He had crayons, true, but nowhere on which he could lay a picture. Had he been wearing a white shirt (he had actually thought about it) he would have used it. Still he drank in the scene's other attributes - the banter and camaraderie and the real ease of being oneself, and realized at that point that the world continued beyond the corner of Belmont and Norfolk streets or even his very own hideaway on Growers Drive.

Logan's shanty - in all honesty it could not be referred to as a house - lay almost concealed among trees and a large bush at the back of the workshop. A dirt yard/parking lot separated them. Strewn about this lot several completely stripped wrecks lay among legitimately repairable motorbikes and others that had obviously been recently repaired - some cleaned and polished to a glorious shine. Not all the newer additions were new. Nor of recent manufacture. Nortons and Indian Scouts, BSA's and Triumphs shared the same area as tiny Honda-125's, Yahamahas and Kawasakis. It was here, Elwood thought, that life began for some and ended for others. Here life was not only art, but the effect and performance of art.

It was here too that Elwood devised his traveling show as the answer to his great problem. He could indeed run away without actually leaving. How clearly he saw it! Each detail of the solution complete with it's own solution including the mechanics of the venture; that of adding bags to the bike and filling the bags with paint accoutrements, at first too much, then too little. But he finally arrived at a happy medium, taking with him those supplies he would need for immediate use and eliminating everything he could easily purchase or acquire for refinement or completion of a work. Of course the assignment was given to Logan who screamed his delight then quietly discussed with Elwood the reasons for and subsequently the solution to his dilemma.

Logan's first suggestion was quickly discarded - that he build a type of glass-carrying apparatus that would stick out as a severely 'A'-framed house at the back of the bike. "The whole idea is to conceal rather than advertise," Elwood explained. At which Logan retreated to the inner depths of the shop and retrieving a book opened it on the nearest saddle and pointed out certain suggestions. Elwood attempted to explain what was necessary and from his attempts it slowly dawned on Logan that Elwood was a painter - of sorts.

"A artiss'," Otis suddenly exclaimed. "Now I know you. Lucien! You know, I say to mehself I see you somewhere." He then turned to Logan: "He want them saddlebags you make for Trombone."

"But ah see dem here," Logan slapped the book. "Look here; is dese you want, right?"

And Elwood knew even from the oil-stained and creased catalogue that the shape, size and colour would be everything he wanted. He asked Logan to order it for him and look after the installation on its arrival. The three then had a beer and discussed bikes and Elwood's in particular. Logan was overjoyed at his new client, especially, as Otis pointed out, one who could afford 'catalogue' bags from Harley-Davidson for his Harley cousin.

"Is a sweet bike man," he exclaimed loudly. "Doh have nobody else fix she, nah! Ah go put meh obeah on you," he laughed in his friendly, boisterous way. "If yer starvin' an' cyah pay meh, still bring she in for a fix-up. Ah tell yer. Yer could have a bike like dis forever, if yer take care of she. Doh forget. I eh want to see nobody put they han' on she. Only me." He clapped his hands and laughed loudly hardly able to keep the spittle from his words. "Da's meh obeah."

CHAPTER -19 - Woody and the deer

HIS VERY FIRST RIDE into the unknown, his bags packed and his tank filled, had taken him into the mountains north of Arima. There he discovered Asa Wright, the bird sanctuary, but was soon disenchanted by the sense of tourism and the heavy influx of naturalists and bird-watchers into that part of the Paria landscape. He was more satisfied on subsequent trips through Lopinot, his bike easily handling the broken dirt track as it skirted the mountains and valleys of the Northern Range, finally joining the paved road that led through Morne La Croix to Blanchisseuse. But though he would never completely escape the social or vehicular traffic of the area it was not the inconvenience of travel or the popularity of the spot, nor was it that undefined abhorrence of beauty without character, but perhaps the incident in Valencia that steered him away from naturalism and the treasures of Asa Wright.

That year, it was not a plan he followed but a sign along the highway that said 'VALENCIA 3 MILES' that caused him to whimsically seek to satisfy a curiosity that had not been piqued till that moment.

He had been the other direction with the Metcalfs and knew the low-lands and beaches far to the east. But this time, this first, he thought he should see what led into the hills and the mountains beyond. The road grew smaller as he climbed and though the bike took the strain easily, once the sun breached the range, it began to get hot. He pulled off the side of the road onto a clearing of rocks and gravel. A stream ran along the road, and as it meandered in and out of the bush different forms of life too emerged.

He parked the bike and took out his sketchbook.

Across the street the hill rose sharply to a crest thirty feet above the pavement and stretching to where it again met the road perhaps a quarter mile away. The cut, for so it was, could not have been very old for the plants and vines that crawled upon it were small and short. Wild flowers grew in abundance; birds and animals darted among them, cautious and yet curious of his presence. Suddenly the place, through which he had hurried not seeing anything to catch his interest, was alive. He could not settle on any one thing. As soon as he determined this, that occurred. The distractions seemed always far more interesting than any subject he chose. Then the deer appeared.

He had been glancing down the road where a man had just emerged from the forest on his side of the road. The man had looked at him but as he drew near he disappeared again into the foliage. Elwood returned to viewing the crest and the tall trees framing it. He was so caught up in the almost gothic majesty that he almost did not see the deer emerge. It did not appear cautious but rather stood boldly and stately, looking around before dipping his head to feed on whatever lay at his feet.

Elwood was enthralled. This was the majesty of the animal kingdom; not man. Every aspect of its being cried perfection. Inchoate at birth it had risen with every season, every challenge, every victory to a state of physical property only envied by man; never aped nor indeed attained. Man must only kill it, as he has all things attaining perfection. He almost has to. How else can he justify his incompleteness!

The man reappeared, closer this time, and this time Elwood saw that he carried a shotgun. The man waved with his free hand and Elwood was immediately captivated by the image he projected. He was old, first and foremost. Elwood always found great character in age. But there was something else in his dark, wrinkled face; eyes that were light, possibly blue, that peered out from beneath the tired brown felt hat he wore. With his faded blue shirt and oversized khaki pants rolled up to cover he ankle of his boots, he seemed to be as much a part of the scene as the deer upon the hill and before he knew it Elwood felt a kinship and empathy not fully realizing that the two were not complimentary to each other.

"Did you see him," Elwood asked, speaking softly but deliberately so that his words could be understood.

"What," the man whispered back, his hands and lips conveying the message.

"The deer. Look." Elwood pointed.

The man froze, looked, and then immediately went into a crouch bringing the gun out from under the crook of his arm. The deer paid him no mind but went about grazing.

The man slowly moved across the road till he was out of sight then clambered up the bank to disappear on the other side of the ridge.

Elwood felt a surge of excitement course through him as he sketched furiously knowing the deer would soon bolt and hoping he could see it more plainly.

The crack made him jump. The deer was suddenly gone. But quickly it appeared again leaping off the ridge and scrambling down the slope. It crossed the road not twenty feet from Elwood and with a leap cleared the small stream and disappeared.

The man emerged and clambered down the slope.

"Where?" he asked.

Elwood pointed. The old man followed. He was not even breathing hard. Elwood was impressed. He thought of following but dared not leave the bike. Suddenly it seemed an inconvenience and he was annoyed. Their first argument, he thought. And smiled.

Sitting on the gravel and leaning against the front wheel he began sketching again. The man. The deer and the man. The deer in flight. The man aiming. The man smiling. The deer again, proud and free, sipping at the stream.

He had packed up and was ready to leave when he heard a sound. Glancing in the direction of the sound he saw the man perhaps a quarter mile away waving at him. He waved back. But the man kept on waving. Elwood mounted the bike and starting it rumbled off to where the man stood waiting for him.

He was standing where a wide track met the road. He did not have the gun, which Elwood thought strange for just as he was unwilling to leave the bike, the man must have considered leaving the gun a foolish thing to do.

"Did you lose him?" Elwood asked redundantly.

The man shook his head and smiled. "Come with me."

Elwood met Tanté Dru that day. She was the hunter's 'friend'; a woman with several children living in a ramshackle house at the side of a wide river. The children all ran out to greet them as Elwood, with no room on the bike for the man, rode up to the side of the house. The children screamed with laughter and asked the man all the questions they should have been asking Elwood. The man passed on the questions and Elwood answered by asking as many questions as they asked. Then the old lady appeared. She came around the house and as Elwood went to meet her he saw in the shed at the side of the house, the deer, dressed and hung from a rope dropped from a triangulated support under the shed. A rage of guilt now overwhelmed him. Had he been party to it? Had he too, even subconsciously, sought completeness in the death of perfection? How perfect was he?

"You have to stay and eat some deer with us," the woman said. "You ever have deer meat?"

Elwood was so shocked at seeing the dead animal that he was struck dumb. And yet there was something so banal, so normal, so friendly and inviting about the woman that he nodded then shook his head not caring which action would be accepted for which question.

"So you staying?"

This time he nodded. "How do you do. I'm Elwood."

The woman laughed. I am Tanté Dru. That is Samuel. Samuel," she addressed the hunter, "You introduce you self?"

"How you do," Samuel said laughing. Then he said the names of the children, each name bringing squeals of laughter from the group as though they all shared in each name. But although Elwood would confuse the names he immortalized their faces. On the day he tasted deer meat for the first time, he filled two entire sketch books with the faces of the old and young, the house and the deer, the table filled with food, the old lady in the kitchen, the hunter with the blue eyes and the children with round, smiling faces.

Elwood returned many times to the home of Tanté Dru and the hunter. He brought bags of groceries, fish and meat. They feasted him on goat, chicken, Lappe, Agouti, Manicou and when they could, deer meat.

He would not be visiting them that year. Success had taken its toll. Now that he had arrived at the zenith of his being there was just too much to do.

Still, as he prepared for the year's beginning, Elwood remembered those happy times as yesterday - the life realism of the hunter and the deer, the richness of simplicity that poverty offers – and then he thought of the complexity of emotion that ruled his life; hate, love, perfection, and the male libido that brings out violence in all sexual and anti-sexual encounters. What would it take, he wondered, to cause him to step over the line; to cut off an ear, or rip out someone else's throat?

What indeed awaited him that year? There was so much promise to it, in thought. But the night had passed quickly, leaving him troubled without a single cause. Yet as he lay in bed looking out through the curtains and feeling himself drawn to an end over which he had no control, he saw dawn's light blue haze emerge from the darkness and dance above the distant trees, and in the futility of resolution with hardly a wink of sleep, he threw caution to the winds and rose. He was fresh and alive; no one could ask for more. It would be a good year, he resolved.

His first stop would be Carapichaima.

CHAPTER -20- sandals on a motorbike

THE ATTENTION HAD BECOME annoying. One policeman was at least understanding and somewhat sympathetic. He shooed away the remaining passers-by who had stopped to conduct their own investigation. Elwood immediately liked him. At first however the officer seemed more interested in Elwood's motorbike than in carrying out his duty. Elwood could tell he wanted to ask about the motorbike – not only the unusualness of it but the curious assortment of luggage fitted into the pockets as well as the high back-pack strapped to the pylon seat like an unwilling passenger. But after hemming and hawing around the issue, smiling shy smiles and pacing back and forth, he finally took the plunge, first assuring Elwood that everything would be all right as far as the incident was concerned.

"If anyting, you yerself should press charges," he advised Elwood, "buh ah don' know what Bosey an' Emelda go say. Yer know Bossy; is he place. An'

Emelda is de wide waitress. Ah mean she have a big…" he lowered his hand to about six inches from his hip. "Ah tink she like you a lil bit," he smiled and looked up for a response. There was none. "Anyway wen ah ax Bossy, at first he say you was jus' mindin' yer business an' Tony and he frien' start to harass you. Yes? He change he mind after, buh ah tink dha's wha happen. Is jus like Tony!"

Elwood nodded. "Right! But I don't want any more trouble. You understand? I'm just passing through. What's the sergeant doing?"

"Axing a lot of questions. He kinda funny sometimes. He know Tony, y'know. Buh, ah don' tink dey friends. Jus' know him a lil bit. Like he always causin' trouble, but not serious. You get some good licks in anyway," the policeman laughed.

'Licks!' Elwood thought. *'What would they have called it if he had succeeded? Murder?'* For he had indeed lost control of his temper and for a terrifying moment thought he was going to kill the man. There was nothing sportsmanlike about the use of his fists. They had one purpose: the man's death. But then his eyes… Always the eyes – pitiful, painful, pleading.

"Bosey say yer have a good right han'," the policeman continued. "He say yer's a painter! He say you does come dere sometimes to draw an ting[3]."

Elwood nodded.

3 *an ting.*" " *and so on*" or "*et cetera*".

"So, dha's all yer paintin' stuff?" he indicated the tied-up package of rolled canvases and disassembled frame wood sticking out of the saddlebags.

Elwood smiled this time but only nodded without answering.

"So wha'appen if it rain?" the officer continued as though reluctant to let the conversation lapse.

"Oh... I don't travel in the rain," Elwood said, relaxing a bit more in the affable policeman's conversation.

"But like when it come up fas'. You know how it does come up fas' sometimes?"

"I know... I've been caught. But I generally pull off the road and get some shelter. I also have a plastic sheet to cover up the bike and the pockets."

"Oh... I see. Ah hope yer don't mind me axing, but ah never see one like that before."

"It's an old bike, 1951 Indian. I got it off a teacher some years ago and had it restored the best I could. The engine's rebuilt; fitted with over pistons, rings and pins, valves..." He stopped, realizing the information had little to do with the question.

"Is a sweet bike, man!" the constable offered after a pause.

His own *bike* – an old lime-green mountain bicycle, its make and emblem hidden under a thick, not too recent sheath of paint – stood almost apologetically against the curb outside the restaurant. The other two officers had turned up in an old black Ford Escort with as much painted over rust and body repair as there were patches of original metal and original paint. The newest coats of paint were the official police lettering in bold yellow on the doors, trunk and hood. Yet for all its aura of importance, Elwood did not think it half so attractive as the old green bicycle that stood, proud and efficient, scant feet away.

All the policemen were dressed smartly alike in short dark pants and police-white shirts, except that the two officers wore pith helmets and the sergeant, a peaked cap. Elwood made a mental note of all the colours, the clash and rhyme of them, as well as the more salient aspects of the scene, especially the figures and faces of all the players. He longed to take out his sketchpad but thought the move unwise.

"He takin' kinda long," the policeman said. "Maybe ah better take yer p'ticulars in de meantime. Yer mine if ah ax yer some questions den? Jus' for de record?"

Elwood smiled again liking the officer even more for his politeness.

"Not at all."

The policeman had taken out a small black pad and removed a pencil from its small cylindrical pocket. "So, wha'appen... From de time you sit dong. Bosey say you have a drink... a coffee? An' a chicken hot-plate. He does make some good dhal, you know. Anyway, Tony see you an'... wha'appen den?"

Starting even further back than the constable's lead-in, Elwood described the confrontation with the two bikers.

To a policeman who dealt more with early morning chicken thieves and late night drunks, a breakfast melee must have been one of the more unusual stories to cross his pad, yet for Elwood it was the third such incident in two years. It usually began as some friendly enough gesture or comment to which he would respond with a pleasant enough nod before returning to his occupation. This could be either completing his breakfast, lunch or dinner or sketching as he sipped his coffee or guzzled his beer. However, where ninety percent of such individuals did not take offence to being ignored, that other ten percent seemed to follow Elwood around with alarming frequency.

Their follow-up would be an invitation to join the party, buy a drink or to simply carry on the already begun conversation. Elwood's response, of course when he did respond, would be a polite refusal. Then the mood would change and with it comments would begin, tenuously at first then outright, blatant and as intrusive as allowed. Usually they began with an allusion to his 'Sappats', 'Alpagats', and according to one, his 'Godzilla slippers', all referring to his sandals and their heavy leather thongs wrapped around his feet. But even when he wore his half-cut cowboy boots, there was always his straw hat or the earring in one floppy ear or his long hair fixed with a bandanna or his paint stained poncho to comment upon. Then one or other of the members of the group would come over to 'investigate'. There would be a question, a poke or a nudge - even accidentally -

then the inevitable remark concerning his ears. A flick. And finally a response. The rest went according to program.

As he related the details of this last encounter to the friendly policeman, Elwood found he could just as easily change names and places and extend the scene far back into his past; even further back beyond the day when his bike was stolen.

If he could have afforded the honesty he would admit that the bike thing was transitional and that the traumatic loss only gave it greater importance. Since his childhood he had always focussed his entire being on the items of interest that marked the stages of his life: string (anything from twine to rope), wheels of all sizes, comic books, crystals, lizards and finally bikes – all had elicited from him a devotion that everyone but his mother thought very close to psychotic. But throughout the years art had been the constant; the catalyst. Art seemed to bring it all together creating his oneness, his personality, and perhaps because it was art, and because he was who he had become, all quirky behaviour was forgiven.

But perhaps he often pushed it too far. Sandals on a motor-cycle! And a straw hat! Elwood himself knew this was strange, knew that others would see it as such, yet he adamantly refused to dispatch any of his bizarre idiosyncrasies simply to make peace with society. True, he examined them constantly, yet more as an exercise where one seeks the cause of change, the point at which one becomes oneself. He often sought such a pivotal point in his youth to join the others; the ones of his adolescence - his great find and his great loss. And the other... His great shame!

Which was not for casual thought.

CHAPTER -21- Dutchies

AT THE SAME TIME, almost at the very same moment that Elwood Lucien was being locked up in Carapichaima, a light blue, Honda Civic pulled into a parking spot in Le Poui; a little town on the east coast some fifty miles away and almost diametrically opposite to Carapichaima. A young boy of about eleven sprang from the passenger side of the car and, leaving his door open, ran along the sidewalk to a coffee and doughnut deli two car-lengths from where the car was parked. The boy tore open the door to the doughnut shop and was already at the counter by the time the girl had closed the doors and locked the car.

"A dozen," the boy said, hardly able to catch his breath.

"Slow down, Siba," the man behind the counter said. "Where is your sister?"

"She coming. Put two dutchies in, all right?"

"If she tells me."

"No. Is for me."

"Two dutchies? Just for you? Are you paying for them?"

"No. But she not paying for them either. So put them in anyway."

Before the attendant could reply the door opened once more, heralded by a small bell affixed to the jamb and triggered by the movement of the door. A girl entered.

She was dressed loosely in a plain yellow bodice and jeans that defined her shape yet did not cling to the mounds or crevices of her body. She wore white sneakers on her feet and a red bandanna on her head, each fit casually protecting or providing the required function to each extreme. She was slim and lithe and moved with effortless grace across the room her every step widening the smile on the attendant's face till the girl's brother could tolerate his lasciviousness no longer and impatiently smacked his hand against the counter.

"Doughnuts!" he ordered. "Hurry. Da's waiting for them."

"Coming up," the man said and reluctantly left the girl's presence to fill the order. "You want a coffee while you waiting?" he asked the girl.

"No. I had my cup for the day... for the weekend, for that matter. I have to cut back. Da says too much coffee is not good."

"Even if it free?"

The girl laughed. "Free or not. Thanks, but no thanks. How's your mommy? My Ma saw her in church and she told her she had the flu."

"Oh, she's all right. She likes to be sick, I think. It gives her something to complain about."

"And what about Raza. You seeing her, I hear."

"Well... she comes sometimes. I much rather be seeing you but I hear you going with Gerald."

Siba looked up quickly. "She not going with no Gerald Mohammed. He jus like to come over all the time. I don't like him. He always bothering Mary."

"Siba!" his sister admonished gently, "He's not my friend. He's Menin's friend."

"That's what he says," Siba challenged. "But I seen him looking at you."

"How do you see him looking at me?" she smiled and glanced at the attendant.

"Like you look sometimes at that picture in the dining room."

"The painting?"

"Yea!"

"Oh, that's a special painting. Not like anybody I know or love. Not like Da or Ma or even you. Just something special that's all mine and I don't have to share with anybody else. But you can look at it too. You see, it's mine but yours too in a certain way."

"One day I'll paint like that. Not so good; but special. And I'll give it to you and you can look at it special like."

She smiled at him, hugged his head to her stomach and turning spoke to the attendant.

"Make sure you have two dutchies in the bag," she said softly.

CHAPTER -22- Saturday

LESS THAN AN HOUR after his cell door closed and with only half a page of hastily scribbled lines and shadows to mark the experience, Elwood was released.

This was quietly done; the arresting sergeant had disappeared and the guard who had finally opened the cell door muttering 'yer free to go' had said it too casually to be official. The friendly constable too had disappeared. Elwood had the feeling a meeting had been hastily convened somewhere in the old brick building that had been his home for forty eight minutes - by the desk sergeant's time. Elwood was offered a rather tall glass of orange juice which he accepted. It was actually very good orange juice, a point he made amiably upon downing the entire glass.

"Fresh!" the sergeant beamed.

"Thanks!" Elwood replied smacking his lips to emphasize its quality.

At that moment the friendly constable came noisily down the stairs and hailing, walked Elwood out to the compound where his motorcycle was held. They talked some more of the motorbike and Elwood happily answered all the officer's queries no matter how simple or obvious. No mention was made of the original incident, neither the arrest nor the release. Elwood shook the policeman's hand when they had finished re-packing and strapping his equipment to the Chief. The hand was large and soft and the smile on his face wide, toothy and well beyond friendly. Had Elwood any thoughts of returning to the deli, or even to the town or vicinity of Carapichaima, he would have asked for the officer's name and address - or at least his phone number. But he was sure he would not return. It was off the route anyway.

"Ah hear yer does pass in here every year," the policeman said. "So maybe ah'll see yer nex year."

"No," Elwood said releasing his hand. "Too many of the wrong people are starting to expect me, don't you think. It's become too much a joke for them. Perhaps the next guy will have a friend or friends, or a knife or a cutlass... It's not worth it. Besides the highway should be finished by next year and I like small roads. It was nice meeting you though."

He watched the officer go to his bike, mount it and with a wave disappear into the sparse traffic. Then with a final look for memory sake Elwood saddled his own mount and retracing his route back to the incomplete highway, continued on his journey south.

The small town had been his first stop-off that year and ironically he had looked forward to spending some time there with scenes he had scouted the year before. It had promised much. That scene in the deli for instance – not the fight; the woman. She had caught his eye; the way she was dressed, the colour of her bodice which seemed a challenge. Then her form, angled against the counter, her back sloped, her large backside sticking out above the seat, her head forward, leaning hand on cheek while carrying on the animated conversation with the other hand uplifted in appeal and the expression of earnest energy on her face. He had caught too the expression of the attendant who stood behind the counter wiping a glass with a large towel and listening with a frown as though set to offer his contribution to the conversation once she gave him room. He had caught the glass cabinets flanking them; the pastries inside – red and white coconut cakes, tamarind balls, current rolls. He had caught the atmosphere; the familiarity, the pleasantness of interaction and *laissez-aller...* before the other men made their obnoxious presence felt.

The irony was most apparent in that he had begun the day in the dark, in the crisp sweetness of early morning with the promise of a long pleasant day and a full season ahead. He had places to see and people to avoid, but he felt that certain surge of expectation from the turning of the key to the first rays over the eastern Caroni hills. Yet, by the time he was out of the little town, the incident all but forgotten, another great irony had arisen. With it came thoughts of incidents and adventures he had long ago put away. And the day itself; the supreme irony.

It was Saturday.

CHAPTER -23- Alloo
Pie for the road

ELWOOD SMILED AS HE made a wide U-turn and brought the motorbike to a stop. There along the opposite pavement lay the justification for that smile. Outside the San Fernando General Hospital grounds two trucks, a pick-up and a converted window van, were parked up on the curb a few feet from each other. Perched upon the pick-up filled with coconuts sat a man in tattered long pants, a bold striped, close fitting T-shirt and straw hat, in animated discussion with his neighbour. This neighbour lounged against the front bumper of his twenty-year old van with a large sign reading 'ALLOO PIES' effacing one complete side of the vehicle and a large tray set just outside the opened sliding door displaying his wares.

Thirteen years ago the group would have surrounded it on their bikes - Simple's treat of course - and would have feasted under the guise of a challenge to determine who ate the hottest.

In those days however coconuts were sold from a wooden cart pulled by a donkey and Alloo pies dispensed from a little tray carried on the back rack of a bicycle. But although still practiced in some parts of the country by the ancient die-hards who still reasoned that perfection should not be trifled with, progress had definitely taken over the role of the street vendor. Fruit stalls and oyster vendors now banned from certain parts of each city had found alternative methods of distribution. But the coconut was not so easily ignored and its charge not about to be relinquished without good reason.

The Alloo pie itself has changed in shape and size in many parts of the country but Elwood was glad that progress in that arena had not yet reached San Fernando. Or at least not that part of that city. There the Alloo pie remained the deceptively quaint little delicacy about the shape and size of a Greek potato Latke or the East Indian Samosa. Alike also in that it is a flour product, it is fried and kept warm under a large cloth keeping it soft and pliable and retaining much of its taste. The one, present day difference is that preparations were completed at home before the vendor set off to sell his wares. Now, with a propane stove at the ready, it is cooked in smaller quantities and at regular intervals ensuring that hot-off-the-cooker freshness true connoisseurs find particularly appealing.

Of itself the Alloo pie is as innocent and pleasant as a child's warm smile. However the deceit is soon revealed. In an innocuous little bowl at one end of the vendor's tray, itself covered but more to protect the insect and animal life within the area, sits the main ingredient of the Alloo pie. Many swear the ingredients are taken from various explosives and acids, with bee stings and snake bites and, once suggested, the basic elements of Greek Fire. It is however only Chutney - a mango chutney with, the Indian vendors say, a soupcon of pepper.

It was well into the afternoon heat and although the thought of a draught of cool, coconut milk brought Elwood to that stop, the delicious threat of one or more hot Alloo pies made the drink even more appetizing. A tall, sweet lemonade filled with ice cubes might have been better suited to the challenge, but an ice cold Carib beer would have been considered tops. Still, one does not argue against a cool refreshing coconut. At any time.

Removing his hat and poncho then replacing the hat, he draped the poncho over the handlebars.

"Two! Right off!" he told the pie vendor then immediately faced the coconut man. "Medium! Not that one in the sun. Yes, that one!"

The vendor could have argued that the sun would have no effect on the heavily husked fruit, but he simply shrugged, and rooting out the coconut indicated, gripped it by the stem and tossed it lightly feeling its balance upon the one hand. Then, with a short cutlass held firm in the other, he sliced horizontally, deftly lopping off chunks of the fibrous covering protecting its shell. With a final chop he exposed an egg-sized dome of soft white jelly millimetres from the liquid. Very carefully he then made an incision into this meaty sweetness and handed it to Elwood. With one long swallow Elwood accounted for half the fruit then turning faced the beaming Alloo pie vendor who asked innocently: "A lil Pepper?"

"Let me try it first."

Elwood bit into the dumpling sized delicacy, chewed, then sucked in some air.

"Hot enough," he breathed out and took a swig of the coconut water. Another bite brought tears to his eyes. "Oh it's good," he wept finishing the first then draining the coconut. This he handed back to the vendor who split it into two halves and with an extra cut into the husk provided him with a scoop. Elwood wrenched off the chip and, scooping, removed the jelly with which he filled his burning mouth. The soothing effect was immediate.

"One more," he mumbled at the coconut vendor, scooping the meat from the second half into his mouth. "What do you think?" he asked the Alloo pie vendor. "Keep this one for tonight?"

"Nah man. It eh dat hot. Eat dat one dey, an ah gi you anedder one. Free. On de house," he laughed.

"All right. All right. Mind over matter." Elwood unwrapped the second load of culinary dynamite and stuffed it into his mouth. The tears again. "Mama yo! This one is hotter," he mumbled happily.

"You brave, oui," the coconut vendor exclaimed handing over the already trimmed nut. Elwood almost grabbed it and immediately put it to his lips.

This time he took small sips with each sucking in air and smacking his lips. "Hoooeee," he sang. "Hot! But good."

When he had emptied the coconut shell he again handed it back for the rest of the performance. As the coconut man, laughing, sectioned the fruit, Elwood took some bills from his pocket and paid for the Alloo pie. "One for him," he pointed at the grinning coconut vendor.

"Oi! You tink I eh go take it. You keep dah one for me," he warned the other. Both laughed as the Alloo pie vendor made an incision into the soft skin, filled the cavity with the hot mango chutney then stuffed it into his own mouth.

"See man! It eh hot." He then filled two others and handed it over to Elwood. "For later."

"For later with a Carib too. A cold one."

He paid the coconut vendor and smiling with anticipation packaged his carefully wrapped prizes and fitted them into his back pack. He would have an Alloo pie feast later when he found a suitable bar or perhaps a motel to rest for the night. Next, folding and strapping the poncho to the pylon seat he mounted the Indian Chief and with another wave, rode off.

The burning sensation remained with him though not uncomfortably and definitely not as long as the memory of the taste. The scene too stayed with him. The faces of both men begged happiness; not the impact a more impoverished aspect would elicit, but one of impish joy he himself would relish.

It had certainly been some time since he enjoyed such an atmosphere of friendship which, though severely limited in time and numbers, did not suffer for lack of expression. Usually he found greater fulfillment in the portrayal of pathos; in desolation and pain. Such satisfaction came from a certain honesty which seemed to give suffering greater export and expression. Yet perhaps it fell to the craving of his eyes and his heart, to see unhappiness before the strokes which then would follow as the mood dictates. Still, as he made these imaginary strokes, filling out the daring smile and the touch of evil lurking within, he found credibility in the image. The coconut vendor would be a backdrop; but one that heightened rather than would lend stability and perspective. He too would smile and his bold stroke of the cutlass would provide movement against the underlying slice of acid housed within the proffered Alloo pie.

Yes! That would indeed be credible.

He made a mental note to return to that spot the following year and try to recapture his feeling. But he resolved to do so before he once again sampled the deliciously dreaded Aloo pie.

CHAPTER -24- Stop-off to trouble

THE SUN WAS ALREADY setting when he gave up on his search for a bar. There were simply none on the route he had chosen. He settled instead for a single storied motel adjacent to a gas station on the outskirts of La Brea. He had used it once before - a late sleep and early awakening - and found it to be just on the right side of acceptable.

The service however, was bad; a family run operation with only one member of the family, the father, displaying any cordiality or showing any respect to patrons. It could have been the right method for locals of that area but with an obviously recent paint job and an unused and still unmarked parking lot Elwood was puzzled at the evident success of the establishment.

On that evening an older son sat at the front desk and never once throughout the sign in procedure did he break off from his telephone conversation. He indicated two things; with a pen where to sign, and with his finger the rules to follow. Elwood waited to ask a question but a couple had entered and not wishing to seem obtrusive simply took the key the young man slid across the counter and left in search of room eleven.

In its favour the room was clean, the bed tidy and the hardwood floor swept. Also in its favour was a back door to the rear of the building where, a galvanized awning covering the first six or so feet, a large well-lit compound extended to a grove of trees. It was almost up against this back door that Elwood rode his bike. It would be well protected under the awning and he would not be far from protecting it himself.

Stripping down to a light, tattered T-shirt over his jeans he wedged the door open as he unloaded his bags and brought them into the room.

The owner's house, a large white-bricked mansion, sat well into the grove of trees. It was tall and stately, two storied, with five high, pointed arches complete with spires forming the roof and a balcony strung along one side. In distance it seemed even more sedate, however throughout the unloading Elwood detected quite some activity, at first the ordinary traffic of members scurrying about their business, then an even greater number who seemed more interested in him. Two young girls (somewhere in their late teens he guessed) paid even closer attention to him as he returned from his room. They emerged from the grove along a well lit walk and approached to a point where Elwood could not ignore them.

As the taller, more daring of the two neared to within only a few feet from him he detected a strong scent of talcum and perfume, one that seemed familiar though to his complete lack of appreciation in such matters his only conclusion was that whatever it was, it was applied in customary excess. Confused by her daring however, he searched for an opening line, one of greeting or comment. Yet it was not he who first broke the silence.

"Tek me for a ride?"

Elwood started at the shrillness of her voice and the audacity of the request. "How do you do. My name is Elwood. What is yours?"

"Selina."

He could see her eyes clearly; bright within but in total somewhat haunting between sharp brows and high cheekbones. She continually brushed away the long, black strands of hair that wisped across her face. Like her face, she was in total composition long and very thin as outlined by the light garment flowing about her hips and legs. She seemed to have no breasts under the heavy cardigan she had draped around her shoulders, yet Elwood reasoned she was not as old as she seemed and indeed could still be quite young. Yet the smaller girl standing wide-eyed and somewhat tentatively a step behind seemed more rounded and shaped though she appeared to be younger and far less brazen.

"And is this your sister."

"Fazia. But she doh want no ride. She 'fraid'," then added, "...of everyting," and laughed somewhat tauntingly. The other responded with a shy smile.

"Well, you get your dad's permission and I'll take you for a ride. But bring him back with you."

"I doh need no permission."

"Well, you'll have to ask him, no matter what you say."

"No! He go say 'no'!"

"Then I can't take you. Where's your mother then. Ask her."

"She go say 'no' too. They doesn't like me to go out the house."

Elwood smiled. Obviously she had no intention of fetching her father. He tried directness. "Do you know where I can buy some beer? Cold beer?"

"Carib?"

"Yes, as a matter of fact."

"Ah could get you one. An' you don' have to pay. If you take me for a ride on yer bike."

He laughed. "Oh no, no. Where's your brother?"

"Which one. Ancil or Rodney?"

"Whichever. The older one."

"Ancil in front. He cyah leave."

"Rodney then."

"He workin'."

Elwood took a deep breath and was about to ask where Rodney worked when there came a screech from the white house.

"You have Fazia there?"

"Yes," Selina screeched back with only half a turn.

"Who is that?" Elwood asked quietly.

"Da's Jean. She always want to know everyting. Don' talk to she."

"Who is she with?"

She looked quickly around. "Karisha."

"Are they your sisters?"

"Yea!"

"Come inside now," another voice ordered. It seemed to Elwood of the same screaming texture as the first, yet the response was immediate. Both Selina and Fazia turned and, giggling, fled back across the compound to the large house.

Elwood watched them dart around a tree, disappear for a second or two then emerge at the bottom of the steps leading up to the balcony on which now stood three figures. There seemed to be a conference of sorts then the figures dispersed. Elwood returned to his room.

The pangs of hunger taunted him as he lay so close to the small packages of Alloo pie. Finally folding away the diary he opened one package and tasted. He finished it quickly and rose, filling a glass of cold water from the washroom. More from thirst he drank it all then brought another glassful to the bed. Yet he found it unnecessary. Not only was the pie now somewhat greasy, but it had lost much of its spiciness and as he chewed, not once did he weep nor even shed a tear, much as he would have liked to. Perhaps life was such, he thought. But why? Why is life so much better enjoyed in heat, and pain... and sin!

Making several sketches of the scene outside the Hospital Elwood, propped against the headboard and thinking of the Alloo pie, cold and soggy in his bag, suddenly felt the urge to sketch the house amid the trees. He ripped off the page and began using a general outline of what he imagined the house to look like without the trees.

Then he stopped, suddenly losing interest or perhaps overtaken by another. Absently drawing circles he looked into the mirror opposite. Then as absently he reached into the pack on his bed and withdrew his diary. Leafing through, pausing upon certain dates and memories, he looked again into the mirror and thought of the big white house and the plenty all around. Could one ever be lonely here, where family meant numbers, sharing, interference, bickering, perhaps competition and some envy along with other such lesser sins and as well, he imagined, a very secure love that can withstand it all?

He finally came upon a blank page.

CHAPTER -25 - a night of Selina

ELWOOD'S EYES WERE HEAVY. The diary had awakened him at first, that compelling urge to record his life for posterity, but the events of the day were beginning to take effect and even memory would not be enough to overcome sleep. There was a noise and this time as he opened his eyes he became aware that the diary now lay on his chest.

The knock was so soft at first he doubted it. It came again, a gentle rap against the back door. Then three taps - paced. Moving off the bed he laid the diary on the side table and quickly strode to the door. Opening it, he was almost bowled over. He caught a flimsy dress - a nightgown - and the heavy scent of perfume and talc. Obviously Selina, he almost protested. She however leapt for the bed and scrambling over it turned off the light so that the room was illuminated only by the persisting high floodlight from the compound which continued to throw a rhombus of filtered light over a small patch of floor.

"Doh stand there," she ordered with a little laughing squeal, "come!

He smiled; a superior and self-complacent smile, one smug, aged and wise and above such as she offered. He smiled too at the irony, that his first offering that year should be dared by the likes of her. For, like the cold Alloo pie that had lost its appeal, the tasty attraction a woman might have commanded seemed completely lost in this slip of a creature with large eyes and only a weak hint at feminine allure. He pushed the door and turning folded his arms as the door closed behind him.

"Do you do this kind of thing often?"

"You fraid of me?" she taunted.

He stepped toward the bed. "Tell me why you think I should be afraid. You should be the one afraid. If not of me then your father or your brother. Where's your little sister, Fazia, or your big sisters... I don't remember their names. But shouldn't you be afraid of them."

"Why I should fraid dem? You think I should fraid you? Fraid for dat?" she pointed. "I cyah even see it. You some kind of mammy boy?"

"No! But I don't like little girls either."

Quick, her hand reached out and clutched him

"Hey..." he began, jerking aback and away from her grasping fingers. Yet his quick, responsive movement slowed, perhaps intentionally, perhaps hoping for her success. Something deep and psychological anyway.

But there was no mistaking the prickling arousal she must certainly have felt as a man transmits to a woman. Puzzled and not a little pleased at the quickness of the still growing response he moved closer as though daring it to happen again.

The room now bathed in the suffused light from the compound as it filtered through the curtains rested upon each image in such a way as to render it almost indistinct. In it the sharp thin lines of her face and form were transposed to a higher plane of acceptance. Her eyes too under the softened light now became alive and sensual, a fact that must have had some bearing on her confidence. His stomach turned in pleasure. His mind urged: 'take her!' with the urgency of one faced with a very tenuous, very dubious opportunity. Yet, confounded by the flow of unanswered questions, suppositions and fears Elwood cautiously approached the ethereal figure now lifting the thin garment over her head. Still amazed and somewhat delighted in his own excitement he caught the hand now extended toward him.

Exposed, she proudly thrust out her small breasts and taking his hand placed it on one. In the same fluid move that somehow defied balance she turned without needing the support of either hand and reaching for his belt undid it with a skill that answered at least one of his troubling questions.

"How old are you," was another of the questions that seemed somehow hinged upon the first.

"Twenty two! I'm too old?"

She had no cause to lie, he felt, searching for justification. Twenty-two is never quoted in a lie. Moreover it is a proud age for one who is indeed twenty-two.

"No! Not too old. But perhaps... too easy. Too..."

Her mouth was on his. A very woman's mouth with expertise and demand. He was glad that decision was taken from him. It was not the time for honour or the pride of heroes. He crushed the kneeling figure to him. The sensation though sent waves of guilt through him. As her bony arms encircled his neck a strong feeling of dissimulation and detachment assailed him. He was suddenly too old for this nubile, free spirit whose age had no bearing on time or wisdom. And the soft, hungering texture of her lips belied the fragile, child-like dimensions of her arms and body.

"God help me," he muttered as his passion diminished. "God help me," he groaned as he tried to rekindle it. Perhaps with another thought. But it was the wrong thought. He pulled away wanting to cry in frustration yet, without a sympathetic and understanding ear he could only slump defeated on the bed and hope she would leave.

She had other ideas.

Pushing him back against the pillow she continued to tug at his pants. What lay within was now a challenge she would not refuse. Nor would she concede defeat in spite of its limpness. Kissing his chest and belly her nimble fingers worked him into an erection again, then impatiently mounting fitted him into her. He slid in too easily. This was no child.

"Oy! Yes! Oy," she moaned.

His eyes covered under the crook of his elbow, he groaned in pleasure as she slid in delicious rhythm upon him. Now mesmerized by pleasure and expectation he felt his body respond. The seizing of opportunity again seemed paramount. However real, the dreamlike quality of her insistence carried with it the very definite threat of cessation. Yet to whom was this opportunity of greater importance? Who was taking whom?

"Oy, oy!" Her tempo gradually increased in meter and ferocity. Suddenly he felt a testing surge of sweetness and with it an enormous pounding guilt that wrenched from him a deep groan.

"No, God!"

"Oy... not so loud. Ahhh... so... yes."

Without realizing it, he had seized her hips and now thrust with all his might into her. He felt her flinch and yelp with the sudden stab then let out a stifled groan throwing all to abandonment as he climbed toward the selfsame peak at which she had already arrived. Limp and tossed as a rag doll tied to a bucking horse, her ensuing cries and moans were as breath caught in hesitant gasps devoid of pain or pleasure within which a long, aching acceptance now sought his completeness. The pause and strain of pleasure came in pulsing waves as her face, now contorted in the duplicity of sin and sweetness, she succumbed to exhaustion and collapsed upon him.

Her breathing was heavy, more gasps within an insane, panting laughter than something of natural joy. His sound was different; groans, racking his frame, then a whine of grief as he once again covered his eyes beneath his elbow. She touched his shoulder. In a flash he had her by the neck and for a moment she thought it desire. But he squeezed and instantly her eyes registered fear. But she did not resist and it was perhaps this that caused him to stop. He released her and turned away.

Realizing he had begun to sob she caressed his face.

"Is all right! Is all right. Doh feel bad," she implored carefully withdrawing herself from him. Though yet clearly confused she then hurriedly found the nightgown and slipping it over her head tried to embrace him. But it was awkward, not being able to encircle him. She looked at him for a moment then turning, quickly left the room.

Elwood remained so fixed within this netherworld of dream and fancy catching his breath with each stifled sob, his arm over his eyes, and, in varying forms of sadness, wept till he was spent. Then languidly covering his nakedness with the edge of the blanket, he remained thus, gazing out through the curtains as memories again flooded his mind.

Valencia, he remembered.

It was the place and the time of his first happiness. And his first premonition. Yet of what... he had not a clue.

CHAPTER -26 - Mrs Golan's guest house

AS HE RODE THROUGH Guayaguayare on a patch of new pavement that lingered for miles, the warm, brine filled wind whipping his hair and tugging at the corners of his eyes, Elwood was so wrapped in thought that he went past his favourite stop-off point and had to slow and turn back.

The day seemed atonement and forgiveness all at once. The gloomy, exhausting sadness he felt upon awakening at noon was quickly dispersed under the brilliant blue sky that greeted him outside. He remembered glancing furtively at the white house among the trees hoping in that obtuse way of not wanting to see what looking sought. Then as he turned the key to begin his journey he felt something lift from his heart. He felt renewed. It seemed he had slept for twenty-four hours instead of only five. Yet he was no stranger to this phenomenon for as he had noted before, when sleep comes uninvited it brings a completeness that has little to do with time.

He headed east having as his direction the well risen sun and a vague sense of location among the towns and cities he had visited years before. Passing through Fyzabad, Siparia and Penal he had been conscious of none of these towns except at the very end of the road leading out of Penal; and that only because the intersecting road of crushed rock went south before it went east again. This winding road, more suited to dirt bikes, nevertheless eased him out of the transition begun in La Brea. He asked directions and chatted with children, farmers, sugar cane workers and a bus driver who had confessed stopping to relieve a bladder infection that had caused several such stops along his route. An oilfield worker on his way to a two-week shift in Pointe-a-Pierre told him of a short cut to Guayaguayare. This turned out to be a dirt road; yet it was even smoother than the heavy pitch surface constantly maintained by work crews from the Department of Roads and Transportation.

On the beach side at the point where he turned back there was a small house tucked into the bushes. It was not easy to see from the road; a sandy but well used driveway as the only indication that it existed. However Elwood thought it must be at least easy to see from the beach. On an impulse he entered the driveway.

The path curved but then opened to a wide area where an old blue and white Studebaker and a green GMC window van sat side by side in front of a small wooden house. The Studebaker was supported without wheels on cement blocks, its hood gaped open and its roof covered with a heavy, faded green tarp that hung halfway down the windows giving it a somewhat forlorn and neglected look in spite of the wilderness of beauty all around. To its right the beach opened to running mounds of sand over which the distant sea stretched. The actual shoreline was not visible but Elwood had the feeling it lay just beyond the dunes.

Close by, several people were gathered around a table on the side of the house closest the beach. Children played in the sand; their noises shrill and loud as carried by the incessant wind. Three young women in brightly coloured form fitting bathing suits glanced up, startled, then fell silent. Three obviously older women too stopped their conversation. These women wore light coloured skirts flowing almost to the ankles and loose blouses which the wind tossed high, exposing their brown bellies and white braziers.

The men hardly interrupted their talk as they stood in odd assortments of bath wear some tight fitting allowing distended bellies to overhang the meagre rim, others large and ballooning or clinging wet to backsides and groin. Dark brown, long necked bottles flourished, packed in groups on the table and interspersing with half-emptied paper plates and mounds of fruit – slices of rich, red watermelons, ripe mangoes, yellow, dark spotted bananas, oranges and tangerines - and covered dishes; the half eaten contents of which lay evinced upon the plates. Elwood immediately thought of Cézanne, his *Les baigneurs au repos* - Bathers at Rest – and for a moment pitied the French master his meagre subjects. A man and a small boy arose simultaneously and approached him.

The man was wide and very dark. He wore sunglasses, a wide hat and a pair of large polka dotted trunks over his skinny legs. His expression was one of not knowing whether to smile or frown. The child, gangly and rail-like, had a smile wide enough for both of them.

Elwood switched off the engine.

"I'm sorry," he hailed, removing his sunglasses and wiping at the tears earlier induced by speed and the salty air. "Am I interrupting?"

"Nah, is all right," the man said taking off his own large sun-glasses. "What I can do for you?"

"Well, I was hoping someone could tell me if there's a boarding house along this strip. I've been passing this way for two years now and I was told a Miss Roland ran a little..."

"Golan," the man interrupted. "She name is Meg Golan. Yes, she's a old Indian lady who live on the plantation about two miles back. Just were you make the turn... when you firs' see the shore. You know where that is?"

"Yes!"

"I know is not easy to see. She don't advertise and the sign is a little post you cyan't really see unless you looking for it. All kind of people come up from the city to stay there an' is always full so she don't need to advertise you see. She's a nice old lady with some grandchildren and a son-in-law - Stan. But I don't think Stan there now. He have a job in Rio Claro, but you will see him sometimes on the weekend."

"Thanks," Elwood said offering his hand, "I'm Woody Lucien by the way.

"John Samarach..." he said taking the hand in a firm, sandy grip, "...and this is Binky and over there is my family. We have a little Independence party going on. Come on over an have a drink."

"Oh thanks, but I'd better check out Miss Golan's place first. It's getting late," he glanced at the sky, "and my next stop is Mayaro. But I'll drop in again if it's all right with you. And again, thanks."

He waved at the two young women who had left the group and had waved shyly as he mounted the bike. It started easily and, as he made the turn and gave a little wave before the bend, he wished with all his heart he could be a part of the gathering, not only to capture the form and colour of the individuals, but to share with them the wonderful sense of family and friends he knew he could never again have.

On the road the images remained with him for a long time and as he drove somewhat reluctantly along the sand-covered road he had to convince himself that it would be better to investigate the boarding house where he would not need an invitation to put up for the night. As well, he liked fixing images with borne-out truths and not leaving them to vague descriptions. And without seeing what had been described as a pleasant little retreat he felt he would perhaps attribute greater importance than may be worth. Or he could just as easily pass up on a good thing.

He accelerated to the speed limit.

The little sign-post was indeed on the turn and now looking, found it easily. The entrance through bushes and high reeds was hidden on the turn from the Rio Claro road however, although, unpaved and unmarked (but for the little sign) it would be easily found from the other direction. The sandy driveway was not wide and he drove carefully. On both sides tall coconut trees stretched into the distance, their line ending almost at the narrow road tracks. However the forest thinned as the road widened to a clearing with the river on one side and a well kept, two-story house on the other.

Elwood could not compare the house with any paintings in his stock of memories for it had a stately independence of its own. It stood on an embankment from which the beach and shore line were clearly visible. Three small cars lined up at the front. At the back and side of the house furthest from the sea, several acres of land lay cultivated with rows of plants that at a guess could be various vegetables as well as a watermelon vine, and in the far distance, a blanket of yellowish green indicated rice in paddies, or corn if not.

The building was obviously one of the manor houses overlooking that which, at the turn of the nineteenth century, would have been a copra plantation. He had come across them in Mayaro, Manzanilla and Matura but none so elegant as the one before him.

It was painted white with a deep red trim over doors and windows and along the edges where the eaves met the walls. The banister ringing three sides of the building was also painted red. In spite of this simplicity of scheme Elwood saw as well this principal image against the backdrop of the distant fields and imagined it stalwart against the strong winds from the sea and bathed in the fierce brilliance of a morning sun. He drew in a deep breath and approved it.

As he switched off the bike, the crash of breakers penetrated the afternoon stillness. After a pause, the sound came again. He did not immediately go to the house but listened and smiled, enjoying the rush of cool air, the myriad fragrances and the one definitive sound he would try to capture in a rage of colour.

The front storm door opened and a pale, fair-skinned man in his later years emerged from the house and hailed.

"Are you lost," he inquired.

Elwood walked up the few remaining feet to the little elevated porch and climbing the few steps removed his sunglasses.

"No! Not lost! Enthralled. I'm Woody," he held out his hand.

The man hesitated, glancing suspiciously at the motorbike before limply taking Woody's hand. He immediately struck Elwood as one of those English types whose own social landscape would have little to do with the healthy outdoors over which they lorded. With his delicately trimmed moustache and cropped haircut, his posture, as well attesting to some military training, was vastly more suspicious as his early adulthood might have dictated rather than the friendly, casual demeanour which would have been more conducive to the present time in that incongruous place. He quickly removed his hand; a reaction that did not displease Elwood.

"Is Miss Golan about?"

"Yes. Inside. Are you expected?"

"I'm never expected," Elwood smiled. It was lost on the elderly gentleman. "No! Are you a guest or perhaps..."

"No! Yes... I'm a guest. J. Marcus Simpson."

The door opened again and a small Indian woman emerged. She was dressed in white bodice and long slacks over which hung an apron with which she furiously wiped her hands.

"This is Anna," the elderly gentleman said.

"Can I help you," the woman asked.

"Are you Miss Golan?"

"No! You want to see her?"

"Yes, thank you."

As she turned, the door opened again and two other women emerged. They were both grey haired and overly tanned but smiled at least. The small Indian woman re-entered the house and called, her shrill voice abruptly muffled as the door closed behind her.

"This is Woody," the man introduced. "This is May and Audrey. May is my wife, Mrs. Simpson."

"How do you do," Elwood smiled taking their fragile little hands. The thought of running away had occurred to him as he watched their weighty eyes lose the effort of their smiles. He had even considered using the magic word 'Metcalf' which he was sure would immediately sweep him into their world. He resisted; even such an end would not be considered pleasant.

Once more the aluminum door opened and another woman emerged. This one too was elderly and fair-skinned though slimmer and her features more finely chiselled than any of the others. The red dot in the middle of her forehead quickly identified her as one of the Hindi castes. He had seen men with the strange markings of either a Vishnava or Shaivite - he had not sufficient knowledge to tell. But he was reasonably certain this dot was decorative being low on her forehead and not the sign of marriage that would normally be high at the hair-line. However he had no doubt at least that she was the owner, Miss Golan.

"Yes!" she inquired.

Her voice was firm, her bearing almost regal, yet there seemed something missing from that final crown of superiority. Elwood offered his hand. There was no hesitation, but she nevertheless took it slowly.

"I'm Woody Lucien. I'd heard much of this place and since I was passing through I thought I might see what accommodations you might have available."

"Oh," she smiled very gently, "we don't usually have people popping in, but... you... seem somehow familiar. Have we met?"

"I'm sure not."

"Come inside, please."

Elwood followed her through the door which she held for him and closed gently as he entered.

"I do know you," she said immediately. "You're that artist, aren't you?"

"Yes... I suppose. But..."

"I know Sue Metcalf very well. She's your publicist, isn't she? Of course it's been a long time since we talked, but my late husband and hers were good friends at one time. Isn't this a small world? At first I didn't make the connection, but it's strange how things hit you all of a sudden. May I offer you a drink? Beer... wine, or perhaps something harder, or softer... Limeade, soda?"

She had led him to a large but now quite empty dining area around which on two sides an unbroken line of French windows looked out at the rolling swells and crashing surf and the little rocky islets that valiantly tried but failed to break the sea's rush to the wide, foam-swilled shore.

"Limeade, with bitters and a cherry," he said, taking a chair with his back to the wall so that he could look beyond the room.

"And a dash of Bacardi?"

"On crushed ice if you please."

She smiled and left the room. He could see so much of Mrs. Metcalf in her he wondered if the pattern came with the era or with the standard of wealth to which they both ascribed.

Of such was the room all around him; the high colonial beam ceiling, wainscoting with elegant mouldings, the papered walls and bric-a-brac adorning narrow shelves. All show.

One of the windows was particularly wide. It was to this one that he walked and standing before it drank in the view framed by a wooden porch below and a striped awning above. He had calmed somewhat though now felt he would not enjoy an evening with either the host or her guests. They would not consider their inquiries intrusive nor would they accept his reluctance to talk as anything but boorish. He on the other hand would also not seek their conversation. He wanted only to walk out to the water's edge and wade in the spent surf. He felt that beyond the trees which cut off his view there must be an interesting coastline with craggy black rocks and trees other than the multitudinous palms that created an image of mass without distinction. Broad-leafed almonds and perhaps a mangrove at the end of the river where it met the sea would break the traditional beach scene and perhaps introduce him to another side of the ocean's face. In any event to give up all this promise and exploration to just sit and talk seemed a travesty. And that, he feared, would be on the immediate agenda.

He returned to his seat and immediately heard some whispering. It was perhaps a quality of the old house and its thin walls, but the sound was carried easily from another room where the guests might have gathered daily; a library, television room or even another dining area. Elwood had been too engrossed in the scenery to notice the suppressed chatter which had at first been taken as simple white noise. But once progressed beyond whispering, certain words were now clear and distinct; words like 'Lucien'.

"I tell you it's him," a male voice said.

"But what would he be doing here? It can't be," came another, its gender unclear.

A clearly female voice inquired: "Have you seen him? What does he look like?"

"Just like him, but very tanned."

"Is he black?"

"No. I don't know. I never asked."

"He's good."

"Have you seen his work?"

"Oh yes. Quite the thing."

Elwood rose again and moving closer to the window pushed it open so that the hissing of the sea, even distant, could drown out the buzz of gossip from within. There was a round table close to the window and he sat where he could enjoy a more fully panoramic view. From the table he picked up a small leaflet. 'Thursday', was the simple heading, then it went on to list the day's menu: Breakfast - waffles, cornflakes, ham and eggs; Dinner - Prime rib, swordfish. There was no local fare here. And that too was unfortunate. Dejectedly he looked out the window again. Two birds skimmed the water. Immediately his face relaxed. Pelicans! They curved and headed out to one of the islands where both disappeared, blending into the rock upon which they had obviously landed.

Elwood sought to remember and thought it might have been the same rock he had seen many years ago, the first time he had visited Guayaguayare but from far south of where he now stood. If he could just picture a rise, the same as he had mounted, from which he had seen the still ocean, layered with several shades of green from turquoise to amber, it could be the same. And the loneliness. It was the first time he had wept, truly wept, since the event of his precious bicycle. But it was the solitude that gave him that right and privilege. And once acknowledging it he remembered the release, the long, hours even after he was spent, just looking out at that lonely rock, strong against the buffeting sea, but alone nevertheless. Alone. That night he had slept on the sand; a sleep he described to his diary as the cleansing of his soul, though not of his mind, and the following day he had sketched till long past mid-day when finally hunger had moved him on. The resultant painting, he remembered, had sold for several thousand dollars. Although it seemed more surgery than sale, he remembered he was glad to see it go.

The pelicans rose from the rock and headed further south disappearing behind a grove of coconut palms. Elwood almost changed his mind about staying. If there were two pelicans there would be others.

"You like our view?" Miss Golan asked. She had made no noise upon entering and he started a little as one guilty of taking a privilege not quite extended.

He turned to face her and took the proffered glass. "It's beautiful. Is this a part of the larger beach? Or is this hidden from it."

"There is a point of land to the north that cuts off access from Guayaguayare itself. It's not inaccessible, but you would have to go around the point. Very slow going, since it is quite rocky and the rocks very slippery."

He took a long swallow as she spoke, almost draining the glass. So there must be another rock to the north. It was a comforting thought. Loneliness is often comforted in likeness.

"Oh that's beautiful," he smacked his lips and looked at the glass. "You do have the touch; everything balanced just right. Perhaps next year, if it's acceptable to you, I should like to spend a week here."

"You're not staying then?"

"No. Not today. It seems you're full up anyway."

"Almost. All very old customers. They've been coming here for... a long time. My husband died eight years ago and they had been coming long before that."

"I'm told you have grandchildren. Yet you seem so young yourself. Is it customary to marry very young in these parts?"

"I was married at fourteen," she giggled girlishly.

It did not soften her features nor was there allure in the expression; however he smiled perfunctorily and accepted the sharp change in her demeanour as perhaps an extended welcome for the next year.

There was no doubt his interest was piqued. But the scenes of splendour were fast becoming marred by the very human element that had the uncanny knack of discovering and treasuring them. He caught a glimpse of an elderly couple making their way through the trees. It was natural. Yet outside the window, the wide porch with deck chairs seemed to indicate a preference for many other guests who would spend much of the day sheltered by the awning or the large umbrellas attached to four of the tables on the periphery of the platform. Perhaps in twenty or thirty years on this very spot there would be a ten story hotel with a swimming pool. And they would call it progress. He shuddered.

"I'd better be off," he said.

"Well, it's a pity you couldn't stay. When you talk to Susan again, please convey my regards."

"I will."

"Oh, Mr. Dupres," she looked as she turned and met the gentleman Woody had first encountered, "this is Mr. Lucien, the artist."

The old aristocratic face underwent a rapid change and he quickly thrust out his hand.

"Oh, I'm very pleased to meet you, young man."

Elwood did not match his enthusiasm but nevertheless took the hand offered. "How do you do!" he responded.

"I thought you looked familiar," he stated which presumption of recognition Elwood did not quite believe.

"Thank you," Elwood responded unable to induce some warmth into it. He moreover would have liked to leave more quickly but the old gentleman stood in his way and going around or through him would have proved awkward or far too abusive. "I have to leave now," he said addressing Mrs. Golan as he released the frail, white hand. But the man stood his ground.

"I have been meaning to get a portrait of my wife for a number of years now," he volunteered with the obvious hint of a commission.

"I'm sorry," Elwood said quickly, "but I don't do commissions. I paint what I feel."

"But of course you do," he contradicted. "I've seen..."

"Only what I feel," Elwood said icily. "I really must go." He brushed past.

"My God!" the old gentleman exclaimed in affront, "what manners!"

Elwood did not heed him. Mrs. Golan stepped back, holding up her hand in mute appeal, but Elwood strode out the door without looking back, not caring that every eye might have followed his every move, from the quick little circle he made upon starting his motorbike, to the slow, almost dignified crawl along the sandy road leading north and finally through the phalanx of thick, grey trunks supporting a crescendo of heavy coconut fronds that all but blocked out the sky till he disappeared among them with only the departing sound of his bike to attest that he had been there.

CHAPTER -27 - the community at Mayaro

MAYARO, IN TERMS OF weather at least, was indeed the better choice. It was October; but not cool. What there was of a gentle breeze was hot with the still pleasing scent of brine and decaying sea-weed. Although the little town sat on the very coastline, its main road ending on the beach itself, that day a soft wind blew from the south-west, more or less from the land, more or less just ruffling the water beyond the small breakers.

The tide had ebbed to its lowest point and now the beach was wide; the sky, open and free with gulls, terns and pipers swooping and flitting about or racing along the tidal pools for small crabs and the herring that had been trapped by the departing sea. Where the town meets the Atlantic, Mayaro bay, Mayaro (like New York, New York) is a seven mile strip of beach along the eastern ridge of the island. At low tide the gently angled slope of that part of the coast makes the ocean-front so unusually wide that at times it is difficult to see where the tidal pools end and the sea begins. On any other day it would nevertheless have been filled with visitors; tourists or city families making use of the pleasant weather.

The region, a prime tourist area has remained unchanged since just after the Second World War when access was made easier by the installation of ferry service over the wide Nariva River flanking its northern boundary. The construction of a bridge and subsequent improvements to it and the coastal road did not in any way amend its attraction. The town itself is quaint; a quaintness easily marketable by its very ghostly, unpainted appearance. The few painted establishments as a matter of fact seem out of place there.

But such a backdrop provides a very saleable atmosphere for trade in the home-made foods and crafts tourists find irresistible. In the middle of the little town there is a bakery owned and operated by the same family for as far back as anyone can remember. Since the town was a village at least. They produce and sell coconut tarts, sweet breads and specialty loaves. But in the main they sell Hops bread - a Kaiser style bun that is an island staple. Everyone goes to the bakery from two in the afternoon till six o'clock when it closes.

Though it is scorchingly hot few wear shoes. The street is wide and covered with sand. In patches where there is little gravel, the asphalt is soft and melting under the unrelenting heat. In spite of this, few townsfolk bother with any form of footwear for no matter what precautions are taken, the sand always seems to get inside and cause bigger problems - sores, blisters, jiggers etc.). Those accustomed to barefoot travel are not concerned. Others could be seen jumping toward the clumps of grass that offer some respite from the searing earth.

Outside the bakery the ground is packed tight with dark soil. It is cool, unlike the hot, white sand and the blazing asphalt of the roadway. Too, a little trickle of water runs alongside the crude exterior of the little shop where a line-up is constant. The children play in the water. Some adults too; but for different reasons. Cooler toes, for one.

There is a rum shop (bar) further up the street. One of its specialties is fried shark and hops bread. The bread comes from the last run at the bakery and the best time for the treat is at six-thirty to seven on any evening of the work week.

Whenever he was in Mayaro, Elwood Lucien always made it a point to be at Rico's Grill (the bar) at seven in the evening. He purchases the shark special and with two bottles of cold beer, sits outside the pub and looks down the street toward the sea and the darkening sky.

On this day the sun had ceased its constant flickering through the coconut palms straddling the town and already completely disappeared behind the western hills. But darkness had yet not come. He knew that when true dusk comes, it falls as a curtain upon the earth. Not like the view from

Filette or Macqueripe where the sun sinks into the Caribbean Sea as a slow, sensuous descent till it touches the horizon, then culminates in a frenzy of colour; swift and short lived. *The sky performs here*, Elwood once noted of Macqueripe. *With the flouncing display of a peacock, it seduces the night.*

"Mayaro instead is that gentle, comforting caress you give a baby, just soothing her brow before she closes her eyes," he told Sam Ramadin in that shy, reflective tone of his, as though Sam had been there at Macqueripe for the display that inspired the epiphany. Ramadin was one of the regulars at Rico's.

"Yea," Ramadin agreed, delicately sucking on the glass of rum with connoisseuric appreciation.

Sam was small framed, his arms tight with muscle and sinew and little else; not any semblance of fat and even the burnt skin covering his body seemed paper thin; crinkling and lifeless. Sharp faced and unsmiling he seemed intense and deliberate in all his actions from the slow, cautious lifting of the glass to his lips to the quick, stuttering delivery of words from an expressionless face.

"A-a-ah know what you mean. Where you stayin'?"

"The unfortunate thing," Elwood continued, ignoring Sam while still subconsciously comparing the two bays, "is that too many people don't know such beauty exists, and those who do, don't realize how fortunate they are."

"Tha's right. You... you g-g-goin' by Miss Leery or you s-s-stayin' at de hotel?"

Elwood took another bite of the sandwich. He had laced it with pepper sauce and was feeling the sting. But as usual he sent a swig of cold beer gulping to the rescue.

Adrian once wrote that the Swiss did a curious thing. They steamed themselves to the point of cooking, then rushed out into the snow or plunged into freezing water. Adrian wrote that he told them they did it back home on the Island too; with hot peppers and cold beer. But Elwood felt the Swiss would know as much about pepper sauce and beer as he knew about steam and snow. Still he thought about it. Every time. It was difficult to get Adrian completely out of his thoughts. He was there with painting and with shark and hops bread. And other things.

"This is the best," he told Ramadin between bite, beer and swallow. "I've never seen you eat here. Why is that?"

"Na, man! A-a-ah come here for a lil grog. Why I should eat! The wife have some k-kind of c-cook-up at home. One day you and me. You mus' c-c-come and tas'e what she m-m-make."

In the four years since the discovery of Rico's grill and the subsequent meeting of Samuel Ramadin, the invitation had been extended at least a dozen times. Elwood had accepted. Once. But he was soon to discover that Ramadin's invitation was little more than drunken banter. He had never been to

Ramadin's home, had never met his wife and had never tasted any of her 'cook-ups' - neither pigs feet with okra, salt beef with black-eyed peas, or chicken pelau with Zaboca. But it didn't matter. He was not starved for local fare.

Miss Leery, the straight-laced, middle-aged spinster who ran a little boarding house closer to the coastal route, cooked these dishes as well as curried crab and a liver roti; two dishes seldom found anywhere else along the coast. Her fare was not bad, he had told her, but he had tasted better. He suspected she tried too hard to please everyone's taste and ended up with a subsequent blandness that pleased no one. Still, she had not copped out entirely as had the hostess of the plantation manor on Guayaguayare. It was indeed curry and there was a lime/pepper sauce that she offered to those who dared. Elwood dared; but kept all daring to her culinary artistry. He suspected that she also knew who he was but was not quite sure and her Elizabethan upbringing would not permit her to ask such questions of anyone. He would not offer to verify what she suspected one way or the other.

In recent times, more to avoid Miss Leery's suspicious glances than his desire to paint, he had stayed at the Erthig; a small motel on Erthig road used more for its libidinous acrobatics than to provide rest for the weary traveler. The often loud encounters never ended before two in the morning and often there were humorous exchanges between rooms. Occasionally too, there were screams, often irate, always female, followed by stomping out, crashing doors and heartfelt pleas to 'stay'. The police were frequently there. But somehow nothing ever came of their visits.

In the middle of it all Elwood would paint. In some peculiar way he found an abundance of energy amid those surroundings and at that time of the night. And at the price he had no guilt for the dabs of colour or the smell of the oils nor did he have any compunction over his use of two, hundred watt bulbs to assist him. However on this evening with few sketches on hand, he had decided Miss Leery's was the way to go. He never painted at Miss Leery's. The whole atmosphere was different. More staid - prim and proper. Too, with supper included in the price he felt it inappropriate to permeate the room with the door of turpentine or tack on the energy from two, hundred watt light bulbs and the disruption they could provide in an area where one forty watt bulb per room was light enough.

"I'll be at Miss Leery's," he answered Ramadin finally now hardly able to see his face. "You all fishing tomorrow morning?"

"Yes man."

"What time?"

"Early. 'Bout eight... n-n-nine o'clock. You go come an' g-g-gi we a han'?"

"Of course!"

Rohan, another fisherman, joined them at a little after eight. He was a large, robust man, not old – perhaps in his mid thirties – but with a pot belly pushing his short khaki pants to the very borders of decency. He pulled up a chair and turned on the parasol light commenting as he did so:

"Ah hope is because you lazy and not because you chupid (stupid)," with his customary broad smile to no one in particular. "I was talking to Blaze and Roony and the rest of them over by Tessa place. She say she ent see you in a long time. I know you was here because ah see your bike pass this morning. You went down to Guayaguayare?"

"Yes," Elwood answered. "I just dropped in for some breakfast."

"You painting down there?"

"No. Just some sketches."

"Some boys was looking for you."

"Trainers?"

"Yea. Ah don' tink they too happy wid you."

"True."

"So what you go do?"

"Avoid them. And stay away from dark corners."

Rohan laughed, his pot belly jiggling. "That Tessa is too much trouble man."

"Can't blame her too much. They just don't like me."

"C-C-C-Cola say you run him off the road," Sam spoke up.

"Well, who do you think tried to run who off the road?"

Rohan laughed again. "Cola too damn boderation[4]. An' Tessa don' even like him."

---

4 Bothersome

"That's his problem."

"Well he have a bigger problem. How long you stayin' here?"

"Oh... not too long. Why?"

"Tessa say she want to see you." He laughed salaciously, betraying Tessa's intent.

"Tell Tessa... No! Don't tell Tessa anything. I'll see her next time."

Rohan continued to laugh. "Ah, when you young," he exclaimed, though he was not much older than Elwood. "An' when you rich!" was more to his point, "...all the women want you. Right!"

Elwood shook his head. "Only the ones you don't want," he smiled, "or the ones you can't have. Anyway," he shrugged, "I have to sleep early tonight. Don't forget what I said," he directed at Rohan, "don't tell her anything. And do me a favour. If you see Cola, don't tell him Tessa wants to see me. You guys like too much... what is it? Bacchanal?"

Rohan, smiling, lifted his beer in response. "A lil tailaylay [5]is good for de soul, man. Buh, he eh go hear nothing from me. Da's a promise, right Sam?" He patted Sam on the back.

Sam said nothing. Only sipped his rum.

---

5 A much deserved rest

CHAPTER -28 - a visit to Toronto

IT HAD BEEN AN unusually calm day that other day in Mayaro way back then. A memorable day, yes. But not for anything special that would happen. It would be a memorable day for what did not happen. It was the day Elwood did not go to New York.

It was the day he should have been looking forward to basking in the adoring eyes of the Long Island art society, fawned over by matrons with long names, millionaires with ready pockets and a calculating progeny with batting eyes and elastic ambitions. Instead, on that memorable day back then, he found himself stretched long legged on a plastic chair overlooking a dusty street in the company of a fisherman who, with hard callused hands and a week's growth of stubble, could care less about the refinements of art or its place on the world stage.

But what was particularly remarkable about that day was the art that flowed from his fingers without any encouragement from the artist who, listening to the mundane ramblings from his subject, heard not a word, saw not a line and chose not a colour. His mind, you see, was absent; gone to another place where another world had unfolded in a slow cadence of regretted moments; moments he would remember with not a little shame. And yet, he would often wonder if what happened might have been avoided if he had gone to New York instead. Or what happened was destined to happen no matter where, whether in the frying pan... or the fire.

As perhaps an apology for not going to New York, Elwood had conceded Toronto; though more through ignorance and trust than conscious, informed choice.

Yet, Toronto, Mrs. Metcalf's alternate choice, had been more than anyone could have imagined. Including Mrs. Metcalf. In coaxing Elwood to 'trust them' (she and Lombardi) she argued that Toronto did not have the overwhelming awe of New York. Also, she confided in him, Lombardi did not live there. And although some of the artwork would be shipped to his New York gallery, Elwood himself would not be asked to make the trip. Only a photo of himself. The tease before the storm, Lombardi had smiled. But she had at least wrung from him the concession that they would leave New York for another time.

The majority of his work would be in Toronto for the week-long exposition. But they themselves would not <u>*have*</u> *to do anything. They would have fun. They would visit all the famous Toronto hot spots as well as the not so hot spots - the AGO and the ROM, and if he liked they would go to the Opera at the Hummingbird. Toronto had all New York did, she promised, but without the stress.*

But even the all-knowing Mrs. Metcalf did not know everything. She did not know that Lombardi's arms and legs were as long as they were. That he could reach out and touch anything and anyone, and, without ever showing his face, make his presence felt. The little joke he dropped on his visit to the island, (that he could make Elwood the first truly Pop Star artist) was now a very real threat. Toronto, she suspected, was his concept of 'Off-Broadway', a first stop to test the market and iron out the performance.

From the very first day, (they arrived at a little after seven the night before) the millionaires and matrons were out in force. Lombardi's hand, she suspected. Some jumped the gun. With a gall unparalleled in all the years of her experience two such groups crashed the little late supper the weary travelers had thought up on the spur of the moment. Appearing to offer their services and hospitality they proposed several changes in Elwood's itinerary - the chief being small dinners with a few special guests. They brought with them three young tittering teens, hardly out of pony-tails and obviously not there for the art. It took an Olympian effort in diplomacy to turn down their offers. But surrounded, and with no time to get their wagons in a circle, the two were soon separated;

Mrs. Metcalf to the lounge and Elwood to the bar where a band called 'The Seven Elves' ended all conversation. It took forty minutes of gyrations before Mrs. Metcalf herself rescued him - just as he was getting his rhythm.

Breakfast too was an event. But this was on the itinerary. They both met with John Haggard, the Gallery director who brought neither his wife nor his offspring. But Elwood understood these types of meetings. Social appointments would have to be kept and the exigencies of trade addressed. Yet as they went down the list, Mrs. Metcalf crossing off many of the events Elwood suspected were more 'show and tell' than meet the artist, Elwood began to appreciate her more as his friend and protector than the mother of his good friends and as the day progressed that became more and more apparent.

Only Mrs. Metcalf would know and be able to protect the shy, withdrawn twenty-year-old from the hubbub his art created, the demands on his time and patience. She was well aware that he would not be pushed, that his temper though petty and childish at times, was decisive and too vastly independent to be threatened by deep pockets or convention. She had promised to keep a close eye on him and to be his first line of defence. But it was a scenario rife with unforeseen pitfalls; an Eden overgrown with forbidden fruit, each now ripe for the picking. And even the all-knowing Mrs. Metcalf was unaware of the danger.

On the second day Lombardi himself turned up.

Wealth, in sufficient quantity, has a voice not easily stilled or compromised. Mrs. Metcalf understood this only too well. When Lombardi announced his coming to Toronto she immediately understood the problems that could arise if dissension arose between the two. Elwood's attitude to the demands of wealth and Lombardi's attitude to the duty one owed to it was in effect on a collision course. It was unfortunate for Mrs. Metcalf that she could see and understand both points of view. The danger of being caught in the middle was a very real one. But at any rate, it would not be Lombardi who would need protecting. With her own nodding acquaintance with wealth and the wealthy she felt it important that she have a word with the entrepreneur. He had to understand that Elwood's independence was a part of that very personality in which they both had invested so much. She had to make sure he understood the role he would have to play to ensure the young artist's trust. Because without it, she was sure, the tour ended here. There would be no New York.

Her decision to have a private supper with the businessman however did not please Elwood. She had spent the last days before their trip promising a great adventure, yet on the second day of that adventure she would be running off on a date. It didn't matter how she explained it, that image became fixed in Elwood's mind. He was quiet when she told him about it, quiet through her return and repeated attempts to get him to open his door. She called him a silly little fool at one point. She also begged his forgiveness.

"Woody I had to... don't you understand? Please open up and let's talk."

There was something so cooing, so musically plaintive in her plea Woody found it unfair of her to use it. Confused by this ability to circumvent his anger he now became more angry at his weakness though he nevertheless refused to submit. She persisted almost to tears - another very unfair tactic, he felt. Had she next uttered a single word in that vein he would have surely capitulated. But 'silly little fool' gave him back his self respect, his strength and his anger. He put the pillow over his head after that and sometime later - much later, after listening to ensure that she had indeed given up - he fell asleep. The next morning he was first up, knocking on her door loudly. Still sleepily tousled and angrily tying up her robe she wrenched open the connecting door. He curtly reminded her that they had an early breakfast and a meeting at the 'Y' at nine. Her 'why didn't you answer when I knocked last night' was met with cool indifference and a 'hope you had fun' retort. Already dressed he turned with a 'see you in the lobby'. He smiled when she slammed the door.

They did not meet in the lobby as threatened but in the restaurant. She stood at the entrance when their eyes met and as she walked slowly toward him both began to smile. At the table she came to a stop. Grinning at him and tapping her feet she folded her arms.

"You bloody men," she almost laughed.

He raised his brow in that shy but confident-in-himself look that was just on the right side of arrogance.

She slid into the booth facing him. "Let's get the apologies over with, okay?"

"I accept yours."

"You little devil," she reached for his ears.

He grabbed her hand. She struggled.

"No, no, nooo," he chided playfully. "I'm not little skinny Woody any more."

But he was more than a little surprised that her hand was so small and that his own strength was so assertive.

"Woody, you let go of my hand," she threatened looking over her shoulder. He did. "You've grown really strong you know. That hurt."

"Sorry!"

"I accept your apology," she grinned.

"Hey! That was for the hand," he protested not losing his smile.

"What hand. I don't have a problem with any hand."

He was grinning too hard now and he hung his head and finished the smile.

"All right!" he held up his hand, inviting a hi-five. "Peace!"

She slapped his feebly as one asking the question: 'did I do it right?'

But that day, without either knowing it, both had left their little confined space of reigned in promises and hesitant politeness and almost simultaneously stepped into a new and dangerous world: Familiarity. But that was only the first step.

They enjoyed Toronto. Not as a prelude to New York as was intended, but in the very nature of the Canadian city. Young - by world standards - Toronto appealed to Elwood on several plateaus; in its very location beside a great lake, its tall buildings and bustling activity from Yonge Street to Spadina, and especially in its multi-culturalism. At the ROM (the Royal Ontario Museum) every second face was a different nationality. A stickler for nuances he detected strong differences among those of the same racial category - Asian, Negro and Caucasian. And in the thousands of sub-categories he marvelled at the independent differences within each. It was Trinidad - though on a larger scale - and, but for the idiosyncrasies of language and culture, he could very easily have been back home. When he eventually chose to remain home rather than visit 'the Big Apple', he was consoled that at least he had seen the world.

CHAPTER -29 - Mrs Joan, gossip about Elwood

IN THE WORLD OF Art and the politics of Fame, Joan Mathias was now important; not only as the mother of a famous artist, but as a font of information pertaining to her son, an opener of select doors otherwise closed to the clamouring public, a holder of secrets, a teller of histories, a woman of resource, of point and counterpoint. Important!

In truth, Joan Mathias could now not only afford the airs that gave her greater import as the mother of the famous figure but she often shared insights with members of society who previously would have regarded her with pity; a sentiment more in keeping with her previously woeful appearance. This too however had changed - the usually heavy application of make-up and regular visits to the salons out of walking distance transforming her from the bed-ridden misbegot to a somewhat envied swan. She now wore regular clothes too; gowns, dresses, in styles demanded by Vogue, Flare and

Elle as seasonal, and determined more by the time of day rather than the limitations of a pocketbook. As a result of this she had grown younger too and in this new-found youth had netted at least one ardent admirer from whom she diligently hid her age and consequently, her son whose age would somehow betray that most protected aspect. The fact that the middle-aged gentleman asked constantly about Elwood and seemed to know a considerable lot about him did not impinge upon this guardianship. She retained her reticence as a strength of character as well as a principle that her life was hers, her son's his, and never the twain should meet. Aunt Tina and her circle of friends, who met constantly at the house, had different principles.

And of course there were other less important figures involved who had their own reasons for regarding Elwood's mother as special. Mrs. Metcalf, for instance, who had heard a rumour that Elwood was involved with a girl and wanted to know whether or not the rumour was true. Not that it was really any of her business, Joan thought but did not say. After all, Mrs Metcalf did have a stake in the young painter would have some rights. And of course if anyone should know about it, it was only natural that Elwood's mother would be the best source. Little did she know!

But although it had taken the first five minutes of the phone call to get to the point and in spite of the fact that Joan Mathias was the least person in all the world to know anything about her famous son, she had enjoyed every second's feeling of importance.

The call had come at an inconvenient time - interrupting a most important part of her soap - and even listening to only one part of Mrs. Metcalf's 'inquisition' she could make sense of only half of both distractions. However by the time she was finally allowed to hang up she had lost all patience with the insistent Mrs. Metcalf.

"Who was it," Joan's sister inquired breezing into the drawing room with two other 'girls' in tow. Mrs. Ann 'Peak' Beasley of the Beasley School of Etiquette and Marguerite Lo, recently widowed wife of Justice Bryan Lo, had been Aunt Tina's friends since high school.

It was only recently that the group had come together after the many years and diverse positions that had separated them. This new assembly might too have been seen as a direct result of Elwood's notoriety, but in fact he was never considered a healthy subject of conversation, or at least, not in terms of his scandalous escapades. Or did this all come about because of them!

Marguerite carried a tray of tea with four cups and saucers and 'Peak' carried one with folded hand-cloths and a small pitcher of milk. Aunt Tina carried herself directly to the couch on which Joan sat and directed the girls to the coffee table around which other chairs and a divan were tightly clustered. The three friends were both of and very much for society and clung to all the graces, frills and pomposity it required. Their cumulative advice and unabashed interference into Joan's life were neither limited to propriety nor even to very basic good taste. Suggestions were always regarded as taken and inquiries never left unanswered.

"That woman again," Joan answered, now hopelessly deprived of the Soap's story-line from which she had hoped to resolve by logic or perhaps some matter of dialogue that would reveal what happened throughout all the interruptions.

"What did she want this time?" Aunt Tina continued seating herself on the couch on which Joan now curled drawing up her feet to give her sister the room her wide posterior demanded. Marguerite had in the meantime placed the tray on the table and had begun to pour as Ann passed along the cups in their saucers.

"Wants to know what Elwood's doing of course."

"What did you tell her?"

"Nothing! I know nothing. He never calls, you know. I see him once a year, if that. She sees him more than me, and I'm his mother. Was on the tip of my tongue to make up something, but..."

"But what?"

Joan sighed. "Oh, she said something about Elwood and some girl... some woman in Mayaro."

Mrs. Beasley squealed with delight. "Something juicy?" she asked.

"Oh, quiet Ann," Aunt Tina chided. "I hope it's nothing disgraceful."

"At least he's not in town," Ann persisted, not completely losing her inquiring comportment.

"And at least he's not getting into fights," Marguerite Lo observed. "Maybe he should get married and stop all this nonsense. If Pudge was still here I would have asked him to talk to the young man. But..." She sighed and left the sentence unresolved though as in some continuing thought reflected: "I miss the old sod."

The others afforded her the little tour of memory. These had become less frequent now and in spite of the common knowledge that she did not think much of the afore mentioned Pudge when he was alive, they allowed her the pretence of affection now that he was dead. None of the others would add to it of course. It was the only demonstration of its kind any of them had displayed toward any of the men in their lives. It would have to suffice.

"Cribbage?" Tina asked expectantly.

Marguerite removed the board from its enclosure, a small hutch within the side table. She herself distributed the pegs, allowing each of the others to place them in their starting positions.

"She thinks Elwood has a girl in Mayaro."

"Oh," Aunt Tina exclaimed simultaneous with Ann's little catch and Marguerite's sharp look.

"Yes!" Joan continued as though an unimportant tidbit had escaped her lips. "She thinks he might have told me. When has he told me anything! Oh, children!"

Marguerite shuffled the cards; a slow, absent activity that, had the game been in progress, would have been met with some impatience.

"Do you think there's something to it?" she asked.

Joan shrugged. "Could be. Last time I visited he had a bag-full of letters from all these... y'know, little miss hot stuffs with their... You have no idea. I could never see myself saying those things."

"You read his letters?" Tina asked.

"Some. Must have been thousands there in a big garbage bag. Stuffed. He put it in the bedroom... my old room... in a corner. A lot of them not even opened. Could you imagine? And the things they said. And photos..." This was said almost aside accompanied by a severe, knowing glance with which she hoped to explain the nature of the photographs.

"Nudes?" Ann asked demanding the clarity or at least some form of elucidation.

She nodded.

Marguerite dealt the cards. "You keep score," she directed at Ann.

Ann may very well not have heard her. "Did you ask him what he's going to do with all the letters?" she asked.

Joan shrugged. "Not my business."

"But..."

"Let's play."

Joan put her feet on the floor and leaned on her knees.

"Children!" she scowled, offering it as a seal of closure on the subject.

CHAPTER -30 – A call to Mrs Metcalf

ELWOOD WENT TO BED but did not sleep early. When he saw ten o'clock had come and could not remember what was on the page he had last read, he arose and went downstairs to the old Mansion's foyer which Miss Leery used now as a reception area. All the lower rooms were large. The old living room in particular was now a parlour in which two of the guests, an old couple, looked at television. There were at least half a dozen large, deep single chairs and two similar divans, two desks (presumably for writing letters), a somewhat lavish coat and umbrella stand and a large bookcase filled with books. He passed through the room and nodded at the couple who both nodded back each with one of those knowing smiles that always annoyed Elwood.

Miss Leery was at the reception desk shutting it down for the night. However when she saw him her eyes lit up. That too annoyed Elwood. He smiled though weekly and nodded.

"May I please use the phone, Iris?" he asked. She had insisted he call her by her first name and rather than make an issue of it, he had extended the same courtesy.

"Of course, Woody. A private call?"

"Yes, if you don't mind."

"Shall I dial the number for you?"

"No. Don't trouble yourself."

"Give me a second then..." she busied about, closing the door to a little safe into which she had placed the register and other items from the desk. Then with a little skip, danced out of his way and entered the parlour.

Elwood dialled the operator and requesting a 'cost-of-call' gave her the number. During the early rings he second guessed his decision. The time of night was not one of his considerations. He had often called even later and had been happily received. However as he had placed more importance on his own schedule, he had found it more and more difficult to take even a few minutes to make the simple call. The real problem however was not in the time but in the complexity of the call. Any call. They often ended in tears. Compounding its difficulty was now the infrequency of the calls themselves. He wondered how this one would be received... if she answered. On the forth ring she picked up.

"Hello!"

Her voice was not sleepy, as though she had been expecting him to call. Another annoyance.

"Hi! It's Woody. Did I wake you?"

"No!"

It was rote; except that in the early days she would ask him to speak softly because she *'did not want to disturb the tall stranger sleeping next to her'*. It was a playfulness he once found attractive and familiar and he would respond by telling her the voluptuous girl in bed with him was just a child and he needed a woman. But all that had ended long ago.

"I should have called yesterday but I painted all night."

"Joseph told me you called him."

Joe now ran the gallery, though not fully. He was no art connoisseur. However he did have a natural head for business which was further augmented by three years at the business college in Canada. Her words however did not mean that Elwood should not have called Joe, but that having the time to call him, he should have found the time to call her.

"I had two works I thought you should see."

"Couldn't you have brought them over?"

"No. I finished them both in Rio Claro and shipped them. One is a simple house which an old man is painting. I sketched him and then with his permission I decided to paint there and then. His wife kept bringing me drinks – shining bush tea and limeade – and there were small children, curious at first, to see what I was doing, but they did not bother me much only asked a lot of questions. The old lady insisted I sleep inside on an old bed of husked coconuts. Now there was a subject for art. I thought of it, but didn't. Just sketched it. Next day I finished the painting and moved on. But I could have stayed there a week. I gave them a hundred dollars; I must remember to tell Roundtree – expenses, you know. Although I hope he doesn't expect me to get a receipt. The old lady did not want to take it but the man did. The other painting: men at the pitch lake. I exaggerated the blacks as usual but managed to capture the individual figures; even their eyes and noses. I'm proud of both."

"I saw them."

"...And."

"You know they're good. You don't need me to tell you that. You haven't needed me to tell you anything lately."

Woody breathed hard. "What do you want me to do? Give up and come home?"

He could hear the little gasp on the other end as she tried to calm her voice. "No! Don't be a fool. But... Oh Woody. I have these feelings... You know! Oh, I'm so jealous now. Who is...? Oh, I don't want to know. All these rumours! I know you don't have anyone, but I can't think of you without thinking you're with someone else, someone young and pretty, doing all those things with her that..."

"Stop! Please! This isn't doing us any good. This is why I can't come home yet. I think of things... I want to be inside... This isn't doing us any good. Please tell me something else. For both our sakes. What... what are you doing with the paintings?"

The pause and sniffing meant that she was composing herself again. "I'm... going... to send '*The Old Man and His House*' to Adrian. I don't know about '*The Pitch Lake*'. That man in it is so haunting. I should... congratulate you. Is it what you intended? No! I'm sorry I asked. Of course it is. But there's so much of you in him. It makes me sad to think of you that way. Incidentally, Adrian sold '*Little dog on a log*', he called it. I think we should start sending all your major works to him."

"What about New York then."

"You know what he wants. You don't care anyway. You're not going to give in. Neither am I. Besides, Adrian should come first."

"Did you tell him what I said?"

"Yes. But he can't come, he said. He said the business is doing so well. He said 'when he gets a chance'."

"He's been saying that for three years now."

"You don't have to tell me that."

"Why don't you go to him then."

"Oh Woody, it would break my heart. He would be happy and I would want him to come home. And I would want to come home. To you. Oh Woody, is there any truth...? Oh, come home... tonight. Just leave everything and come."

"Please..."

"Don't you want to anymore? Why must all the men I love leave me? Oh why? For loving? For loving..."

He listened to her cry then and his eyes reddened for her sorrow. He would have told her that her sorrow had made his heart heavy but she already knew. And she would repeat again her regret for calling him a *'reckless child'.* He did not want to hear that but he thought of the irony; that in his control and resolve he was now the adult and she, through longing and loneliness, the child. And there was nothing he could do to salve her pain.

He stayed, long and silent but at least there on the line. Till he heard the gentle 'click'.

The single forty watt bulb softened his face in the mirror as he sketched. Even so he detected the hard lines that reflected more than age. *Frowning makes you look like an old man,* his mother said a long time ago. *Guilt,* he remembered thinking at that time; *not frowning.* Now he did not frown nor did he feel guilt. But the effect was indeed there. Frankie Biggs! Strange how his face suddenly came to mind. The mirror perhaps.

It seemed a million years ago when he looked into that other mirror. But he remembered crying then as he saw his face in it. Frankie Biggs! Only Joe had called him Frankie. Then he died in that terrible cycling accident in Couva as he and his group were training for the Olympics and he became Frankie to everyone else. And it was with the thought of the diminutive sounding 'Frankie' that he had wept into the mirror. He did not paint that face then, interesting as it was. It was too unflattering, he thought. Besides, how would it help Frankie to paint an ugly face? Yet even in sorrow then it was at least young. He was twenty-three.

Now he was days away from his twenty-ninth birthday. And the face reflected back from that mirror was, not the young face that wept for Frankie Biggs, but the face of an old man who had wasted his years in guilt. The end would be soon, as old men saw it, not the warrior death with all life coming together in one glorious finale, but slow; an unfolding period of mornings and evenings filled with life, and nights filled with longings and sorrow, loneliness and regret, as a rehearsal for that final full-blown performance of death.

All with a sweet and bitter sameness; the sameness of memory.

CHAPTER -31 - guilt! Painting Mayaro

Warren Toth's report gleaned from Diary notes of Feb. 2nd and Feb. 5th.
Speculation based on such facts.

For weeks after they returned from Toronto she could not look into the eyes of her sons. Yet still, in spite of the guilt, the hunger remained. It seemed that imbedded in the very shame itself there was such excitement that logic and reason had no place. Nor could she find blame. Blame would require analysis and to analyze one would have to go over in detail the entire encounter. In past attempts she had gone only so far as to realize what had indeed happened: his reaching, the madness and incredulity of his closeness, her hand pushing at first... But against what had she pushed. Not a boy, but a man. Shoulders, sweat, passion, that agonizing, belaboured breath that should be confined to the throws of death rather than to the surge of life. When did it happen, that spring to adulthood? And where did she lose her own status? In his competence, his intensity, his anger, his superior skill, his impatience with error, his honesty with himself? And what stayed her? The flattery of his desire? She could have turned her face away but instead met him, hoping instead to falsely argue away the consequence of her decision. He needed her. That alone was reason to hold him. But her nakedness beneath the robe would betray any pure intention. They were alone in the apartment. It was late. No one would call. Saturday night. The black shroud of concealment demanded she taste the fruit. And his need. To grow up... No! It was her need.

The truth was as a slap across her face.

She crumpled pleading to the floor beneath him, paradoxically pulling at him yet with conflicting denials, watching him impatiently fumble at his clothes, then she, opening... inviting...

SUBSEQUENT NOTES.
A WOMAN IN TURMOIL:

Twenty-two years separated them - but the human heart is impatient with age. Her own husband was eleven years her senior. Yet even then! One would have thought that in those days eleven years would not matter much. But it did. At seventeen she had felt so much of life calling, begging her to explore her own talents, enjoy her own freedom and wildness; it would soon be over anyway. Yet she had been a creature of society; that demanding animal, the pet she had toyed with all her life, so that when the social step was offered, she would have to take it. Her own mother encouraged it. That was enough. Mom was, after all, always right.

She got seven full years out of it. It was more than many of her Convent school chums would ever see. She packed into it three boys, comfort, wealth, trips abroad and of course the Gallery - her life.

She had one affair. Louisville, the visiting French artist/playboy had entered soon after Jonas' ascendancy to the Ambassador's staff and his subsequent departure. His own indiscretion might have also contributed to her weakness (or was it her pride) and ultimately the incident, but, when it was over, and quickly, she was glad. Still, all that week, drifting between the flattery of a long, overdue attention and the guilt of carnal exercise, all she could see clearly was her sons' mother succumbing to passionate kisses and embraces in the shame of intercourse.

The early morning was cool. Elwood had been there for the sunrise, had even fallen asleep in the sand and been awakened by the gulls for the display of splendour as the sun emerged from the sea. It had been a clean rise. Just one little cloud, albeit long and low on the horizon, had blazed orange with a cadmium brilliance as the sun peeped over the shimmering distance. The wind was back on course. It blew in from the south but was gentle enough to allow the fishermen to put out into the bay with their cargo of seine piled high in the middle of the boat. Those on the beach anchored one end of the huge net as the boat circled far into out into the shimmering green among the white-splashed waves, letting it peel out along the arc.

The tide was high; not the high/high that occasionally brought waves as far up to the ridge where the boats were beached, but the usual low/ high that just covered the flats as it swarmed up along the gentle slope. The culprit moon almost directly overhead hung impishly from the sky, its crescent form barely visible even against the clear, brilliantly blue canopy.

Upon the embankment well above the surging sea, Elwood sketched furiously. He wore his usual Van Gough straw hat and hiked up jeans but no shirt, not even the beloved poncho in which he loved to wipe his oils as well as his hands. This instead lay on the sand, a rest for his keys, wallet and box of charcoals. Leaning against the prow of an overturned boat, the Indian Chief motorbike sitting majestically dark amid splashes of chrome and well back under protection of an almond tree, he cut a curious figure; one, had another artist of similar determination passed by, he would have felt the need to commit to a large canvas.

From time to time he wandered down the slope to capture a face. The fishermen ignored him; they knew he would prefer it so. But some of the others, especially the women and children who came to 'pull seine', tried often to talk to him, inquiring what he was doing and wanting to see it. He ignored them. Some took it as a curiosity; others did not. He ignored even their petulance. However when the boat returned to shore some distance away and the signal to pull was given, he quickly put away his sketches, cramming them into a large canvas bag which he strapped to the bike's backrest, and returned to help, happily joining those whom he had ignored only minutes before.

Lines formed on both ends of the seine; regulars from the town, passers by, joggers, beachcombers. First the rope, then the mesh was seized and, patiently but with no less force, tugged with uncharacteristic zeal. Progress was painfully slow, imperceptible to those not accustomed to the process yet to the initiated no more than a simple test of patience. Although it seemed at first that their combined efforts were in vain, experience dictated that as the two groups toiled they drifted closer. Hands only detected real progress. One slowly passed rope or netting to the other then sought what was passed back by the person in front. Now conversations were easier. Those who had earlier asked where he was from, what he was doing, how he did it, why he did it, did he truly enjoy it, and how could anyone make a living from it, found his replies ready and friendly - even when he was out of breath.

These were the same questions he would have liked to ask of those surrounding him. But did not. The images spoke. Waist deep in frothy water, hands touching, bodies bouncing against each other, the women squealing, the men joking, the children dancing in the surf splashing at each other, mothers yelling at them to be careful of sharks and rays in the net, they themselves bouncing seductively against the men, happily parrying their sexual innuendoes. Elwood longed to sit above them, close enough to see every pore of their skin in colours ranging from gleaming ebony to coppery yellow, and every healthy drop of sweat breathing through it. Instead, as a second choice, he worked, slaved as one of them knowing that, unlike them, he did not depend on the catch for his survival nor would he take any fish though they would again offer one as they offered to all the 'pullers' who had earned it.

This alone would make him strange. In their eyes he was a 'haunt'; a ghost who visited them from another world. They had told him so; as a joke of course. But in reflection he found the label fitting. As if to give further credence to the label he volunteered nothing about his life and seldom answered questions about his person. His age for instance. Though many would guess, and correctly so, that he was not quite thirty he would only shake his head and laugh.

He knew what the men would have asked but did not. He would have liked to tell them though that although he was not gay, they need not fear him for their wives or girl friends. But he would have to extrapolate without revealing any truths. Rather he would cling to mystery; it seemed to please both sexes. For this reason he found it difficult to refuse the attention of the women (some quite young girls) who flirted with him and whose curiosity often went beyond good manners. He could tell the men would have resented it if he had been the one making passes. However, in his own refusals they themselves exhibited caution. In that part of the country, there were no grey areas; everything was black or white. You either liked men or you liked women, slept with one, or with the other. A man who slept with neither was a 'haunt'.

A man he knew only as Matik sought him out when the two groups of pullers came together and the catch hauled up on the beach. It was a good haul and the fishermen were generous. Matik, gingerly holding by the tail a small shark about three feet long and still squirming in his grip, hailed him as he walked away.

"Tessa want to see you," he yelled loudly.

"I know," Elwood replied though not as loud. "But I have to go."

"No man. It eh about that," he assured him. "She have some pictures about the Turtle nest you an she talk about."

"Oh! She told you this?"

"Yea. She tell a bunch of fellas. They tell she you don' like girls, but she say is none of they business and she still have to see you."

Elwood smiled. Matik did not mean anything derogatory in his statement and Elwood would not take it as such. But an opinion was clearly being formed. In their eyes, Elwood was losing his greyness - but in the wrong direction.

"All right. I'll have a talk with her. Is she home?"

"Yea. What happen! They din' gi you a fish?"

"Didn't want any."

Matik waved and headed off in the other direction.

Elwood watched him go, but having promised, he was now re-thinking Tessa. If he went and if the pictures were good he would have to remain. A courtesy dictate. But if he remained for any length of time he would have to stay overnight. She could invite him, but accepting her invitation could have complications. If on the other hand he rented a room at Miss Leery's he would definitely be staying, no matter if the turtles were good or not. Then he would lose a day.

With images of the seine-pull fresh in his mind, he needed to paint. The sketches would help, but the excitement was there, now. He needed to capture it in full, rich colour, not settling for what was approximate. If he left it for one day he would fret and worry at his mixtures, doubting them for lack of excitement. Then he would be tempted to leave it for another day when his memory was refreshed. Then he would have to return soon. Procrastination did not work for him.

Or he could return to the 'Hotel'.

He decided it was the better choice.

CHAPTER -32 -
painting Tessa

TESSA, FORMERLY MRS. LOOMAT, who was widowed when still in her teens, was once a beauty contestant who was cheated of the crown. No one doubted that she was cheated. There was little that anyone in town did not know about her, but that she should have been Carnival Queen was the most well expressed of opinions concerning her. In Mayaro at least, she was queen. Her royal subjects pretended she was one of them and could relate countless incidents of her childhood, that is, before she went away to become beautiful, but neither men nor women reacted toward her as they did to others. Elwood was different. He saw her for her beauty, true, but more for her childlike simplicity above that regality. But ignorance was his excuse. When they met on the beach two years ago not only had he never seen her before but he knew nothing of her. Yet rather than feel slighted, she suddenly found the young (actually she was three years younger), serious artist a challenge for her charms.

The former Mrs. Loomat was not only a tease; she was an accomplished tease. Often, people don't regard teasing as a skill. Not till they see the likes of Tessa at work. Eyes, lips and fingers dance as though they were clothed in veils of seduction and moved to the music of flutes and cymbals. Words are not so much spoken as intoned, their messages insinuated. She flaunts her youth with the expertise of an old whore and the enthusiasm of an athlete. And to all this is added a well tutored intelligence. A rapacious wit honed by the seasoned devils of the city where she was schooled was no fair contest for the simple housewives, fishermen and farmers of the area. Even Elwood, city folk as he was, would have been no match for her. Nor was he interested in a fight. At first.

If there was one thing about Elwood that bordered on fanaticism, it was discipline. Like the Saturday mornings of his youth, his life was planned not only on a day to day basis, but taking the unforeseen into consideration, hour to hour as well! Though he had the common sense not to expect people and circumstances to fall into his rigid schedules, he nevertheless tried his best to stick to the itineraries he planned. His work season, for instance. It began with the end of the rains and ended when they began again. The dates were definite; but the rains were not. Still, on the first of December he would leave home and by the thirty first of the following year's August he was prepared to call it a day. Not that he would stop painting altogether, but during the rainy season, he would cover only the north east and regions immediately south of that. And only on bright, sunny days.

In the early days these forays began as daily trips where he would leave home early in the morning and lose himself for a day to return that night too exhausted to follow up on his sketches. On the days he painted he was often interrupted and on occasion the delay would last well beyond common sense or politeness so that, at times, he could be found finishing his work on a beach by the light of his motor-bike – a special contraption wherein light was supplied by a 12volt extension lamp connected to the battery. But, the lesson learned, he found this system far more enjoying and productive.

He usually began his season in the south – Marabella, San Fernando, sometimes passing through the oil-fields of Point-a-Pierre and sometimes going as far as Point Fortin. Then he worked his way across the island, through Rio Claro and down to Guayaguayare before moving up the east coast to Toco and Grand Reviere. When he found something of great interest he would immediately paint it or, if impossible under time or weather constraints, return to that area and, still sticking to his schedule, eliminate another less important venue completely or at least shorten his time there.

Each locality had its attractions; Mayaro had two - the seine fishermen and Rico's grill. Until Tessa. And then there were three.

On that memorable day he had been resting in the sand against an overturned boat when a group of girls invaded the beach, their loud almost shrill chatter preceding them. When they appeared, scampering among the dunes, and along the water's edge, making hard, unpleasant sand-balls and throwing them at the young men who frolicked in the surf, Elwood sat up and took notice. All wore swimsuits, (string suits, he called the girls' attire for indeed they were nothing but string with little patches of modesty.) Tessa Loomat however wore a large hat and a long, white, diaphanous garment flowing over her equally revealing suit.

Elwood sketched her. Eventually she noticed him.

Curious that his eyes followed her as he seemed to 'write' upon a large pad, she investigated. He denied her access to the work. She insisted, teasing, flirting it seemed with every sinew of her sensuous body. Then, suddenly pausing, she took off her hat.

"Are you drawing me?" she asked though more as a demand.

"If you must know, yes! Do you object?"

"No! But why don't you show me then?"

"Because it's not finished."

"When it's finished then will you show me?"

"If it's good."

"And if it's not?"

"I'll start again."

"What will you do with the bad one?"

"Probably throw it away or destroy it."

"Oh, that is a terrible thing to do. Why should I let you draw me then?"

"You don't think it will be good?"

She pouted and her eyes softened. "Will you give it to me if it is bad?"

A slow smile creased his face as he felt the energy and strength of the last plea. This tone was now childish and yet not innocent. She had plucked it seemed all the strings of an instrument she played with such ease and confidence it fascinated him. She had employed not only the craft of language but the very basis of communication - a communion of thought, above and below the surface of banality, reaching into essence and touching upon frivolity with just enough of both to make it familiar and perfectly acceptable. He suddenly wanted to start over, to paint that pout and destroy the frolicking creature about to throw a sand-ball.

"All right," he agreed, "if you let me paint you."

"Yes. I'll let you paint me."

When he was finished the sketch he deemed it bad, gave it to her and remained in Mayaro for almost a month, sketching her till he found what he sought. The principal piece - the brooding almost plaintive image of a young widow looking out to the lowing sun - sold for six thousand dollars to a buyer from New York; the other two for fifteen hundred apiece. She was angry with him that he did not give her any of the paintings (she actually wanted all of them). But she was furious that although he was paid so much for them, she had received nothing. Following a rare outburst of anger from her as he presented himself at her house (her invitation,) it took him almost six months before he returned to Mayaro, but when he did, she had cooled. He suspected that she had begun to see him differently, as the artist perhaps, the one now become famous.

She did in fact make a special effort to ingratiate herself with him. It was a condition the 'circle' (the townsfolk close to her) found curious. With his every visit they probed, offering gossip and insight in exchange for some of his. He would not play the game. The young girls and even the more mature women teased him with suppositions and conditions of Tessa's attraction to him. Based in part on these and what he knew of himself, he formed a picture.

He was different, he concluded. As a man or at least from the men she knew. In spite of her taunts, he would not fight with her. He smiled when he was insulted, refused when he should accept, and flatly turned down what other men would die for – or said they would. Finally however she had stumbled upon his Achilles' heel. He loved what was out of the ordinary which growing list included many items ordinary to them; Rico's grill, the stone bakery, the seine fishermen – and just possibly, turtles. These she promised him if he consented to do one more portrait of her.

"A grand one," she said, "like the Mona Lisa."

He smiled and promised, though warned her it might be his last.

"I don't care."

But she might.

CHAPTER -33 -
goodbye to Tessa

ELWOOD WAS COMMISSIONED ONCE – almost forcefully so – to do a portrait of Mrs Matilda Dubonet who offered quite a lot of money and prestige and the promise of grander things to come if Elwood could make her famous and eternal. Elwood painted her on the toilet reading a newspaper. She was affronted and outraged, but the painting was indeed a work of art and though she threatened to destroy it, she never laid a finger on it.

It might well have made her famous had she ever showed it to anyone, but she never did, and so she was never quite famous.

Still, she paid for it.

On this Wednesday in Mayaro, Elwood pulled up outside Tessa's house with her *Mona Lisa* firmly strapped to and hidden within the folds of his Indian Chief. He knocked on her door at a little after two in the afternoon. He had planned the rest of the day in increments of allotted time, giving her two hours, with an hour and a half to Rico's grill and the rest of the night to the fishermen. Still, his knock had been tentative, betraying perhaps a lingering fear he'd harboured of her since their first encounter and her last fit of anger. She opened the door quickly and pulled him inside.

"I hate you," she said smiling. "You make me beg you. Why are you so bad to me?"

"I'm not," he protested meekly.

"Yes, you are. And why do you tell them you don't like girls?"

"I never said that. But it could be true."

"No way. You could hide it from them but not from me."

"And you're so sure of yourself?"

"Since the day I met you."

Elwood's eyes raised in surprise. He remembered the moment. Yet how could she tell. Perhaps when she put her hand on his shoulder. Perhaps that was her little trick. But how could she know that he was aroused. He was seated, his knees high, his back against the boat and the work on his lap. Yet, had she not wanted to see it, or pretended to. And even clutching the pad to his chest had she not wrestled him a little, falling on him, even lying there for one agonizing moment. He did not think about it then but now he smiled.

"So, all men are in love with you?" he conceded playfully. "Except me, perhaps."

"Oh, ho, I know," she sang out. "Now you have to pay me a price for the turtles."

"What price."

"You have to hold me and tell me you don't want me."

"You little devil. All right," he dared, but as she came to him he knew he would fail the little test.

"Oh ho, I know," she squealed before he could lie. "Now you have to kiss me."

He should have protested the little game but he was already bending to her face and feeling an elusive flush on his own.

"No!" she laughed and spun away. "Now, you have to suffer."

He laughed with her but his head spun. "You are a devil."

"No, don't say that," she pouted, "it's bad luck. I'm very nice. Would you like me to show you?"

"Maybe you're a saint then!"

Her smile froze. "Don't you say that to me? Never. God will not forgive you. Me neither." And then as quickly she flashed a smile. "Would a saint do this?" And she swiftly cupped him.

"Oh," he squirmed, his brow puckered, "why do you do this. I should not have come here."

"Come... see the pictures. Maybe that will cool you down." She ran laughing into the dining room and through to another room.

Now this was art, he thought. Not the crude demands of a dark energy expressed in a Motel room. Not some secret shame confined to hidden hours or based on a pathetic weakness one could hardly call a game. Here was true excitement; the sparring of lovers, the jousting of friends, and all within a framework of coy innocence one could easily label as harmless. Still, he followed slowly, a lingering doubt in his better judgment as the residue from that encounter with Selina persisted.

He had been told Tessa lived with her grandmother. He prayed it was so, yet not so. But it was. Yet as he passed the old lady, nodding and mumbling words of greeting at her, she did not look up to his face or even at the by now obvious bulge in his pants. Her eyes looked straight ahead unseeing and seemingly unaware.

"Is that your Gran?" he asked when he caught up with Tessa.

"Yes! Did she speak to you?"

"No!"

"She is angry with me again."

"She too! Do you like people to be angry with you?"

She stopped before a huge cupboard and turned. "Only those I love."

He stopped. For a frightening moment something dark passed over her eyes.

"Tessa you must stop this. Or there will be great sadness in your life."

"Are you scolding me?"

"No! I am telling you this for your own sake," he said gently, putting his hand on her arm. "There is great sadness throughout the world. I do not wish yours on my conscience."

She looked at him more intently as though the game had gone out of her. "You are scolding me. But why? I only wish to have fun with you. Why do you wish to be serious with me? Everyone knows I play. I don't wish to be serious with anyone. Come then, if you must be serious let us look at the pictures." She had removed a folder from the large cupboard and proceeded to spread the photos on the table.

"Can I see them in the sunlight?"

"In the back yard. Come."

She gathered them back into the folder and hurried through a corridor to the back which opened to a sheltered patio. She placed the folder on a picnic table at the end of the patio and spread out the pictures again. He picked up the very first; the beach covered with little dots which he examined closely. Another must have been taken at ground level, the little creature inches from the lens. Still another showed eggs broken and in disarray among the leaves and twigs on the sand.

He could not tell whether they were Green or Leathery turtles. Both species nested on that part of the island though he doubted in the same area. The ideal scenario of course would be for him to see the actual laying of eggs. He had an image already in mind but as with these photos, it was one-dimensional, created out of balance and light. The life was missing. Still, it was better than nothing. It would hold him till the fulfillment of the promise.

"How did you find them?" he asked in wonder.

"The children find them. If they born in the night they go down to the sea without too much trouble – you know, from the birds. But if they born in the day, the children put them in buckets and take them."

"Did you do that?"

"I used to. But I don't like how they feel; rubbery and squiggly," she laughed.

"Who took these?" he asked holding up one that showed an egg with an eager chick emerging, its doleful eyes already aware of the marathon of death that lay along its path to life.

"A friend. He's from Matelot. He works for his father who has a camera store where he takes passport pictures."

"You just asked him?"

"Yes. He said he would do anything for me. I just put him to the test," she laughed. "What would you do for me?"

He laughed but did not answer.

"He is a good photographer," he said taking another from the folder. "I would like to pay him. Ask him how much and if he could send me a receipt – for my accountant."

"Pay me if you have to pay anyone. He has his pay."

He looked sharply at her. "Are you just teasing again?"

She laughed sharply almost clapping her hands but not quite letting them meet. "Mama," she called still laughing, "you hear me?" From the front came a faint, "yes... what... want?"

"Bring some tea!" then softer, "would you like a beer?" she asked Elwood.

"Tea... is all right," he answered politely, not condoning the way she spoke to her grandmother, yet not interfering in what he deemed an accepted form of communication between the two. "Bossy," he observed.

"Me!"

"You. Even to your Gran. Does she know you're a tease? That why she's mad at you?"

"Oh no, no! I'm not a tease. Why do you say I am? Do you want me to give myself to everyone? I'm sure you don't."

"Touché. Still, I do not entice others the way you do."

"Then why do I want you? Why did you make me go through all this trouble just to get a kiss from you?"

"You did not. And it is you who denied the kiss."

She smiled and her eyes lit again. "So you think I teased you? Do you want the kiss now?"

He shook his head as he smiled and looked back toward the house. "No you don't! I do not wish to become your slave, to stand outside your door with all your other suitors, pining for another kiss... or more perhaps. I'm sure that's why they hover about you, hoping... even running all the way from Matelot just to do you a favour. Perhaps when I'm old and death is looking in on me I can take the chance to think of you and pine for you because I would then have a chance against you. But not now; not today..."

Throughout all this she smiled as proudly as if he were complimenting her on a victory. He had more to say but the door opened and the old lady came out with a tray. Elwood stood up and took the tray from her hands. She tugged a little, not expecting his action, but released it somewhat shyly.

"Hello Gran, I'm Woody," he said putting down the tray then quickly extending his hand. The old lady tenuously accepted it and nodded shyly, smiling. "Come and join us," he invited.

Her shyness increased as with a bashful laugh she shook her head and sought to release her hand. "Oh no..." she protested, "no thank you. You young people enjoy youself." And suddenly becoming free hurried back to the house.

"Oh that was so nice," Tessa said and he caught a warmth in her eyes that he had not seen before. "She's going to talk about you all night you know." She set about pouring and preparing the tea. "She doesn't like the others. We had a fight over a man my husband knew. You know my husband died a long time ago?" He nodded. "He was his lawyer and he came up to see me. Gran, as you call her, never liked him. He said my husband owed him money and hinted at... things. I suppose I should have just told him outright that... well, I was not interested, but why should I hurt people. Tell me?"

"You are strange. But your 'Mama' is right. She knows more than you think... even with your wit and your wiles." He took the cup she offered and sipped. "You should listen more to her. And... I'm sure men like that, even men like me, deserve the hurt they get."

"Why men like you? You are not like him."

"I am a man. I'm shocked to say it, but I've seen me in the mirror and I know what I am."

"You say it so sadly."

"No. Not sad. Just a truth."

They sipped and looked out at the heavy growth of the back yard, the greying shrubs and sparse fruit trees that must have once looked kept and orderly as they flanked a stone walk that now disappeared into their wilderness.

"It's late," he said putting down the empty cup and shuffling the photos into the folder. "The sun is going down. What a pleasant afternoon. I didn't think I'd stay this long."

"Now everyone will think we have made love."

"How so?"

"They will ask me and I will not deny it. It's none of their business anyway."

"But what of the men you have loved. Will they not be jealous?"

"Which men?"

He looked into her eyes. She smiled.

"You have not slept with anyone?"

"I am not saying that."

"What are you saying then? That you have?"

"I am not saying that either," she laughed, yet more as a little girl with a big secret.

He nodded. "Tessa, you are playing a dangerous game. There are young men out there who will not play your game. They may even have a game of their own."

"You are saying they may harm me?"

"Yes! It is possible."

"How? Could you harm me?"

He shook his head slowly. "Not for my life."

"So, you love me too, then."

"Yes... In my way. Yes! So you have me too. Does that make you happy?"

For a fleeting second he caught what he construed as alarm in her eyes, and then it was gone.

"Paint me. For me alone. Not to sell. Will you do that?"

"Yes," he sighed. "Yes. But you must do something for me in return."

"What is that," she cocked her head.

"Release me. From whatever hold you have on me now. From whatever could be. Toy with me no longer. Let us only be friends. Your game must be just a silly exercise to you, but it's imprisonment to men like me. That's what I meant earlier, that's what I want. Will you do this for me?"

Before she could reply Gran opened the door and called.

"Ojay and Doro waiting outside for you," she said. "They say you going to the movies with them."

"Tell them wait," Tessa said, and as the old woman retreated inside once again Tessa returned her attention to Elwood. She looked into his eyes, smiling, and approached him, peering intently yet not lessening the smile till she was close. Then reaching up and pulling down his head opened her lips on his. Shocked and dubious at first, he nevertheless responded. His arms encircled her and secured her to his body. He was young again, truly young, before knowledge and pain, the excitement of promise and the immediacy of pleasure commanding his young, ripe being to dip into ecstasy, taste the fruit Eve offered; first taste, first fruit, all firsts, birth, awakening.

He raised his swimming head yet unable to lift his eyes from her sensuous mouth.

"I will release you," she said. "Never."

Laughing, she skipped away and entered the house as Elwood took deep breaths and followed. As he entered the living room he heard Tessa and the other girls.

"This is Woody," Tessa said upon seeing him. "He was kissing me in the back."

The three girls laughed at Elwood's discomfort not realizing his budding anger.

"You want to come with us?" Tessa asked teasingly.

"Tessa!"

"You see," she continued, still smiling "he's my slave too."

It might have been said in jest or coquetry but Elwood's eyes now steeled though his shy smile remained.

Instantly, Tessa knew she had gone too far for while he might have forgiven anything were they alone, she now could not retreat in fun without loosing face with her friends. She walked up to him and was now sure of the damage.

"Sorry," she whispered, taking his hand. "Come with us."

"No," he said, still smiling but removing her hand from his. "You go enjoy yourself. I have to get something." And nodding to the girls he strode out the front door. Bated moments later he reappeared with the 30 X 21inch covered canvas and presented it to her.

"As promised," he said, then turned and walked out.

As tears sprang to Tessa's eyes, even as she fought to keep her smile and her daring, she knew it was over. She had finally come to know Elwood Lucien and she knew he would not be back.

"I'll put this down," she said and hurried to her bedroom. But she did not return and when the girls eventually went to see what had been taking so long, they found her weeping uncontrollably in the arms of her Grandmother and on the bed an angelic image of herself as a schoolgirl – pure and chaste and innocent.

And when the girls tittered, though they quickly stifled their smiles, both knew that Tessa would never again show that painting to anyone.

CHAPTER -34 - Joe and wife at the gallery

“WHO WERE YOU TALKING to?” Lucy asked as she emerged from the end room in the basement of the Gallery.

Lucy, was the former Lucinda D’Antonio, who had brought a new dimension to the hate that pitted the brothers against each other, Joe often accusing Pete of being jealous, of never having a woman of half the worth or striking beauty as his Lucy and Pete responding with every weapon at his disposal. Pete’s main weapon was Woody, suggesting by innuendo and at times outrightly so, that Joe’s only attraction for the vivacious Lucy was that he knew the famous Obzocky. Wasn’t it the reason she took the job at the Gallery in the first place? It was a claim Joe staunchly denied.

Sporting a new Van Dyke beard over which he bubbled shamelessly, Joe, upon returning from Canada, had taken over some of the duties at the gallery and with it the importance of the office. Much of what Pete said might have contained a sliver of truth, but Joe was not buying it. As in the past, Joe knew that Pete's only sense of the truth was that which he could twist to suit his way. It did not matter that to everyone else, Joe's sense of Truth did not exist beyond his new found importance.

That day, after talking briefly with Elwood, he had returned to the basement where he would continue packaging some works for shipment abroad. Over and above his thoughts of the beard, he was buoyant enough speaking with Elwood yet he could not hide his puzzlement that upon announcing Elwood, his mother did not rush out to inspect the newest works as she usually did. Which might have caused Elwood himself to hold back on his own enthusiasm. But it was all this back and forth reasoning that had caused Joe to delay answering Lucy's question. Though eventually he did. If still somewhat distractedly.

"Elwood!" he said. "He's going to see Mom. I asked him what he wanted to do with the yellow canvas. He just shrugged. You know how Mom always says it's not finished? Well I think it is. I think I even know what it is."

"What?"

"Eh! Well, something he's ashamed of, I think. I think he can't paint it. Yellow. I could sell it. Put a nice frame on it and I could sell anything Woody paints. But Mom says 'No'. Anyway I thought you left."

"No. I have this box of stationery for your mom. I thought it was him talking to her."

"Why didn't you come out and say 'hello' then. You shy with him?"

"No! He doesn't like me."

"Elwood! You must be crazy. He likes everybody, you think he's not gonna like you? Everybody likes you. It's Pete who doesn't like anybody. You have some dust on your shirt."

"Where?"

He dusted her sleeve.

"Don't make it worse now."

"Here's the brush. You want me to brush it off."

"No! I'm sweating. It will smear."

He dusted the top of her shoulder with his hand, but continued on down to her breast.

"What are you doing," she smiled thrusting out her chest.

"Nothing," he said now caressing the one breast, "just seeing if everything's all right."

"What do you think?"

"Yes... So nice and soft," he continued then undid the buttons at the top.

"And this," she touched him, "is getting nice and hard."

"Ohhhh, don't do that." He slid his hand down her blouse and unfastened the clip between the cups.

"Ohhh, you're going to get into trouble with your mom if she comes down here."

"Nah, she and Woody'll be talking about art and shit for another hour I'll bet." He now caressed both breasts as she expertly undid his belt and zipper letting his pants fall. Now she played with him till he suddenly lifted her skirt and in one motion stripped her panties down.

"Why don't we wait," she suggested gasping out the words.

"Are you crazy...?"

"...Not the wooden box," she said quickly as he lifted her. "Splinters!"

"Where?"

"The table." She pointed. Wriggling from his grasp she stepped, shuffling out of the undergarment though not completely and, dragging it and him as he dragged his own pants with one foot, led him to the table. He kicked off the pants then quickly lifted her and as her legs came up, thrust once lightly then deep into her. She threw her head back then brought her mouth to his, rubbing his face and beard with her free hand.

"Ohhh you make me... yes... You look so sexy now," she moaned, "Yes, it turns me on... Yes, harder, hurt me... yes... no,... No, you pig. Don't you dare... Oh fuck, you pig," she hissed at him still trying to pull him into her. "You pig! Don't take it out. Ohhhh."

But it was done. Sheepishly but happily he leaned against her as she beat on his arm.

"I'm never going to... You're never going to..."

"I'm sorry. I didn't mean to come," he apologized slipping from between her legs and hurrying over to where his pants lay. He dusted it then put it on, losing his balance and falling heavily against the box.

"You Fuck! You useless fuck!" she sneered. "That's you all over, Joseph Metcalf. Your father's imprint. Thinking only of yourself! You're good for nothing but useless things like this place... And it's not even yours. Lord only knows what you'll do with something... important!"

Joe's eyes grew cold and an empty look seemed to envelop him in an impotent rage even as he clenched and unclenched his fist. It cautioned Lucy and stayed her fury as the next words that might have further expressed it. And then he smiled and seemed to be Joe again. But his smile did not seem altogether happy; more like the smile of one who had uncovered a secret no one else knew. Or would like to know.

Lucy closed her legs tightly and leaned on her thighs. "Get my panty," she ordered. "You're not working late tonight. You've got another job when you come home."

Joe grinned as he handed her the garment. She snatched it from him though it was obvious, at least to Joe, that she was only frustrated not angry.

"Yes dear," he said.

CHAPTER -35 - at the gallery; news of Adrian

MRS. METCALF HAD BEEN crying. Elwood had been suspicious when she greeted him with sunglasses on a dull, overcast day. But the cool greeting that took place in her office at the gallery convinced him she was hiding something. Joe had been there and, as he mentioned, Lucy too, 'somewhere around'.

Elwood had interrupted his trip, returning to the gallery which was his custom to deposit his finished pieces and re-stock his supplies. At any rate, this is what he told Joe. Of course it could have been handled otherwise but as he explained to Joe, he needed the long ride to clear his head and regain his focus. This obviously puzzled Joe but as usual, Joe would not seek clarification. Joe was always afraid of knowing too much.

When Joe went down to the basement, Elwood relaxed and turned his attention to Mrs Metcalf. He had been worried since that phone call from Miss Leery's boarding house, had detected something in

Mrs Metcalf's voice when they spoke and although his own mind and conscience were clear there was still some doubt that their secret was safe and not about to be unravelled. This thought always unsettled him and although there was nothing about their present relationship that could not be explained away, he was cautious in his words with Joe, even unhurried to end the conversation though when it did end he could not hold back the deep sigh that seemed to expel his worry.

"Something is wrong," he said softly with a touch of fate and not a little hope.

But Mrs Metcalf shook her head.

"Adrian," she said, the name strange and anguished, "in Canada... he wants to give up art. His father is financing a gallery in Ottawa and he wants to run it full time."

"I'm sorry," Elwood said and looked it. She seemed so small then, so helpless, he would have embraced her even as he had done his own mother at such times, yet with Joe around it would not have been advisable.

So much had changed in the last few years. When they returned from Toronto he had avoided her as best he could, but the fear that so radical a move might cause suspicion caused him to formulate a schedule – a business routine – and stick to it. Still their meetings, as few and necessary as they had been, had kept the door open. But at times the tension of desire and guilt had been so oppressive that the strain had begun to tell on both.

She had nevertheless used every opportunity to urge him to at least visit New York and though adamant about going and leaving behind the security and familiarity of his life and work, he had at least acknowledged her desire to be a part of his life. In the past year he consented to shipping out some of his pieces, allowing even more to be put on display. Yet she had gone even further (for his sake, she said) and shipped out all she had, even pressuring him to submit more works. Finally she had confessed her intentions and, proud of his success, even to the point of arguing with him, pleaded with him to *seize the opportunity.* He had refused. He had felt betrayed at first by her confession then, later, disappointed through all the talk that she was using him to expand her business. No matter her explanation, he would not be comforted. But even that had abated, though now it seemed it was she who needed comforting. Her last appeal to him was almost desperate; now he understood why.

"Lord knows those two (Joe and Pete) will never amount to anything," she lamented in that distracted way that always worried Elwood. However it was not a statement reserved only for him though when repeated to her friends, they excused it for the sadness that had befallen her. Moreover they were quick to point out that it was said lovingly of her sons and with a touch of gratitude that they at least still remained with her. The rest remained an open book to friends, family and enemies alike. And of course to Elwood.

Joe himself had wanted to study business and had enrolled at the Julliard in Toronto, Canada. And the fact that he had not chosen to go to Ottawa, that he would therefore not be with his very influential father, offered her some comfort. Yet it was Adrian who concerned her. He had talent, she still insisted. Yet now he had taken a step that not only disappointed her, but would take him away from her forever. Joe on the other hand was forever.

Before going to Canada he had hastily married Lucy and if she did not love him, she had at least shown some gratitude that Mrs. Metcalf had welcomed her in spite of the fact that Mrs Metcalf had only recently confessed to Elwood that although Lucy was a pretty girl, she was sly in both countenance and manner; a disposition too many others regarded as shy. But even in this attitude there was some consolation. For that shyness notwithstanding, after only a first few weeks of strangeness she had made herself at home and though spending as much time with her own mother now provided Mrs. Metcalf with a certain warmth and promise to fill the void of Joe's departure and the assurance that he would return. The downside to all this was a big argument Joe had with the righteous Pete over the incidence of Lucy's pregnancy – the actual cause of the hurried marriage. Not that Pete needed a cause to bait Joe.

Pete had moved away to a friend's place outside the city and Mrs Metcalf seldom saw him now; a situation she looked upon with conflicting acceptance; a trade-off perhaps of peace for longing.

Pete had found religion some years before he left school. It was not one of the accepted religions where 'turn the other cheek' or 'forgiveness' was practiced, but rather a rigidly strict discipline performed in a tent and dependent upon the Reverend Alfred Rooster for its very flexible and interpretive rules.

Mrs. Metcalf had not minded at first. She often complained to Elwood that it was his father's influence, or rather the memory of his father that had influenced him. She was, admittedly, far too pig headed to be religious herself, though she once tolerated it in her husband and now in her son. And yet it troubled her. At times, often in the midst of a silence when Elwood thought she was looking at his work, she would suddenly ask a question on religion, more a challenge perhaps, on the assumption that Elwood had absorbed a great deal more from his years with the priest than he chose to admit. There were even times he would steadfastly protest his ignorance while giving his opinion, yet she suspected these were questions he dared answer simply because there was more street philosophy than theology expected of the query.

These desultory moments were not frequent however. Moreover Elwood had come to expect and even welcome them as relief from the business of Art, the tension of other subjects and even from the widening gulf between himself and his benefactor.

"It may not be as bad as you think," he offered.

"Or it might be worse," she countered. "What am I to do? Is this the price I pay for loving too much? No! I'm sorry! I'm just overwhelmed. You're probably right. He asked for you again. Adrian. I so wish... I'm leaning on you too much, I know. To solve all our problems." She unconsciously removed the sunglasses and unwrapping the protective cover over the work, looked at the new pieces.

Elwood looked at her.

She had aged; if not in years then greatly so in tragedies seen or imagined. There were now definite lines about her eyes and the pallor in her cheeks had greyed. Yet her chin was still strong, her lips still firm and the cascading hair, even with telltale strands of white, soft and feminine. "Wonderful!" she muttered, then, her voice catching, "Oh, Adrian." She wiped her eyes. Elwood placed his hand on her shoulder without even a backward glance. She covered his with her own tiny hand. "What would I do without you!" she mourned.

"*Where do you want these*?"

Lucy had come up softly with a box and some papers and her inquiry startling Elwood. He withdrew his hand abruptly.

"Just put them on the desk," Mrs. Metcalf said coolly, stiffening but hardly stirring. "It's just pencils and stickies," she told Elwood. "Could you give Lucy a hand? Put the box on the shelf."

Elwood turned, avoiding Lucy's penetrating eyes and taking the box, easily put it on the top shelf. He then turned and stepped boldly over to Mrs. Metcalf.

"Don't worry," he patted her shoulder, "everything will turn out fine." She did not respond. Had she seen through his condescension? Did she suspect that he was saying goodbye?

He turned again and not bothering to look at Lucy, strode out the front door.

PART II

CHAPTER -36 - Fauna

ELWOOD GAZED OUT AT the eastern sea and the smile that settled upon his face widened with acceptance.

Above, skies ranged from egg-shell to a pastel blue with wisps of hurrying cirrus clouds. From the ocean, warm fluffing breezes that tossed and soothed hot hair, caked the cheeks with salt and brought sweat to all covered parts of the body. Underfoot the ground moved constantly; a burning, powdery sand mixed with small pebbles. But where the lapping water met the land there were only pebbles that seemed below the water a predominately xanthous shade of translucency. However upon closer examination he found them multi-coloured; chalcedonous stones, glazed as of fine china, agate and burnished crystal quartz, no two alike either in size, shape, texture or transparency, each an art form, yet in their great numbers sacrificing their wondrous individual uniqueness to the mass becoming as it were a living carpet, carelessly shifting, loose and friendly, offering comfort and threatening pain.

The morning sun seemed almost to create that sensation of fulfillment few in the entire world would know and fewer still could fully appreciate. Here the hedonistic as well as the aesthetic would agree on the quality of life as a whole as well as the individual qualities themselves. Heat accounted for the physical sense of gratification but colour, as true and clean as a clear sky could offer, presented the glory of being; the rich green coconut palms graced and stately held aloof by their long and slender, greyish-brown stalks; the sculptured earth with its burnt grasses leaping over mounds of yellow sand - hot and dry - leading further to a cool, gently sloping beach, smooth and brown against the vibrant white foam of the ocean's spittle.

His mind mixed colours furiously, his imagination laying dabs of Cerulean on Titanium white and lacing Terre Verte with lines of Cadmium yellow pale. The long, ribbed stalks, begging of Payne's Grey deepened with Raw Umber, would stand out against the deep dark interior or against the mountains of Indanthrene blue that stood pasted and pale in the background. He felt the urge to make it actual, to bring out a canvas and apply to it those ingredients of art that gave palpability to the spiritual. But he dared not move for fear of losing the composition and its relative temper.

Elwood dug his toes in the sand and looked out longingly at the flaked white surf and the swirl of titanium just dirtied enough with a light Naples yellow. But pigment could not compete with reality and he sighed wistfully.

It was still too early in the day and therefore still too cold for a swim. He looked around and thought of sketching the rocks in the distance or the grove of trees behind him. But there was no hurry. This little nook would remain untroubled for another thousand years.

Two things he now regretted. He should not have returned to Port of Spain, and he should not have completely avoided Mayaro; at least not this year. If he could face the truth, it was Tessa he should have avoided. Though, as his libido now suggested, not completely. Her kiss had made its mark upon him, unsettling him, confusing him throughout the entire dry season and well into the rainy. Now she rode his memory as did so many others as wisps of longings flitting by from time to time.

But the rainy season had come and gone and he had chosen this year to begin at the other end of the Island. Perhaps he could start all over with a different view of things; a different city or town, perhaps a village with adobe walls, a stream running through it. He had ridden through and passed the little town called Le Poui and was disappointed that it had no Poui trees. The garage mechanic and the owner of the little deli that sold doughnuts both told him there were indeed Poui trees around – the golden yellow and some pink - but he could find none. Moreover they had told him that the late showing in September was not as beautiful as the spring flowering at the end of the dry season. He did not believe them. He also did not like Le Poui. There was too little life to it.

The irony was he had avoided the south because of the trouble the year before; too much life. He had sought peace and could find none and though he had regretted his words to the policeman who had arrested him, that he would not return to his town, he might still have returned – but for his promise. He could see by the policeman's face that he did not believe Elwood would not return. But Elwood had to prove, if even only to himself, that he was a man of his word. Besides, at all costs, he had to avoid Tessa.

He had called her once from the City, a long process involving several long distance operators and several wrong numbers till one such wrong number knew her last name. She had been surprised and as far as he could tell, pleased. Then she had accused him of not playing fair and she even cried as she begged him to take her away with him. But it was too like her and though his heart yearned for it to be true, he could not believe it and laughed when he so accused her. She hated him, she said... But all the words were the same and the expressions too. Still, when he hung up eventually, the longing remained.

He rose and dipped his foot into the clear water. It was indeed cold - like the Basin. He remembered Adrian's very first letter to his mother, the part where he talked about dipping his toes into the Mediterranean and the shock of learning how cold is cold.

"Yet not so cold as the pebbled beach of Brighton, or Dover and the English Channel... a disappointment in terms of weather as she frowned upon bare backs and bare feet yet provided in sadness and history what the Basin could not."

Elwood remembered Mrs. Metcalf had read him the missive excusing it as more a description of Nice than a report on his health. He had sent photographs too, she said; some of his paintings and charcoal drawings. Sad! Adrian had of course included no mention of a show but again invited Elwood to "drop in for a visit." Mrs. Metcalf too had still hoped. She hoped too that Elwood would accept the invitation, even offering to pay his expenses for such a visit. Perhaps he should have accepted. Hindsight! Yet now so long ago he found comfort in his sadness and delight in the loss of a full memory.

He removed his pants and shorts and donned the brief-like trunks he doubled as an oversized swim suit worn more for comfort than style. Though made of cotton and would take longer to dry than regular trunks they offered as well the ease of wandering and clambering with more dignity when he ventured off the beaten track. Folding the pants carefully he placed them on his boots. These were not the tall, cowboy boots he originally wore when he first purchased the bike but more comfortable half cuts with high heels, though the heels were now badly worn, jagged in a rounded pattern at the back. He left the little pile and walked over to the bike which sat on hard ground, protruding like a proud panther from the tall grasses some distance from the rocks at the bottom of the hill.

Removing his shirt and hanging it on the handlebars he took out a large towel from one large side-pocket and slinging it over his shoulder, returned to his clothes where he threw it onto the little pile before running and diving into the invigorating pool. A deep trough extended from the beach to the first of many rocks encircling the cove. He swam to the rocks but felt the tug of a swirling current which almost panicked him. But he stood upon the rock and checked the rip in the water and saw that it went nowhere. He retuned to the beach. But as he dried himself with the towel, slinging it over his back and rubbing vigorously, he noticed, out of the corner of his eye, a figure descend from the rocks high up on the beach and approach the bike.

By the long black hair being tossed about by the wind he could tell it was a girl, a fact borne further by the rhythm of her step and the unmistakable curved form that moved within that rhythm.

Immediately Elwood felt relief and consternation at the same time. That it was only a girl offered no threat to his being there. But that it was a girl, one who so boldly strode up to his prized machine, examined it carefully then hurried along, kicking up sand as she skipped toward him, puzzled him. The dress she wore was long and flowing, almost properly high necked, long sleeved and more business than casual. Proper too was the band around her head that did not adequately restrict her long hair. As she drew even closer, he noticed a pair of sandals she held lightly one in each hand.

She was not as he had first thought her; not too young, nor too small, nor in any way unattractive, yet her ingenuous demeanour clearly indicated to him that she was not in any way fearful for her own safety. He had seen this attitude in many of the very young children of the region. Young boys often challenged him, demanding to know what he carried in his box or his bags, and in effect what he was doing on their territory. Young girls were even more daring. They often had more personal, more intrusive questions about himself, even volunteering information on themselves, their parents or siblings, their homes and school, what they liked and what they did not. Elwood waited.

"What're you doing here," the girl asked when just within earshot though once speaking, she did not come any nearer but rather turned and faced the sea. Now in profile, the wind blowing against her and the hair though ruffled, straight back from her face and neck, he noticed how un-childlike she was. There was something too about the profile, something familiar and he could swear he had seen it before. He tried to place her in a car or in a deli somewhere, among friends, in different attires... Nothing worked.

"How do you do?" he ventured hoping the sound of her voice would add memory to the visual image.

"How will you get out?" she asked ignoring the introduction.

The voice was not familiar yet he wondered at its sweet texture and the form of her words, the vowel sounds and crisp consonants. He was sure he had not heard it before. Why then was it so...

"I'm Woody. What's your name?"

She was silent.

"Have I seen you before?" he asked outright.

She looked toward him intently then said askance: "You can't get out, you know. It's easy to get down but impossible to get back up again."

Elwood looked around. The statement itself nudged at some fear he'd had on descending the hill to the beach. Though he had dismissed it then it now worked its way back into his consciousness to unsettle him.

"I'll get out," he replied defiantly and somewhat smugly.

"No you won't. Even my brother couldn't get out and his bike's smaller."

"What's your name?"

She thought for a while and he thought he detected a suppressed smile. But whatever it was, it was brief.

"Woody?" she said as though reinforcing an earlier knowledge he had simply confirmed.

He nodded.

"All right. My name is Fauna. Do you like it, or maybe you think that's a silly name?"

"Not at all."

"My father liked it. My mother wanted to call me Mary but... You like Mary?"

"If that's your name, yes."

"That's a cautious answer. Or maybe you're not afraid any more and now you can only see a poor little girl who's dared to look at the great man. Why are you looking so at me? Do you think I'm pretty?"

He nodded. "Fauna! Do you know me?"

She was silent but there was that little suppressed smile again. "They say you're gay. But I don't think so."

He was immediately conscious of his wet suit but refused to react, either to turn away or look down. But he had to challenge her smile.

"Will you let me sketch you?"

"No! I was just curious. Now I should go."

"Please," he said hurriedly. "Not yet. I'm harmless, believe me. Did I...? Have we met...? If it's something I once said or did, somehow... I apologize. There is so much I want to ask."

"Boy, do you have a guilty conscience. But no! It's nothing you said," she assured him with a light smile. "I'm on my way to work. I saw you ride off the road and I knew you'd be in trouble. But, it seems I was wrong. You have everything under control. Besides, I like Cocoa beach... That's what we call this one. It's nice and private... for people walking.

No cars; no traffic. So I have no problems with people like you having to learn the hard way."

"What?"

She did not reply but looked toward the bike. He followed her look.

"How did you get here, then?"

"I drove. But I'm parked on the road."

"It's a long trip down."

"It's going to be longer going up."

Her words were final as she turned sharply and hurried back along the sand. Suddenly, and with a certain desperation, he did not want her to go. He sought the appropriate words that would make her stop but somehow knew that nothing he could say would be adequate. And then again, did he want to see her stop? Her presence had been compelling enough, but now, as she moved away there was something so erotic in her manner; her form and movement and the confidence of her step as she drifted past the bike and up the rocks where she replaced the sandals on her feet. Then dodging behind a row of Almond trees and low bushes, and not even turning to look back at him, she disappeared.

CHAPTER -37 - Cocoa Beach; stuck

THE WATER WAS NOT warm. A deep pool eddied and swirled just beyond the quick surf. Beyond the pool he discovered a deep channel between rock walls that rose from the sea-bed like two great halves of a cleaved pineapple, their flat tops worn and staggered and concealed just below the surface. The water churned in that area where the waves sped through. But hardly pausing, the swell pushed on to the abrupt rise before the beach, rose quickly, lipped and crashed on the narrow beach then hissed up its steep incline.

After some time the buffeting foam energized and invigorated Elwood to the point of fatigue. By noon he found himself hiding from the sun in the cooler water but when the surf increased in height and ferocity and the wind blew harder and with a bite from the ocean against his wet skin, he retreated to the comfort of his towel then to the shelter and security of the grove of coconut palms pushed into the hill. This little area he investigated further, for not only was it cooler than the rest of the beach but to the left of it there seemed to be a small stream emanating from somewhere between it and a rocky wall that extended along the beach and well into the sea where it had been broken into mounds of weathered boulders.

Following the stream he came upon its source. And smiled. Immediately he thought of the Basin, for high above the ground, seven or eight feet, a spring squeezed through the cliff face, leaking in sufficient quantity as to splash upon the lower rocks and collect at the bottom into a small pool about six feet in diameter. He noticed too that there were other leaks along the fissure at the back of the grove. All contributed to the stream, though none so closely resembled the falls of the original Basin as this first 'Little Basin'.

All around it bright shrubs, small plants - lilies, crotons, wild herbs, graceful weeds - of deep greens, vibrant yellows, blues, browns, meandered throughout the base as a thick leafed vine leapt from the overhanging awning and cascaded down the steep incline as in the framing of a shrine.

He followed the stream as it pushed its way through long persistent grasses that bordered the base of the hill and around buttresses of large boulders and stones that protected it from the influence of the sea, till he came upon a plateau of pure, white sand upon which he sank cross-legged and contemplated the wonder of this tiny paradise and dreamt of remaining there forever a part of its splendour.

Now he gazed about, re-evaluating and re-assessing the dell, wondering each time it rose in magnitude till it became almost numinous if not for the reality of its separate parts.

At first it had seemed somewhat messy. Coconut branches, twigs, logs, rocks, were strewn about. But where he first thought the arrangement by carelessness he now saw how carefully the high tides, the winds, the rains and the sun had orchestrated its present structure. He patched it out; each square a masterpiece – if he could capture it. Leaves, grass, the scum left high on the slope, little landslips exposing an almost cadmium pale redness; every aberration as every logical movement seemed in order. And then as though he could hold no more within his limited, very mortal, very fragile brain, he lay back and contemplated the racing sky.

When he had rested enough he unstrapped his paints and sketch-pad from the jump-seat of his bike and sketched his discovery all afternoon till the sun was low on the horizon. He then packed everything back on the bike and leaving it, hiked around the base of the hill in search of an easy point of exit. There were none; that is, not an easy way out. The only possible escape began some ten feet up a steep incline. This was blocked off by the small stream at its base, no problem in descending to the beach, but the ground upon which it ran was too loose and unsure to offer any hold to his tires. And without any kind of runway, it prevented the jump and momentum necessary to take him up the incline.

The soup flask was not quite empty and he drained the remaining spoonfuls which more added to his hunger than satisfied it. But he was not worried. It would not be the first time he had been stymied either in situation or in the threatening lack of sustenance.

Two of the coconut palms were heavily laden with fruit. He started to climb the one that had an easier incline but halfway up the trunk he slipped and slid down to fall the remaining four feet into the soft sand. Not hurt he nevertheless weighed the danger of hurting himself and decided the risk was not worth it. Perhaps if he got truly hungry he might try again.

He washed the empty flask in the salt water and rinsed it and himself under the 'Little Basin' then drank heartily from another cold trickle forcing its way through the dark rock. Hurrying now he gathered twigs and sticks and dragged a log to the plateau of loose sand just outside the grove of Coconut palms. Smashing the log against the trunk of one of the trees he gleaned the brittle dry remnants and short logs and assembled them on the perimeter of the clearing of soft sand. Triangulating three of the heavier pieces and filling the hole with twigs and dried leaves he lit a small fire just as the sun descended behind the western hill.

Then the bike. He easily rode it over and set it against one of the trees in the grove.

Showering once again under the too cold water-chute he towelled vigorously then spreading his wet laundry on a vine and a beach towel on the loose sand before the triangulation of wood and now leaping flames, he dressed in his riding gear - long jeans and jacket - knowing from experience how cold beaches got at night. He did not wear his boots, though. He could never sleep in any form of shoes - even sandals. Socks would have to be enough protection.

Darkness descended quickly. It was a pleasant show and he tried to sketch with his back to the fire; but it was too awkward. Even lying on one towel his head propped by another he found uncomfortable and the light insufficient.

As he struggled for a better position he thought he heard cries in the distance. This was not unusual. It seems a characteristic of such places, a mixing of surf and wind through the fronds to produce wails or whimpering. However this time they seemed constant though indistinct. He listened to the surf. It was angry against the outer rocks but not so against the shore. Still, the new sound seemed to ride above it with a deliberate and persistent urgency he found difficult to ignore. Returning the pad to the saddlebag and adding more fuel to the flames he could hear the sounds more clearly. Muttering.

Then a call; sharp, something like “Hello there” but tenuously sing-song and unsure.

Two flashlights flickered in the distance. He was considering turning on the bike’s lights when the ray of a flashlight and calls of ‘Halloo’ drew close enough for him to make out quite clearly the two figures approaching.

“I told you,” came out of the dark, the voice unmistakable; more so since he had suspected it could be the girl he had earlier encountered.

“Yea...yea,” he replied happily but with a touch of sarcasm. “You know you’re pretty snooty for your age! Who’ve you got with you?”

Immediately in front of her, coming into sharp view was a man, large but smiling.

“My brother. My father’s up the hill with the car.”

“The whole army,” he joked.

“Hello, I’m Hasim,” the brother said holding out his hand.

Elwood took it. “Hi! I’m Woody. What did she tell you?

“Nothing,” she answered for him. “Hasim’s my buddy... my favourite brother,” she bounced against him.

“She told us you could not get out,” Hasim said. “Did you try?”

“No! Not really. But I saw it would be difficult. Maybe tomorrow it will be easier. Sit down,” he invited moving from the towels.

"No," Hasim said quickly, "we have ropes in the car. If you would like to get out tonight, we could..."

"Oh... that's all right. Thank you so much. I wish I had something to offer you. You are very kind. I never thought..."

"Hasim, maybe first thing in the morning," the girl suggested.

"Yes," he agreed. "Come with us. We don't live too far from here. Just outside Le Poui. You must have passed it some miles back."

"Yes! I know it. But it's not necessary, you know."

"Where've I heard that before?"

"Oh, it's no problem," Hasim persisted. "It gets really cold here you know. And nothing will happen to the bike. We could help you bring your bag and... whatever else."

"This is quite a nice surprise," Elwood, obviously pleased, nevertheless sought to preface his protest. "But I really don't mind staying here. I do this quite often."

"The tide will be high tonight.

"How high?"

"High! It will cover the beach."

"High as here?"

"No," the girl said quickly, "unless the wind is from the east, and strong."

"Will it be strong?"

"By the time you know that for sure, it will be too late. And even if it is not strong, it will be cold."

"You said that."

"At least you must be hungry," Fauna added.

"I've been hungry before. I just hate to leave the bike here."

"Curry goat and chickpeas with some dhal?"

"Ah... How did you know..? You sure we haven't met before? Did someone tell you..?"

"Maybe," she teased.

"Yes... You know," he smiled, "I'm going to accept your offer."

Hasim bellowed with laughter, only his clean white teeth now indicating his presence. Elwood too laughed aloud and rubbed his hands.

"Curry goat and chickpeas - and dhal, right? Never let it be said that I turned down dhal with curry goat," and kicking sand on the fire he prepared to leave.

The talk of food and motorbikes continued as he, with Hasim's help, unstrapped his paint-box and the large back-pack from the rear carrier then the saddlebags from their place astride the rear wheel.

"Truth is I was looking forward to a nice meal in Matura tonight and the thought of all that goat curry going to waste is just too much to turn down."

"Come on Mare," Hasim ordered, "grab something."

"Mare? As in Mary?" Elwood exclaimed.

"Never mind," Fauna shyly bumped her brother while looking at Elwood. "Long story."

CHAPTER -38 - invitation to sleep over

THE PATH TOOK THEM through and over the rocks to a slim trail leading up the hill. It was quite a long walk and reminded Elwood of the rill above the basin - forever ascending till a wide clearing suddenly appeared. He had not seen it on the descent because it was to the far northern edge of the ridge and he had taken the far southern entrance. Just above the plateau a man stood in the half light outside a small car, a four door SUV that had been driven off the road to sit at a dangerously steep angle on the shoulder.

The man opened the front door and light flooded the interior, incidentally lighting his face as well.

He was short and wide, his features overly rounded, cheeks, nose and chin like little bubbles on his face and not at all resembling his slim, handsome children. He wore a suit complete with waistcoat and tie which in such a warm climate seemed incongruous at first or without knowing the reason. But at least he was smiling.

He hurried to the trunk and had it already open as Elwood reached for his outstretched hand.

"How are you, how are you, hee hee," he chuckled as one with a secret no one would ever know.

"Hello, I'm Elwood Lucien," taking his hand and the enthusiastic pumping it provided. "Thank you so much for your kindness."

"Oh...oh, I'm Dr. Carrington," he beamed. "You coming with us, yes, hee hee."

"Yes, thanks."

"Yes Da," Hasim replied almost simultaneously as he carefully laid the paint box and saddle-bags on the coil of ropes piled high in the trunk. He then helped Fauna with the sack she had toted. Elwood had not been allowed to carry anything but his sketch pad and towel.

Fauna led him to the front seat but he, insisting, opened the door for her then got in the back with Hasim. The father chuckled all the more at the little proprietary two-step then, accepting his own role, tried his best to ignore them, got in, started the car and drove off.

"Do you people do this often?" Elwood asked Hasim but in such as way as not to exclude the others.

"No... Not really. But last year it happened to me and I just could not get out."

"What kind of bike do you have?"

"It's a 250cc off-road. I thought I could do anything, go anywhere, but that hill stumped me. Finally I had to walk home."

"Then the ropes?"

"Yes. From the other side, you can drive down the slope... you know where you entered the beach... before the drop. Anyway, from there to the beach is not very far."

"So you stretch the rope and... You'll still need a few people to help up the..."

"No. Unless yours is really heavy."

"No. Its a cruiser, great for touring, comfortable on the long stretches of road but it's light enough for off road. I like high handlebars and big saddlebags so I guess that makes it look bigger, heavier than it is really."

"I dream about owning a Chief. My uncle rode one. The old work-horse, he used to call it. No electric start - just crank. But sometimes he would crank and crank... Sometimes he wouldn't even bother. He would just push-start it down the hill, then jump on and... pow! Big bang and lots of roar. But I loved it. How's yours run?"

"Great! But I had it rebuilt with all the bells and whistles you get in modern engines. What about the Harley?"

"No. That's for rich people. The Chief's a Harley frame anyway. But the Harley's got the name. No! The Norton and the Chief! They're for bikers."

Elwood smiled. He thought of another biker - Cola, who 'walked the walk' and incessantly talked of it, expecting that those who did not, had no right to ride such as a 51 Indian Blackhawk Chief - nor did anyone else. And he figured that of Elwood in particular, no matter his own chances with... anyone else. But what particularly irked him was that Elwood wasn't into bike talk. Therefore he was either an ignorant wanna-be or a wuss and not deserving of the metallic blue and chrome treasure or ... anyone else.

Nor would Cola be alone in this attitude.

Elwood did know the language but the assiduous dedication was always beyond him. It was one reason he avoided rest stops or delis where bikes were parked outside. Invariably though, no one else reciprocated this need for privacy. His own bike parked outside these establishments seemed to act as a magnet for single riders or even groups of bikers with that 'brotherhood' need to know. Moreover their inquisitiveness often went far beyond the bike. It seemed the brotherhood gave them no sense of propriety in either their questions or their manner. They felt it no intrusion to enquire of where he was going or what he was doing, even suggesting more often than not that he go and do it with them. Nor did avoiding them or refusing the invitations in any way prevent or stem the questions on the machine.

Often he would protest that he was not truly mechanical and though he was aware of its performance features, he could not say how well his own compared with other makes, models, sizes, shapes, power characteristics, ease of handling, sleekness of styling or even choice of colour. In any case no matter how many motorcycles he had, no matter the retro-style design, gross engine output, roll-on power, loading capacity or ride ability, no matter if the wheels were hollow-cast or the shocks had five-position spring preload adjustability, his heart was still with his little ten-speed buddy - his blue and silver Raleigh. Everything else was just afterthought.

But that was history; his history, his special time in this life where he would forever see his purpose and dimension come together, full and rich, not necessarily happy or regrettably sad, but there nevertheless. Besides, the Chief was the best, for comfort, style and reliability. He researched it and stood by his findings. There had been only one flaw - age. And he had seen to that.

CHAPTER -39 - the house among the trees

THEY TURNED OFF THE main road where a large sign read, “Le Poui - 5 miles.” But they did not travel the five miles. Not along the Le Poui road anyway. They turned into a narrow lane hardly wide enough for two cars and traveled in a continuous arc, over a high rise, through a valley then down into a heavily forested dell. And then the house.

It was tall.

It seamed to appear suddenly, a hint through the trees, then in full majesty at the end of a driveway. Elwood knew it immediately as one of the copra estate mansions built of wood though this one was elevated upon a brick foundation which seemed to extend upward supporting its second story. There would be many rooms; each high and wide, with small, shuttered windows, heavy beds and wash-stands in the bedrooms and dark, solid woods in the living and dining rooms.

Outside, there had been some improvements - the brick perhaps being one of them. Another was an upper balcony ringed in by a wooden balustrade with, it seemed, access only by means of the upper rooms. This practical addition did not compromise the stateliness of the manor but added a dimension of comfort and domesticity to it. The wood too; though painted with what the little light allowed could be white, was at least not compromised by the aluminum siding common to all the housing developments constructed in the latter third of the last century.

Though the sun was now completely gone behind the tall forest surrounding the area, two high lamp-posts on either side as well as several patio lights and luminance from within the house itself, adequately lit up the exterior. The car's headlights showed this to be a wide, flat area but broken into several sub-sections; two sheds - one quite large the other quite small, a scrub garden with indistinct boundaries or rows, a patch of grass obviously not mowed for some time, and what could be a large coop or a pen just showing at the back.

They parked between two other cars, one a Honda Civic, the other an old Austin Westminster, antique but in acceptable condition. Both seemed carelessly thrust into the clearing a little way from the house. A thick grove of shrubs separated this area from the house. Through it a stone walkway covered with gravel from the edge of the path led to long, wide steps, perhaps half a dozen, which ascended to a large, exposed front patio stretching the width of the house.

"This is it," Hasim said casually more as a signal to exit the car than an expression of pride in the quality of the structure.

"Where do you keep your bike?" Elwood asked as he stepped outside.

Hasim grinned. "I don't live here any more. Just visit a lot. I keep the bike home," he pointed to somewhere along the road, "but I do all the fixing over there." He pointed to the large shed. "I keep all my tools there. Show you in the morning. Feed time now. I hope you like curry."

"It's my favourite magic word. Beats abracadabra." He caught Fauna's smile and returning it followed her as she, bouncing up the steps, led into the house. Turning as he mounted to the wide porch Elwood looked around to see Hasim bringing out his backpack.

"You don't have to," he called out. "Leave the other stuff anyway."

Hasim waved in acknowledgment.

Two boys in their early teens pushed through a creaking storm door almost knocking into Fauna. The resemblance to the doctor was profound. Both had the same gleeful eyes and rounded features as the doctor yet displayed an ebullience that would seem unlikely in him. The smaller of the two led the way elbowing at the other who tried to move past him. They were both slim and their faces suggested a strong kinship (more than likely brothers) - especially their wide eyes and long noses. The smaller though had a more open smile, free of any reticence and it seemed to Elwood that he would have liked to say much if he were allowed to speak. The other, only slightly taller, had more a quizzical look to his smile. His hair mopped in disarray, contrasting sharply with his more closely cropped sibling.

"Watch it you guys," Fauna cautioned gruffly if playfully. "This is Siba and Dharo," she introduced them holding on to their hair as they struggled against her and with each other. "This is Woody," she completed the introduction and released them.

"I'm Siba!" the one in front dared.

"I'm Dharo. You can call me Tom," the taller boy said proudly.

"Yes, yes," Fauna said patting his head. "Let's go inside."

Inside, that is just past the front door, was an area wider and longer than any two he had ever seen. Though still generally referred to as the Living room, it was divided into two separate areas by a channel rug and two posts flanking it. It was airy; large windows placed around the three outer walls and on the forth, three entrances leading to other parts of the house. The one on the left was a closed door, the middle, swing doors leading to a corridor, and on the right an opening over which hung a thick, unbroken line of dark wooden beads.

The left side (the side with the closed door), though separated from the other by only that path to the swing doors, could have been considered a family room. Fauna said the kids called it the TV room and others the reading room. In it were large, deep chairs where two young men sat (both had risen upon his entrance) as well as a small desk and shelves of books in one corner. The TV in the corner was turned off.

On the other side of the posts, the true living room seemed untouched and untroubled, more a showpiece for special occasions. Here the chairs were dark as the low coffee table and the cabinet in the corner, the walls, tastefully papered and sparsely adorned but for a large gold framed picture or painting.

As he moved to get a better view, something caught his eye; something familiar – an experience perhaps. Then it dawned on him and he smiled with the melancholy of meeting a long lost friend. It was his bike. His first work with the signature almost shyly inscribed:

'Obzocky'.

CHAPTER -40 -
meet the family

THE PAINTING WAS HUNG above a long bureau covered with bric-a-brac; silver goblets and candlesticks, as well as some wooden and ceramic pieces that had distracted his first glance. Still smiling he retreated, but on returning had caught Fauna's smile as she turned away. The two youngsters had noticed nothing. The two, more adult young men from the family room introduced themselves.

"Memin," was small and bespectacled with a thin moustache and penetrating eyes, serious to the point of suspicion. His greeting was perfunctory, following which he quickly, almost impolitely, returned to his deep chair and his large, hard covered book.

"Ansaro," on the other hand more closely resembled Fauna, his features more comely than either Memin or Hasim. He was quite genuine in his handshake and greeting. "I'm a teacher also," he added. "I teach second grade, though. Not like Memin and Mary."

"What do they teach?"

"They teach high school."

"A house of scholars, then."

"When I grow up," Dharo interrupted, "I'm going to be a doctor."

"He likes to cut people up," Siba teased. Everyone laughed. Even Dharo.

"I'm going to be a surgeon like Da," he countered.

"That's fantastic," Elwood said encouragingly. Looking around he saw that Fauna had gone inside with Hasim and their father. For a moment he did not know what he should do and only half listened to an exchange between Dharo and Siba obviously continuing an unresolved argument they'd had earlier. Then Fauna and the others emerged from the set of swing doors. An elderly woman followed. The likeness in Fauna and Ansaro was immediately apparent. He would have guessed her age as in her late forties or early fifties yet there was something not quite right about that assumption. She was still wiping her hands in an old apron with a ripped pocket.

"This is my wife," the still smiling Dr. Carrington muttered in a way that reminded Elwood of an usher with a flashlight showing him to his seat; polite, perfunctory and softly so as not to disturb the other patrons enjoying the movie in progress.

"How do you do," the wife extended her hand after another quick wipe. The grip was strong and bony and Elwood revised her age adding to whatever its truth, years of toil and hardship she perhaps had faced with equanimity and acceptance. Not as his own mother had done with surrender, but with wear and tear from an on-going battle she refused to concede.

She was taller than her husband but her height was not stately; more hunched and meek, her pretty face, sharp but friendly, her hair a plebeian white, almost dirty. Yet from her retiring eyes there came a smile of welcome which sincerity Elwood could not question.

"How do you do, Mrs. Carrington," he offered, "I'm Woody. You have a charming family."

"Oh, thank you," she said shyly, bowing her head. "Please... come... sit," she indicated the beaded entrance.

Fauna led him through the curtain to the dining room; a large room with a long table completely prepared for a feast. To this room there were two other entrances, one leading to the corridor with a similar curtain, the other an exposed opening to the kitchen. From this entrance a young woman entered. She carried a large dish which she handed over to Hasim.

"It's finished," she said to Mrs. Carrington. "Dharo, sit over here."

Hasim placed the dish in the centre of the table then led the woman to Elwood.

"This is my wife, Zora," he smiled as she extended her hand though did not smile and only nodded with a curiosity that was not unfamiliar to him. "We live closer to the town," Hasim continued, "but sometimes we eat here. Zora helps out, especially if Ma's not feeling well."

"How do you do," Elwood smiled politely in spite of her unchanged expression. He wanted to inquire if this was one of those times when Mrs. Carrington was not well but let it pass. The others crowded in as Fauna pulled out a chair for him. Politely he took it but waited as she sat in the one between him and her mother. The two youngest sat opposite with their two older brothers as Hasim then his wife flanked Elwood's other side. Almost instantly, talk began. Rather, from the tone, it had been the continuation of talk. Elwood caught from Ansaro's first remark that another individual had been expected that night but that he had called excusing himself. Something about an old car was given as the reason he would not be present. It was accepted with laughter.

"Gerald Mohammed is an old friend," Fauna explained almost shyly.

"He has this great big Buick," Hasim added, "a V-eight, almost twenty years old. Always gives him trouble. He's a taxi driver from Arima - chartered service. Kinda sweet on..." he jabbed with his thumb in Fauna's direction.

Elwood turned in time to see her blush and turn away.

"Oh, you," she said, covering her face, then quickly turning back, dipped her finger in the glass of water and flicked it at Hasim. Elwood too was sprinkled and thought of retaliating but instead smiled and tried to catch her eye. She looked away, the sleepy blush only slightly dimming her eyes.

"Will you show me how to paint?" Siba said unexpectedly.

"Siba," his mother responded quickly as everyone else gasped. "Mind your manners!"

"Oh... it's all right," Elwood waved. "I'm glad..."

"Well, we didn't want you to think..." from Ansaro.

"Mary told us..." from her mother.

Elwood held up his hand.

"It's all right. And," he turned to Siba, "of course I'll show you what I know."

"We have three of your works," Fauna explained.

"I saw the bike. That's where I remembered you now. From the gallery. You were there with a group. Did you buy it then?"

"Yes! Da bought the others. Before they became too expensive."

"I'm flattered."

"I have a bike," Siba informed him timidly.

"Me too," Dharo said more proudly.

Out of the corner of his eye Elwood saw Mrs. Carrington bow her head and make the sign of the cross. None of the others did. He glanced at Fauna. She did not miss it.

"Mom still believes. She used to be a Catholic," she whispered.

"No one else?"

"No... not really."

"What's your religion," asked Memin, who had heard the exchange and obviously seen his mother.

"I have none. That is to say, I believe there is a God, but I don't think He's in a book or a building."

"But what makes you say, 'there is a God,' then," he continued.

"Memmy leave him alone," his mother chided.

"No! It is good to know these things. Do you mind?" he directed from his mother to Elwood.

"Oh no!" Elwood smiled. "But it does seem strange that very often those who say they don't believe spend a lot of time asking others to defend God."

"So... you believe?" Fauna asked.

"I suppose I must since I truly have no facts but only a feeling."

As he glanced around at the faces, even those having their own discussion at the other end of the table, he thought he caught a little smile from Mrs. Carrington. Her head was bowed though and he thought then that it could have been his imagination. Still, he was sure he had a friend in his own little *credo.*

"But aren't feelings based on substantial knowledge," `Ansaro asked. "Da, you've read Niche's..."

His father chuckled, taking a spoonful of Goat curry and spreading it over the rice. "Let's not bring the old guy into this."

"He's a long ago and far away, isn't he Da," Fauna joked; probably one of her father's predictable lines.

"Sound logic has no era," Memin said as either a quote or his own personal maxim.

"...Nor does it belong to the individual who utters it first," Ansaro added.

"'Do unto others...' First said by Plato, then by Jesus. Who therefore has claim to it?" Memin asked. "Nevertheless it stands, but more as a balance between right and wrong, a condition to the relationships of society. Yet what part of it is superstition and what part logic. Small guy and big guy. Does it hold for the small guy as well as the big guy? What would the small guy do to the big guy that he would like... or not, be done to him?"

"And superstition..." Elwood.

"Avoiding doing or saying or even thinking in a vacuum for fear that something within that vacuum might exist... and do unto you."

"Yes, but..." Elwood had interjected without considering he was in the presence of several teachers and a doctor. But as soon as the words were out, he realized it. "On its own," he dared having really no choice in the silence that expected more from him, "without anyone being superior or inferior, is it not an excellent standard for human relationships?"

"Of course," Fauna immediately acknowledged. "Advice, prayer, or just simple statement; it has great merit, you must agree."

"And don't forget, Jesus said it."

This last came from Mrs. Carrington. As all eyes turned to her as she sat holding up one finger and a fork in her other hand, she too paused, then returned to the plate.

"Authority!" Elwood exclaimed. "It's a good point!"

"What do you mean?" Ansaro.

"Is that what Mom meant?" Fauna.

"A very good point," the doctor once again spoke. "Although Plato said it, did he truly understand it? As your Ma said, Jesus... The Son of God, if you accept his authority, is this not his divine authority talking. If even he says it last, isn't it therefore more the confirmation that Plato needs to add truth and dimension to the words?"

"Wonderfully said, Mrs. Carrington," Woody smiled looking at the elderly woman who hung her head even lower yet failed to shield her shy smile. The doctor patted her shoulder and smiled.

Throughout all of this, dishes were being passed around without any break in the flow of their transportation. Exclamations and interruptions notwithstanding, scooping, pouring, ladling continued steady and undisturbed by the incessant, often overlapping talk and the subsequent munching and smacking of crisp lettuce, steamed rice and curried goat. They ate just as readily with fingers as with spoon, knife and fork, dipping often into finger-bowls and wiping constantly in the abundance of paper napkins and towels strewn about the table. Emboldened by their lack of concern over their own etiquette, Elwood felt expected to dig in with gusto. Which he did.

Challenged with several varieties of hot sauces he accepted and tasted one, suffered, and tasted the others. Weeping and smiling, his ears ringing, his mouth watering, his lips screaming, he fed upon the strange wonder of the food and with every bite, washed it down with cold beer. He thought of telling them about the Swiss but felt he would have to explain too much more. Instead he plunged ahead in an apparent frenzy to see which would fill him first, the beer or the hot food. The beer lost. Long after he was completely sated, he still sipped, if only to soothe his flaming lips.

At Fauna's insistence he carried his third beer to the less formal side of the living room where one conversation continued unabated. Memin had returned to his large, thick chair while Ansaro and Hasim sprawled along a long, deep couch. The subject of discussion had changed and all three spoke at once. The television in the corner was now on but no one was looking at it. Fauna led him in and sat next to him in the large divan. Siba brought a small table, pulling it noisily from another chair and set it next to Elwood's elbow. Upon it he conspicuously placed a coaster. And smiled as Elwood placed his glass on it.

"Siba, your homework," Fauna chided handing him an exercise book and a copy of Dickens' Oliver Twist.

"I know, I know," he assured her though taking them reluctantly. "Only a little left."

"Bring it when you're finished," she ordered gently.

"And tell Tom..." Memin added more severely, breaking from the heated discussion with Ansaro and Hasim. "As a matter of fact," he said rising from the large chair, "let me go with you."

As he led Siba out, Hasim addressed Elwood.

"He always likes to take charge," he said with a smile. "To Da or to the little ones, it's the same."

"What is the discussion?" Elwood asked.

"There's going to be a strike," Fauna explained. "You might not have heard... It's the public schools again."

"Always is," Ansaro added. "And always the high schools in this area."

"But isn't that against the law? Wasn't this deemed an essential service some years ago?"

"No! It was only promised," Fauna said wearily. "So many things promised - smaller classes, more classrooms, more teachers. Do you realize it was twenty years ago that such proposals were first voiced? Twenty years ago. All that's been happening is, somebody uses it as a political statement to get into power, but then once there, it's ignored. That's why teachers leave the island."

"That's why, those who go away to England don't come back as teachers," Ansaro stated, a fact Elwood had heard with some repetition.

"But," Fauna continued, curling her bare legs beneath her and facing Elwood completely, "it's the children who always suffer."

If he could only capture that, Elwood thought. It was the way her face had turned and her expression now earnest and appealing sought his understanding. He nodded; but only half was directed to what she said. Not even half. He felt a blush. But it could be the beer or the long day. He seated himself more comfortably against the thickly padded armrest, lifting one knee toward her and stretching his other leg along its side.

"Here, take off your boots," she said and moving pulled at the one on the floor. Elwood slipped off the other.

"Oh, someone's going to be jealous," Hasim teased.

"Oh shut up," Fauna snapped with some shyness and a smile just pouty enough to lend impatience to it. "I'll put these by the door," she added as she hastened away.

But she did not return. At least, not as Elwood knew.

CHAPTER -41 - a tryst in time

IT WAS DARK. ELWOOD at first did not know what had awakened him then he realized it was the dream again. He arose from the divan and through the dimness as his accustomed eyes could now discern the bodies of the two brothers as he remembered them; sprawled along the long couch, their legs wide, one upon the belly of the other, arms akimbo and heads against shoulders. Memin's chair was empty. The TV was off. Clearly someone had done that as well as switched off the lights. He looked around then walked softly across the room to the patio doors. Opening them gently he stepped onto the porch.

It was as day though with a blue haze masking all but the deep black shadows. That which was lit was clear in form and distinction as though all colours but the same pre-eminent blue were muted. The moon would be behind the house so that its light's vibrancy reached far up the hill and even revealed the road as a winding though broken line snaking up through the overhanging forest.

The plastic chair at the end of the porch was cold. He sat nevertheless and looking over the banister remembered the dream.

She had touched him. Strange! He could never dream as an adult. Always the child and not only the child, but the helpless child. Now he tried to separate the dream from the reality behind it.

"A least you're no Michelangelo."

Again he was embarrassed. But sweetly as though he should have been but immediately became as one forgiven by his own very adult sexual urge. And the logic of age that comes with experience.

"Let me see."

It's strange too how pretty young girls bring smiles, yet with handsome older women, smiling is not possible. Is it therefore an acknowledgment of control that the smile depicts? How old was he? Nineteen! Was he still nineteen! How old is nineteen? How young is nineteen! He felt it. Wide eyed and innocent. A child at nineteen. Everything else had grown up but that. The dream too refused to age, refused to learn from the dream before. It remained in sweet helplessness as one afraid to change or even question, where the change or the question might hold an answer that was more undesirable than the former condition from which it sought to flee.

But was it unfair?

Aye, there's the rub.

Innocence is not confined to brackets of age. That was experience talking. Not the artist. The man. The social animal that knows, and knows the difference, or at least can make the argument.

The thing about it, though, was that her face betrayed nothing. Curiosity, perhaps! But curiosity is not like a question or puzzlement that elicits a frown or a squint, peering into query without any clue to the solution. Curiosity has more the arrogance of a smirk, feeling the answer, even knowing it, yet needing only confirmation for its argument.

She knew the answer. He was indeed aroused.

He covered his face. *God! Why did he have to be the fool? Why conscience and shame when she had only curiosity.*

He would have liked to have his sketch-pad so it could occupy his mind. The shed, for instance. The lines of its roof and corner wall and the intersecting tree that leaned across it. He traced in his mind the flow of lines he could seat within a perfect frame. It had no need for colour or daylight; they would only distract; bring smells and warmth and give it a dimension he could not ignore. But there against the blackness, it was total - perfect.

A woman is not old at forty. He knew that now.

It is difficult to know it though not when your eyes are swimming in pleasure and your breath comes in spurts as delicious waves rolling over you.

On the other hand, is it not possible for the woman to feel the same? Forty says something. Even in the eyes of a nineteen-year old toy, that perhaps was the concept reflected from within. And even if it had begun as a curiosity, perhaps the reality of age had overtaken what was simply a play on daring, shocking words. Arrogant words that should have simply stated that she was above that, or perhaps, not with a child.

Let me see.

It was not a demand. It was simply a playful dare. Had he the courage to show what should have been an embarrassment? But what is it about young men that brings them to their feet when they should sit and cower, when they should run away and cry into a pillow and wait to be comforted by the older, more mature hand soothing their brow and reassuring them that this happens to young men at this time and at this age. But perhaps he had been beyond that, in age and in urge. Perhaps he had been at the point young men reach whose courage is challenged and whose libido alone is left to answer that challenge. He had stood up, not entirely with defiance, but more as one not in full control of his legs or his hands or his mind. He had looked toward her eyes and had seen them fall and the smile wane and the lips open and even in her glance he had felt his power return to him.

Report on Diary entry of Jan. 16th:

He had seen her breast. It was perhaps her fault for wearing only a bath-robe, expecting as usual that he would simply leave the work on the table. But he had ignored her "leave it on the easel" from the bathroom and had remained, wanting her to see it in his presence. The interconnecting door between their apartments had been left unlocked so they could retain some privacy but with facilitated access to each other.

It was moreover the fifth day and he had already sketched enough for a minor exposition. With growing familiarity and a matter of course, each piece had been displayed for her perusal. But he had painted this last, the Basin, from memory, an eight-by-ten miniature that seemed more to match his mood than depict reality. He was therefore curious to see her reaction.

Still drying her hair she made straight for the work. She propped it against the lamp then against the telephone. But as she moved it into the light he had noticed the robe move too far to the left and noticed too that she did not mind or give it any regard. The painting captured her. He knew it as her hand clutched at her pale throat. The robe closed again. As she stood back he turned a little to look at her face in profile. She brought her glasses up to her eyes and bent to look more closely at the water lapping at the marble sized pebbles he had taken pains to describe. There; it opened again fully revealing in its entirety the treasured pink nipple and a fullness he had in the past only hoped was so. She noticed it, something womanly, an instinct, and, almost guiltily, rose. Her turn toward him was slow. His turn away from her was quicker and he immediately sought the edge of the bed and covering himself with entwined fingers almost fell into it.

"Elwood," she smiled with some smugness, "are you aroused?"

The flush burned as a fire, the question exciting him even more and though he dared not breathe, there was really no discomfort. He did not smile nor did he cower. The thumping shame of his own accepted and desired guilt was more a puzzlement, though he could feel nothing impersonal in the strangeness.

"Let me see," she asked, her smile wider, superior and playful, teasing, as she would ask a child unaccustomed to audience to sing a song he knew implicitly yet would not have the courage to execute. Or had she discovered a weakness in his embarrassment that would give her back the strength she had lost in his superior skill and confidence.

Removing his hands, he stood, feeling the stiffness against the material command her attention and, he though, her respect. Her glance up did not deter him. There was redness in her cheeks and her lips had become full and, passing her tongue over the quick dryness that had come to them, moist. Her eyes too. Softened. And her breathing. As his.

"At least you're no Michelangelo," she said though they both knew immediately that the quip was entirely without humour this time.

"I'm not ashamed," he had said. "I want... I need..."

"I know," she said quickly though it was more a gasp. She stepped forward. It could have been an

attempt to pacify, to reassure him that she understood young men's uncontrolled reactions, their strange requests to which young girls responded with alarm and joyous fleeing. But she was not a young girl and when he reached, she did not flee.

When dawn came and the mountain line ending the stars now marked a clear distinction from the softening sky, he relaxed and closed his eyes.

CHAPTER -42 - an hospitable family

HE FELT THE HAND before he heard the voice.

"Didn't you want to sleep in the guest room?"

"What!"

Opening his eyes sleepily he looked up at her face and the smile that immediately captured him.

"We have a guest room, you know," Fauna said, the smile more pronounced. Behind her another figure moved. He glanced past her as she moved to one side but closer. It was her father. The doctor chuckled and nodded his head but did not speak.

"No! No! It's all right. I had a good sleep actually," Elwood protested. "Was I snoring?"

"No! Do you?"

"No! But why were you smiling then?"

She laughed shyly. "Other things."

An erection perhaps, he thought as he rubbed his eyes, left over from the dream and the cold morning. He was not embarrassed though he dared not look down. But who else saw it. Or would she let them.

"Anyone else up"

"No! I came out first and... You were cold and I covered you."

He looked down and there indeed was a blanket. He smiled.

"We'll have breakfast, Da," she said turning to face her father. "Would you tell Mom?"

He shuffled off chuckling.

"I have to tell you something," she said making a face as though there would be reluctance in her message. "You had a wet dream."

"Oh Cheeze..." he started, flustered, then smiled. "Did I..."

"Yes!" Now there was something of a teasing delight in her voice.

Now he was shocked... But more so that he was not embarrassed. He felt a strange excitement almost as though something very intimate, very private and cloaked in illicitness had taken place between them.

"Can I tell you a secret?" he smiled as, with an overwhelming urge to hide within daring and brazen it out, he beckoned with his finger.

She bent closer as on her part almost defying him not to be embarrassed.

"It happens," he whispered.

"You're a wicked man," she whispered back. "Come. I'll lead you to the washroom."

He arose and stretched, then followed her - closely.

After breakfast (he could not believe it was seven thirty) they piled into both cars and headed out to the beach. Elwood rode alone with Fauna. The trip was not long but they had not been private since she had led him to the bathroom where he could wash up and change the offensive garment. He had moreover avoided her shy smiles as he was sure she did. He had begun to realize these smiles are definite signals, often misconstrued, that denoted special feelings where there may or may not be any. Still, it is a clear indication that a conversation of sorts is continuing. It had seemed funny between Adrian and Vera, Joe and Lucy and hilarious between Spat and Eunice. But they had been young and laughter was excused. Now, with nothing but a few hours and an inadvertent ejaculation between them, Elwood did not want laughter to determine the degree to which he had become attracted to Fauna. Apart from which, she was so much in control, so above foolishness, he wondered how much of the scenario was in his mind. To that end he brought up their first meeting.

"The coincidence of your knowing me is too amazing. I'm sure I don't have that many photographs of myself around."

"Are you serious? We all know you up here. How long have you been passing through Matura and Le Poui?"

"On my way to Toco, for a long time."

"Well it has to be more than six years. We see you every time... or at least hear about you. The young girls titter and their mothers cluck and pretend," she laughed a free delightful sound that he wanted to hear again. "You know that little deli on twenty-six? You always have a quiet breakfast there... the little corner with your back to the door. Let's see, second week in February, Saturdays at around eight, or Sundays around nine. Unless it rains. Oh, and you came early last year."

That was acceptable. The townsfolk at the little restaurant in Matura where he created quite a hubbub would remember him differently. It was there he had punched out one of the customers (himself taking quite a beating from two of his friends) over his refusal to buy them a beer. The police had been called in and had the owner of the deli not explained the truth of the matter and pacified all the parties, Elwood would have spent some time in jail. He never stayed in Matura since that time, but always dropped in for a coffee and a greeting before moving on.

He shook his head, his smile wide and incredulous. "You mean I'm that predictable. I've been coming this way because I was sure no one knew me. And, as a matter of fact, not in all the years has anyone even talked to me. 'Cept the cook, the one with the pouting face and the scraggly reddish moustache and, oh yes... the hat. Don't tell him, but I've been meaning to paint him for some time."

"Agouti?"

"Agouti! Oh, that suits him. That really suits him."

"How would you do it? Just sketch him, and then take it home?"

"Maybe. That's how I usually do it. But sometimes I would like to just paint. If I could get someone to sit still." He was looking at her as she glanced around. "Why didn't you agree?"

"Oh that. I was nervous. Couldn't you tell?"

"Yes. At first I wasn't sure but when you went on babbling... asking me if you were pretty an' all, then I knew you just wanted to leave."

"Yes. I must have seemed so foolish."

He shook his head. "No. Not at all foolish."

"You're getting me nervous again." It was a quick glance but said with a smile. "You should stop that."

"What?"

"Looking at people like that."

"Like what?"

"Studying them. Isn't that what you do?"

"I suppose. I don't mean to. But I suppose it's because you have an interesting... face. Your face is pretty. Sorry. You always this self-conscious."

"Well, I wasn't always a schoolmarm. Of course I'm going to be self-conscious when someone tells me.... you know, that I'm pretty. I can't see it myself, but when people say it, I have to believe it or think it's just a very tired line. So if I chose to accept it for honesty sake, I suppose I could regard myself, not just swelled in the head, but, basically, pretty... or at least something someone likes."

"Yes. So do you believe me then?"

"Nope!" she laughed.

But she was pretty. Perhaps too pretty for the canvas and too happy to give her a calamitous or unsettling mood. Tessa on the other hand, though even more classically beautiful, adapted easily to tragedy. She was tragic; though he could think of nothing specific to reinforce that theory. It could be in the disappointments of her past life, secrets she hid with a desperation that somehow hovered about her eyes and certain looks, or perhaps something to come, a disaster with which she flirted, as he had cautioned her, though as yet unimagined. Fauna, with that same ability to flirt - more, to as receptive a suitor - was happy, and destined for happiness. And therefore truly pretty. The conclusion over, he began to enjoy her prettiness.

She was a woman. Yes, indeed young; but there is a stage in womanhood that once passed, a young girl becomes that superior creature weak men find intimidating and strong men find... breathtaking. A woman - not the young girl Tessa continued to be and delighted in being - but one in dignity and respect as well as allure. Elwood had once thought about it as being a part of the defensive make-up of the female psyche. That at least took the puzzlement out of the analysis. But it was no answer to the softening eyes and shy smile and the feeling he now had that he was being invited into them. If he could paint her now he would have imagined the Basin in its mystery and symmetry, both alluring to him, though the water beneath the falls would not be that numbing cold upon first entry. She would rather have been the refreshing coolness after both the midday sun and a swelteringly humid air had stifled him almost to stupor. The towering rocks and the overhanging forest surrounding the pool would be his protection from praying eyes seeking humour in his delight. Nor would they be as imposing or unforgiving to his attempts to scale their heights. And the cascading water! It would be the life he could take forever to capture.

Did she hear him?

"What! What are you thinking," he asked. "You smiled suddenly."

"Nothing," she smiled.

"I'd love you to invite me again," he suddenly suggested.

The words now more request than imposition seemed so natural and familiar that for a moment Elwood wondered how he could have thought it otherwise.

"Of course. Anytime," she replied.

But was it etiquette? Was it kindness? Was it empty?

Now, even with nothing more to discuss he found the end of the drive too sudden. They pulled on to the shoulder behind the other car. Hasim and Ansaro stood outside. The opened passenger door and the leg sticking out could only be Memin reading his book. The doctor remained in the driver's seat till they stopped. Then he got out quickly and smiling widely, waved. Ansaro too was eager and at the ready when they removed the pile of stout rope from the trunk. Hasim attached it to the rear bumper of the lead car.

"Ansaro can go with you and show you," he directed. "Mare, you stand at the ridge and tell me when to stop and go. And I'll tell Da."

The whole scenario took on the look of a quiet get together, but as Ansaro descended the hill dragging the end of the rope, he looked at his watch. It was an unconscious look that suggested impatience but revealed perhaps a time schedule to which they needed to adhere.

"What's the time," Elwood asked as he stumbled after him.

"Pretty close to eight."

"Are you going to be late for classes?"

"No! We'll make it."

He could only mean the three teachers. Elwood hurried now. The glance at the watch had served its purpose. It had been years since Elwood himself had had cause to glance at a watch. He had been so much a part of nature's alarms - to sleep, to wake, to eat, to rest - that he regarded clocks as anachronous. He would so have regarded the people who lived by these timely alerts and directives had he not been sympathetic to their fates. After all it was not so long ago that he himself was so bonded.

The incline was steep but short. The rope followed a straight line cutting at an obtuse angle across the more gentle path on which Elwood had descended to the beach. He reasoned this path would be the objective of the upward climb. If they could get the bike this far (and he still had doubts) the rest of the way would be easy.

It helped that Ansaro had done it before, and not so long ago that it required a crunch of memory. He made straight for a clearing above the little stream where the angle was not as severe as the drop-off Elwood had used.

"Bring it around here," he ordered pulling down the rest of the rope.

Elwood hit the ground at a run and made for the grove.

The bike was even more beautiful framed against the backdrop of ascending stalks and the coconut tree against which it rested. For a moment Elwood paused to commit it to memory. It was lazy. Glistening it seemed wet black amid its chrome pipes it reclined as an enormous elephant seal that had rubbed its back against a large scratching post. Now it slept, not soundly, but just on the cusp of awakening as with only a gentle nudge.

It leapt to life; the one touch of its electric nudge more than enough to rouse it from slumber. Elwood immediately put it into gear and rode it over to where Ansaro stood patiently. Ansaro quickly passed the rope through the lower frame and crash bar and double knotted it.

"That all right?" he asked though more for assurance than as a suggested effect that could be subject to change.

Elwood nodded and revved, urging the machine forward into the stream. Ansaro shouted and waved his hands in a forward motion. Elwood felt the rope grow taut and straddling the bike for balance, his two feet against the giving slope he now let the rope do its work. As it began to pull he let out the clutch and felt the rush of power to the rear wheel. Not too much. He knew he should not force it least it dig a hole into the loose soil. Just enough to assist the climb. Ansaro now pushed from the back. It was a very gentle shove, but it was not needed. The rope tightened to a rigidity that suggested it was at the breaking point. But the bike lifted, and as Elwood let out the clutch and the engine screamed, it leapt up the incline and determinedly gained ground, ascending at a steady but manageable pace.

The root sticking out just below the path did not at first present a problem when Elwood saw it blocking his way. He simply angled the bike and tried to turn the wheel. But the wheel would not turn. The rope from the frame lay hard along the rim preventing any movement to the right or left. For a fleeting moment he thought of calling out, then almost immediately it was too late. The wheel hit the root and jammed, lifting the rear of the bike for what seemed an eternity... then the rope parted.

It was not a new rope but had certainly seemed strong enough for the simple job. And in fact it had done its job. However it was not up to the test the root had arranged. A weak spot, not far from the top of the hill, suddenly gave. The upper part of the rope whipped out across the empty road. The lower snapped back, and as Elwood braked to at least prevent a downward plunge, the rope leapt at him as a rubber band seeking its state of rest. The inert mass though did not come to rest. It folded in the air, gathering weight and condensing to tightly packed unit shot against Elwood with such force that upon contact with his chest it took him completely off the bike and sent him sprawling down the hill. The bike followed, slipped at first then tumbled at an angle away from the route Elwood took.

This last was the only fortunate aspect of the incident. Had the bike followed the flailing, helpless body, it would most certainly have crushed him at the bottom of the drop. Instead it came to rest against a tree, its hooked handlebars gripping the stem as one tumbling from a roof would clutch at an overhang for dear life.

Immediately, (he had not quite lost consciousness) Elwood knew something was amiss with his arm. He had felt the numbing snap as he hit the ground reflexively reaching out for something to stay his plunge. Though the pain was not immediate he instinctively knew what the numbness hid. But that was the least of his troubles.

Air! He gasped for it. It would not come. He now realized that he had not breathed since the rope had made contact with his chest. He struggled, pleaded silently for a help he knew could not come. His eyes opened toward the hill he thought he saw fauna, though his arms (the injured one was now excruciating to the touch) were being pulled over his head. Someone was screaming, ‘Stop’. The voice was light and shrill. Fauna. Then swiftly, a darkness came.

CHAPTER -43 - a bump and a break; rescued

THE MOMENT ITSELF WAS crazy as wild, bright scribblings on black canvas; colours and movement intertwined. And someone sitting on his chest. He was being dragged by his feet through the forest, not along the path but through the rill above the falls. The water was cold and uncomfortable but not so much as the sharp stones along the bottom of the stream. He felt each one as they passed underneath. He tried to kick but his legs were broken. No! Not his legs. But still he could not move them. If he could only push the person off; the one who sat on his chest. Why did he sit on his chest? Joe was trying to push him off. Pete was praying. He tried to call Pete but there was no sound. It was all so deathly quiet. The forest was still except for the feeling that there was a different something, not sound - perhaps noise, the kind of white noise you heard when you opened the window and suddenly you were connected to the outside world. A presence

- not a ghost or anything creepy. An awareness, a dimension you didn't know existed till you opened the window. It was there in the forest. With the cold water and the sharp stones. And someone sitting on his chest.

She was kissing him. He tried to push her off. Pete might see her. He could feel his judgmental eyes even though he had his head bowed. Her lips so soft. Why did he enjoy her lips so much? Perhaps he should just give in and enjoy her. That would be so easy. Yet he must resist. Adrian himself would not like it. No matter what she said, no matter her excuses... Perhaps though, it was because he resisted that she said those things. What needs?

Leave me alone?

He gasped and opened his eyes as Fauna was descending to his face. She drew back, startled.

"Oh God!"

He gulped in the air and weathering the pain in his chest breathed deeply.

"Ow!" he said softly, more a whisper but not moaning, and breathed shallower. "Oh my head! My arm..."

"Yes! It's the ulna, I think, there's a big bruise below, it's either cracked or broken. Broken, I think. The radius seems to be okay, that's why the arm's not hanging. But it could be cracked as well. Though... Ansaro's gone for Da. Just lie still. Are you cold?"

"No! Cool. My feet... my toes are wet. How's the bike."

"Oh you... the bike! Forget the bike."

She was on the verge of tears now and it felt good. Comfort had indeed many faces. Warm sheets and cool blankets, feet up and a dish of balata, and mango wedges sprinkled with salt and black pepper. Sunset after the rain! This was another. Gentle eyes and soft fingers to soothe the pain. If he could only sketch her outline at that moment, everything would be perfect.

"Here," he stirred, "help me tuck my arm into my shirt."

"No! Keep still. You could also have ribs broken. In fact I'm sure of it."

"Then I'll need your help."

"No! Don't. Why are they taking so long?" Her words were as restrained panic, begging him to heed her advice and her suffering. He would have ignored her though, but for the sharp stab under his heart as he tried to move.

"Ow," he said again but indifferently, without emotion, as though the word itself, when uttered, was comfort enough.

"See! See! You're not to move again. Why doesn't he listen to me?" she asked of no one. "Let me do it then. Why are you so stubborn? Let me... Give it to me."

She had managed to help him lay the arm in his shirt and reversing the long tail around his arm and buttoning it and moving it against his stomach, he now rolled to an upright position.

"The thing is," he offered, "if I just wait here, it will become more difficult to move. See! Just support me a little on the other side... yes! You are strong. Help me up the other side... the path over the rocks."

As though seeing the wisdom of his words though not entirely agreeing with his determination of injury, she encircled his waist and helped him toward the rocks. Hasim was there first, then Ansaro and a little behind him the doctor followed with his little black bag. (It was actually dark brown.) But he had lost his smile.

"Let me lift you," Hasim shouted. "Don't move."

"It's all right," Elwood assured him. "We have everything under control."

"Let me see," the doctor said when he was close enough. "When you walk, is the pain sharp?"

"No! It's dull, unless I twist," Elwood reported but stopped and let the doctor feel his side and wrap his arm in a contraption that looked like a Sushi wrapper.

"Good! Then don't twist. Gently now, you may be a little light headed," he said when he was finished and moved aside.

The entourage moved cautiously up the rocky steps to the walk then, Hasim leading and the doctor trailing, continued slowly up the hill.

"I'm so sorry," Fauna whispered, seeking some privacy in the softness of her confession.

"It's all right. I'm the one should be sorry. You're going to be late for class."

"Oh!" she uttered impatiently," screw... Oh! Sorry."

He chuckled; but it hurt a little and he cut the laugh short. They helped him into the back seat of the doctor's car and Fauna got in with him.

"I'm going to the clinic," the doctor said to Hasim. "Take the others to the school and meet me back there."

"Tell them I won't be in," Fauna yelled at Ansaro.

Hasim seemed to hesitate, but the doctor did not wait. He drove off. Minutes later he was turning into the busy little Main Street of Le Poui. He did not hurry but made all the proper signals, turns, stops, yielded to amber lights, waved on pedestrians who had the right of way and, on arriving at the Bailey Clinic, parked outside the main door. Hurrying into the building he quickly emerged with two orderlies. One of them pushed a gurney before him, noisily bumping along the tiles at the front of the building. Both however tried to help Elwood from the car. Their help however, producing more pain, Fauna, screaming, waved them off and gently eased him out the other side.

The 'clinic' though referred to as such, and in spite of the fact that it once was a three room medical emergency unit, was more a hospital, and the only one in the region. There were three wards consisting of ten beds each, two semi-private rooms, an operating theatre and x-ray adjunct, a triage area, waiting room and foyer where patients were received and assessed, and three offices to the right of this large area.

Dr. Carrington had one of the offices. Elwood was taken into this office. While the doctor changed, Fauna led the way to a back room where the three helped Elwood to a sitting position. The men left after locking the wheels. Fauna swung around a little platform and slid it under Elwood's arm.

"When Da has a better look, we'll take you to x-ray. How are you feeling?"

"Pretty good," he smiled. "You do this often?"

She nodded and smiled. "But not like this. You got me in a panic. I never panic. But you almost had me crying."

"I feel better."

"One day I'll pay you back," she teased. "You look tired. You could be in shock. Do you want to lie back again?"

"No!"

Dr. Carrington entered with a nurse who immediately helped remove Elwood's shirt.

"Do you want to stay?" the doctor asked Fauna directly.

She nodded.

"But perhaps you'd better sit for a while. You look pale. She looks pale," he said to the nurse.

"Do you want some water?"

"Yes. For him too. Da, do you think he should come home with us?" she asked, turning as the nurse filled two glasses from the tap and handed them to Fauna and Elwood.

"Yes! But not till tomorrow. I want them to keep an eye on him here."

"But we could..."

"No! It would be better. It's going to be uncomfortable tonight unless he can sleep upright. I'm sure... look at that bruise, the fifth and sixth. Get him to x-ray." He scribbled on a pad and attaching it to a clipboard, placed the clipboard on the gurney. The nurse released the stops and pushed the gurney out of the office.

CHAPTER -44 - the prognosis

THE DOCTOR WAS RIGHT; it had been an uncomfortable night. But the nurses who attended him throughout (a little more closely than other patients, he suspected) made it less painfully so, eagerly adjusting the bed at his every groan. In spite of this he slept, fitfully until almost daybreak then soundly till he was awakened just before noon by very audible whispering and some shuffling about.

"You are lazy," Fauna accused softly, her face little more than a foot away from his. "I kept breakfast for you."

"Hi," he managed with just a weak smile. "That was some sleep! Did I embarrass you again?"

"You're terrible. Have some coffee. By the way, Hasim brought your bike home. I know, I know... your baby's not hurt. He said the handle's a little twisted but not to worry."

"I'm not worried," he mumbled as he took a sip. "What about the..." he nodded toward his arm.

"Da will tell you," she said matter-of-factly then furtively whispered, "it's cracked; but the two ribs are broken. Shhh."

It seemed so clandestine he was tempted to laugh. However memories of the night before stayed it.

"Has Jean and Dinah left already?"

"Jean and Dinah?"

"The two nurses... last night."

"Oh, Jean and Donna Mose... they're sisters you know."

"Oh!"

"Gone since seven. Jean and Dinah! They will laugh... You just watch them, though. They tell each other everything. And their mom too. Bet they won't sleep till all of Le Poui knows about you. Why did you ask, by the way?" "Oh, I pretty well kept them on their toes with my complaining."

"Bet they loved every minute of it."

"By the way, how come you're here and not at school?"

"Breaking biche[6]," she laughed. "Didn't you ever do it?"

"Not as a teacher. Did you get the whole day off?"

"Uh huh. Thanks."

"Thanks! You thanking me?"

"Uh huh. Famous artist fall down, go boom. They had to give me the day to take care of you."

---

6 French Patois - l'ecole biche - meaning to break school or play hooky; truancy.

"I thought it's your... Da, who's doing the taking care of."

"No! Today he's assisting. It's my show. You're coming home with us anyway, right! I'll be looking after you. Till you're better..."

For a fleeting second there seemed doubt and alarm in her look.

"Maybe I'm putting you...." he offered.

"No, no, no!" she quickly stopped him, her voice high, strained and pleading. "Say you'll come. You can't not come. You have any idea how I feel... how everyone at home feels. Hasim especially. It was his rope. And what about me. Be fair! Be a sport! You're not in a hurry to go somewhere, are you? You can't anyway. I promise, if you come home and if you have somewhere to go, I'll take you. There! How many chauffeurs have you had in your life?"

Footsteps approached. She glanced around as almost upon her turn Dr. Carrington entered.

"Da, he's coming home with us," she said quickly not looking at Elwood but standing between him and the doctor.

"Of course he is. How are you feeling?" the doctor asked moving around her.

"Pretty good."

"Have they changed the wrapping?"

"No!"

"Incidentally, you want to talk to anyone? There's a fellow out there from the radio – 1020 News."

"No... no. Definitely not."

"Mare, Honey, tell them he's not to have visitors." She hurried out. "You've two broken ribs there..." the doctor continued, "but the good news is the arm's just cracked... hairline. I hate hairline cracks. Patients always tend to ignore them. You just remember, it's a break. All right? It'll be painful for a while. Good thing you're coming home with us. But do me a favour, will you?" He stopped and looked directly at Elwood. "Don't toy with her." He let the words sink in. "She's kind of special to us. She's lived through viral pneumonia and rheumatic fever. But her heart is good. I couldn't stand it if somebody hurt her."

Elwood stared dumbfounded at the man who a day ago seemed to him a babbling, chuckling idiot with a little secret nobody cared about but himself. Blunt, straightforward, he had just laid out the rules.

"Of course," Elwood mumbled. "Of course," a second time; this time to reinforce the promise.

"Right! Now... we'll check you out a little later. This place is more out-patient than sleep-over," he peeped at the bandages. "Then we'll slip you out the back. Everything's all squared away..."

"You mean, paid for? No!" his soft voice becoming firm. "That's not going to happen. I can pay my way..."

"No, no. It was our fault..."

"Rubbish... Now I want to tell you something. You're not going to pay for being nice to a stranger. I'm just as much to blame. More! And I can afford my own folly. Listen to your daughter. She'll tell you what I cost... what I'm worth."

The doctor chuckled, one of his little idiot, 'hee hee's'. "All right, all right. But… after this, no more talk about money. Right! We will be insulted. I mean it."

"Oh well, I'd say this is a lucky break, then," he smiled, wincing at the pun.

"Yes... though it's a pity it's your right hand. Painting will be painful for a while."

"Not for me. I'm left handed."

CHAPTER -45 - Mrs Metcalf panics; Pete rages

TWO LETTERS CAME THAT day. Although the mailbox was full it consisted in large part of junk-mail and bills. There were also the bi-weekly Time, Joe's GQ, the monthly Glamour and, stuffed on top, a plastic bagged evening paper. Pete emptied the box and the overflow up to and including the slot. Making his way noisily up the steps and banging the door to open and close it he 'Hallooed' loudly. Joe and his mom were in the dining room around the long mahogany table unpacking a number of limited edition prints which would have to be framed the next morning. Mrs. Metcalf extended her cheek for Pete's perfunctory kiss and indicated the table in the corner for him to place the mail.

"And what's that called? Face fuzz two?" he snickered.

"It's a Van Dyke," Joe retorted obviously irked by his brother's tone.

"How long you..."

"Oh just leave it alone. It's my face I'll do what the hell..."

"Joe!" Mrs. Metcalf appealed wearily. "Let's not argue."

Pete pulled up a chair and reversing it sat down heavily. "When's what's her face coming back?" he asked.

"Pete! Be nice!" his mother admonished. "Lucy's gone to see her mom for a few days, that's all."

"Just want to know. You're not pissed, are ya BIG brother." Pete, a full head taller than his older brother often found that funny and worth repeating several times throughout the day. Joe never responded.

"Why don't you two get on any longer?" Mrs. Metcalf asked knowing it was unfair to include Joe in the blame for what was essentially Pete's attitude toward his older brother. It seemed that Pete had been even more impatient of late. His visits had increased but then so had his bad temper, much of which he took out on Joe... and Lucy, when she was around. Joe of course never fought back - he had always been so submissive even with Adrian who never pushed - but Lucy was turning out to be a *Feisty Little Beastie*, as Pete often referred to her, giving as much as she got even from Pete. Perhaps, he accused when warranted, eventually she would wear the pants in the family. Perhaps Joe was hoping for that very thing. Mrs. Metcalf sighed and clicked her teeth.

"Where's Woody these days?" Pete asked of no one in particular. "Is he going to help you and 'She

Wolf' with your costumes this year," he aimed at Joe. Joe shrugged but did not reply nor stop working. "Still going with Barklay? What're you going as?"

"Oh... some metallic thing," Joe finally responded.

"Future world," Mrs. Metcalf clarified. "There... what do you think," she asked holding up a small print, "white oak? Or perhaps maple!"

"Something darker," Pete offered.

"No! Oak," Joe said firmly but more to his mother. "You know the one with mahogany inlays."

"Yes! Is there a package in the shed?"

"I'll see first thing in the morning," Joe said. "I'm sure there's still a box there."

"You going to put it together?" Pete taunted.

"Maybe," Joe answered and rising went into the kitchen. They could hear the kitchen door close as Joe must have changed his mind and gone outside and into the 'shed', the garage no longer used for the car but for some woodworking and storage of art supplies.

"He's getting even more morose," Pete observed cynically.

"Well, I can't blame him," Mrs. Metcalf replied with an edge to her voice. "At least he's trying to be your friend if not your brother. I don't know why you have to be so hostile towards them. They're talking about getting married and it's a big step for both of them. You should be helping..."

"You mean she's talking about marriage. He just moves along with the current."

"That's so unfair, Peter. One day you'll meet someone and have to compromise too."

"Ma, that's not compromising. And don't try to tell me about my brother. He's Dad all over again. Follow the crowd. It doesn't matter what he's giving up - his family or himself, his intelligence, his pride - just do what somebody stronger says. And the strongest has the last say. I thought, 'what a mousy little thing' when he brought Lucy home, so meek and mild... Well, even she's stronger than him. The way she conned him with that pregnancy bit. You think any man in this whole country would have fallen for it?"

"Pete, she was... she may have been pregnant."

"Ma, nobody's pregnant for only two months. Cheeze... Even you. You're reluctant to blame her, blame anybody. You'd think..." He stopped there and seemed to flush. The change was abrupt as he turned and walked out of the dining room and into the kitchen.

The telephone rang.

Impatiently Mrs. Metcalf picked it up and untangling the cord, answered.

"Mrs. Metcalf," asked the excited voice. "This is Simple. Joe there? Did you hear about Woody? Pete there?"

"Simon, slow down. Just a minute." She covered the mouthpiece. "Pete! Simon wants to talk to Joe or you.

From the kitchen she heard Pete yell for Joe. Pete seldom wanted to talk to Simple. Pete seldom talked to any of the old group. Besides there was an extension in the shed. Joe would not have to come inside. "It's Simple," Pete yelled almost as an afterthought.

Mrs. Metcalf hung up. "He's very excited. I don't think I ever heard him so excited."

"Well, it's a good thing I didn't talk to him. When he's like that he's impossible. Remember when he heard about Frankie? I thought he was going over the edge." He had re-entered the dining room and now sat astride the table as she continued working on the prints and cleaning up the shredded paper. Suddenly they heard the hurried steps and the kitchen door burst open.

"Ma! Woody's in an accident. Simple says he's in a pretty bad way."

"Nooo," Mrs. Metcalf wailed gripping the table cloth. "Oh God, Joey, where is he."

"Some place on the east coast. It was on the radio."

Mrs. Metcalf almost ran to the elaborate stereo system where she fumbled at the knobs before it turned on. It was already dialled to one of the four local stations in the area. However there was only music on the first. She switched to the others on the preset. She whimpered with each attempt. But the news was over. Still whimpering she returned to the first. Music.

"Call the station," she yelled at her sons standing dumbly looking at her.

"Ma..." Joe pleaded, "take it easy."

"For God's sake, Pete, call the station," she almost screamed. "Find out..."

But Pete did not move. A cloud of anger masked his features. He looked angrily at Joe who returned his look with one more of sympathy and hurt than anger.

"Joe..." she pleaded, now tears and panic in clear evidence of her state.

But now even Joe did not respond. He looked at his brother as behind him their mother came apart. The message was clear; the communication painful to the extreme. They were both wrapped in Lucy's hateful words uttered during Pete's last bout with her, his accusation that she was sly and manipulative and her spiteful retort: *"You think I'm sly. You better watch that friend of yours with your mother."*

"Son of a bitch," Pete screamed and stomped out, slamming the front door.

CHAPTER -46 -
assignment, Lucien

THERE WAS QUITE A lot of activity at the Gleaner where the news originated. But there was far more excitement at 1020-News Radio, the Gleaner's radio counterpart under the same ownership. (Both media outlets were in the same building and although at different ends of the building and several floors apart, they exchanged news with as much facility and frequency as though they were in the same room.)

Since the last change of ownership and the shakeup of staff, the Gleaner had become a morning paper. That very much put it out of the immediate or continuing news coverage. Warren Toth, the reporter who had stumbled upon the story, phoned it in, then made his way quickly back (his editor's demand), now spent more time at 1020-News than at the Gleaner. His morning submission hung in News netherworld, completely written, yet to be completely re-written before they went to print.

Then it hit the fan.

The radio crew, including radio reporter Brent Lawry, sent to continue the story found the bird had flown - and the story no longer did.

"He's staying at a friend's place," Lawry reported. "He's been discharged... no operation, no critical state, not even a bent motorcycle to show. Staff says he was in and out before they even knew he was here."

"We're going to look like assholes," program director Bernie LaTouche groaned. "Just get what you can and head home."

"Want me to do a phoner from here?"

"And say what? No! We'll just leave it alone for the next couple of hours. Notice anyone from Radio Trinidad or 610?"

"No! It's a small town and not easy to find. Besides, if they even get here, they've missed the boat. Should I still hang around...? Just in case?"

"No... Yes! Maybe! It's late. You're off now, aren't you?"

"Yes. Since four."

"Don't pull anything funny, okay? Send the crew back but if you like, you can stay. We're not going to pay you overnight or anything. But if you want to stay over... at your expense, mind, we'll excuse you from tomorrow's shift. Read me. So don't come back with some big expense voucher... because I'll kick your ass downstairs. (His office was on the third floor.)"

"Cheapskate!"

"Yea, right. Just keep your ears open. There should be a little shit motel there. Give me a call when you get there?"

"Who's paying for the call?"

"Fuck off. Call collect. I guess you don't have any friends up there, do you. You don't have friends anywhere, I'll bet. Did you talk to Warren? Bet he could dig you up a friend!"

"I'm not that hard-up."

LaTouche did not react to the somewhat superior quip. "Don't forget! Call!" He hung up. But with his hand on the receiver he thought of Toth again. (How the mighty hath fallen!) How could such a promising career go down so fast? He sneered. Did that smug little twit - Lawry - ever feel the hand on his shoulder? No! Only the good ones! The human ones. The too sensitive ones. Whose turn was next, LaTouche wondered. He dialled the newsroom extension.

"Downs," he barked at the young writer who must have grabbed it on the first ring, "kill the Elwood Lucien story. We'll play it for suspense for a while. Then at ten... when nobody's listening, we'll tell everybody he's been released and everything's all right. I'm going home now. So you handle it. I need a drink. Lawrey's going to call in. When he does, take the info. Don't bother to call me at home. I'm not going to be in any kinda condition to answer." He hung up.

"Fucking rummy," he muttered crumpling Warren Toth's original report and throwing it into the wastebasket. "Gonna have your ass."

CHAPTER -47 - snake eat crappo

ELWOOD OPENED THE DOOR. His ribs hurt, but not so much now as when he tried to get out of the bed. Still, it would hurt just as much to get back in. He had to get out though.

He'd been lying there in the dark thinking of form; not individual form, but scape - the angles by which nature determines through all the basics of erosion, the relationship of trees, rocks, leaves to the slope of a hill, the force of wind and rain, the sun's burning heat or lack of it. And he thought of pieces of wood under a forest canopy, bereft of sunlight, and settled on one in particular, dank and crumbling with that dusky, mangrove smell you get when you crack open a crab's back or sink your foot, shin deep in black, swamp ooze; a smell that remained as an almost tangible memory for a long time. It was on one such piece of wood that he had found the lizard those many years ago. It was blended into a rich green background of Pommecithere[7] leaves against which the cracked branch had lain for years till the rot and the insects had given it a form and character that would live forever in that one piece of art. He sometimes compared it (not by execution but in subject) to Van Gough's yellow chair; both inanimate objects, yet with a life one could ascribe to as having breath and pulse, warmth and emotion. In retrospect, the lizard seemed attendant. It was then, as he glanced over instinctively as somehow determined by such thoughts that he had noticed the crack in the window get lighter - not bright as filtered sunlight, but just so he could see the outline of the window.

He had to get out.

He knew it was stupid to walk around in the still dark room - he could trip on something - but the chance was worth it. Probably worth it even more to see Fauna get mad with him. Peeking out, both ways, he could see, even in the dim dawn light there was no one in the living room. However, a leg stuck out from the divan on the other side. It was Ansaro's. He tiptoed through the chairs and out the front door. It was cold; the mist, dark grey and heavy and drifting in ghostlike patches down the mountain side and along the road. But the darkness had indeed lifted.

The plastic chair in the corner of the veranda, was wet; not just the cold dampness that threatened

---

7 Pronounced, *Pom-cee-tay* – Golden Apple - a fruit the size of an apple that turns yellow when ripe.

more discomfort than could actually deliver, but one that would actually soak through clothes in seconds and would be dripping and clammy against a bare forearm. Elwood thought better of trying to slide into it. If once achieving it he found remaining there too uncomfortable or too painful, he would have to go through all that fuss and bother to get out again.

His toes were cold too; but somehow the wooden floor was not wet. He looked down and wiggled his big toe.

"Wanna try the yard, big fella?" he muttered aloud. "I Guess not, but you don't have a say, do you. Suffer!"

There were no rails on the steps so he'd better not stumble. Looking down at his feet, he side stepped to the bottom then gingerly placed his foot on the first flagstone. A frog jumped just to his left startling him. It was a small one, but leapt high. Another jumped where that one landed and where it landed several hopped away into the little eddies of mist hugging the ground. The reverse domino effect brought a smile to his lips. He listened; but there were no real discernible sounds, just something distant, a susurrus of reverent notes somewhat as an atmosphere in motion but without distinctness.

He moved along the flagstone walk, his feet in protest against the sharp gravel as well as the larger, rounded stones that would not cut but rather push uncomfortably and at times with some pain against the heel and the even softer, more sensitive instep.

He was quite awake now; alert, to every nuance of sound or movement. Someone had mentioned snakes. He wasn't quite sure if it was at the house or at the clinic - troubled sleep sometimes had that strange effect of creating scenarios out of casually tossed words. But it would not do to step on one - real or other. He would either jump like one of the little frogs, or be bitten by the reptile. Both effects would be painful.

A long, thin stick of wood leaned against the fence. Upon closer examination it appeared to be an old broom handle. He had to step off the path to get it but once in his hand he felt more at ease. Now he used it to poke at large leaves and dark corners. One could not be careful enough. Once on the way to the basin they had encountered a Fer-de-lance among the bamboos. They had been careless and Simple almost paid the price of their folly. They had all passed the spot and he, bringing up the rear, had casually poked at the base of the clump. His squeal and curse galvanized the group into action. It did not flee as most snakes did but rather stood its ground rearing its head as reminiscent of a cobra. The boys in group were not threatened and set upon the unfortunate creature beating its head to a pulp with their staves. It was only later, however, upon describing the serpent as part of the story, that they learned how close Simple had come to a very painful death. His parents never learned of the snake; it was the only story he ever kept from them.

The small shed was locked. Elwood looked at it for some time, his eyes caressing its sloped walls and not quite mitred angles and the character of the wood covering it as a grey, striped skin beneath its galvanized roof. The large door to the other shed gave it a more functional appearance. It was pulled in, not locked, leaving quite a large gap though not large enough to slip through. Elwood tugged at it. However it did not give easily and realizing he would have to close it again, he aborted the effort. In any case, he did not want to disturb anything that might have itself slithered in.

He walked to the end of the drive then returned to the steps. Two steps up he sat and cleaned his feet rubbing them against the bottom step. Next he tried to spot one of the little frogs. He reasoned they must be in the damp grass. This was no longer the tall reeds that had greeted his first arrival but a shortly cropped lawn now extending all the way to the back. It was cleared but for some items that seemed not out of place; a lawn mower left sitting where the user had left it probably the day before, and some toys - a scooter, a soccer ball and some coloured string balled up and thrown in a heap just where he had seen the first frog jump.

The other side of the walk was not as well kept. There seemed more weeds than lawn grass in the area, but there were at least more flowers than weeds on that side, especially pink and white impatience and several varieties of Croton. In any imaginary frame Elwood selected he felt he could paint a completely balanced scene. Against the backdrop of weathered fence wood he pictured one of the small white flowers standing out against the dark bottom of the fence.

Then, movement.

A green slither emerged from the weeds and poking out its sleek head inspected the area. It was a large grass snake about eighteen inches long but thick around the belly. Elwood instinctively froze. The snake emerged fully and crossed the flagstone path entering the grass on the other side. Instinctively Elwood lifted his foot from the bottom step. But he was nevertheless fascinated by the ease with which the snake moved from one spot to another, slithering under his gaze to disappear then reappear a length ahead. Suddenly it stopped and lifted its head just above the short grass. Following its head's point he saw to one side of the steps a large bullfrog clumsily inching its way toward the snake. It too stopped and seemed to gaze at its enemy. Only the child's coloured toy stood in their path. An old saying came to mind:

Snake eat crappo[8]
You [9]*doodoo sweet.*

It seemed to fit his mood, a reminder that he had indeed lost his heart. All that was left was for the play to unfold as nature intended. Grass snakes ate frogs

8 Crapaud - pronounced cra-po - usually identifying an unusually large toad or bull frog.
9 Sweetheart.

as a rule, but this 'daddy-bull' seemed far too large. Yet, he'd heard of stranger things. Perhaps had the snake been even a small Macajuel (boa constrictor) the saying would have been as good as executed. But with a grass snake, even of that size, he would have to see. In any event Elwood anticipated some sort of direct confrontation with at least one victor. Bull frogs had been known to eat small snakes too, but this grass snake had some body to it. As well, both protagonists ate their prey whole, not as other predators of the beaked or sharp-toothed variety by dissecting into mouthfuls. The showdown, probably based simply on territorial claim or perhaps a right of passage, could dissolve into posturing or a series of grand charges. But for whatever reason, it would be interesting to see how the two would eventually solve the dilemma.

Away in the distance a Semp's song emanated from the mist. Other birds joined in, all distant and individual yet in a strange harmony as one, if listening for, can easily detect and isolate each note and character of the medium in the very same way one can tell violin from flute in an orchestra in spite of the one, singular tune they all serve. There was a more pronounced trill over toward the large shed and an answering warble from almost the same area...

But Elwood did not lift his head from the dramatic confrontation that commanded his attention.

The snake inched forward, then again stopped. The frog put out one crooked front member and heaved his bulk forward upon it then too stopped with the other leg grotesquely angled away from its body.

Elwood experienced a strange sense of quickening, as though he had an abundance of oxygen in spite of the fact that his breath was now so shallow he thought he had stopped breathing altogether. The pause in action had been so long now that he chanced a quick glance up toward the hills where a tremendous cacophony of shrills, squeaks, cooing, clicking and the songs of thousands of birds was in progress. The mist was lifting. The tops of the trees were now clearly visible as was the line of the mountain. A light breeze had come up too and was hurrying the mist along. All was movement now; but for the two upon the lawn.

As though upon a given signal, three things now took place. The child's ball of brightly coloured string unravelled - a Coral snake, its red, yellow and black rings clearly visible. At the same time the grass snake slid forward. Almost simultaneously the frog pounced, leaping with an agility that belied its bulk and landing with great precision on the small coral snake. The grass snake paused, changed direction and sped off. The frog with calm indifference toward the highly toxic venom of the small snake, opened its mouth and took it squirming into its jaws.

With a series of gulping snaps the conclusion was over in seconds. The bull-frog turned and after one quick little hop ambled awkwardly till it had disappeared behind the steps. Elwood drew in a deep breath and let it out slowly as he recalled the rest of the old Creole omen:

Snake eat Crappo,
You doodoo sweet.
Crappo eat snake,
You ka-ka fuit[10].

This second part meant trouble. Either he would do something foolish and pay the price, or ...

Elwood returned to bed.

He did not immediately fall asleep.

10 Your ka-ka fuit - death is inevitable.

CHAPTER -48 - recuperating

IT WAS NOON WHEN he awoke propped against several pillows to a lounging position. Outside someone had entered the house and slammed the front door. He heard Mrs. Carrington admonish that someone. He figured it to be one of the smaller children... or perhaps the doctor.

Looking around his room for the first time in the daylight he saw that it was not large; yet, not cluttered with useless furniture or the accumulations of a long term resident, it was more than adequate. He imagined his bags were stowed in the long closet opposite. The bed lay along the centre of the room between the door and the window. The jalousies were folded to one side and a white chintz hung against the panes as the only defence against the sun. Below this window a type of low foot-locker with drawers was braced against the wall. Upon it he recognized his pad and some other pieces from his saddlebag. Flanking him were two side tables. Both supported lamps, but the one on his left – closest the door –

held a tray with a small towel covering it. He peeked under the cover. The tray contained two glasses - milk and Orange juice - and a plate with fruit and some grain in a bowl. He swung his feet over the side of the bed and removing the towel completely and draping it over his leg, drank the orange juice in one gulping draught. Next he poured the milk over the grain. He had never seen that grain before but it was sweet and he detected a hint of oats. There were other tastes too - perhaps cornflakes and farina, but the sweet additive was definitely honey.

Transferring the cereal to his lips was a delicate operation; not hurried in spite of the long trip and the careful wiping of the spoon against the bowl before it could undertake such an accident-free voyage. But the clinking sound was too loud to go un-noticed and presently there was a shy knock on the door.

"Come on in," he dared.

Fauna peeped in. "Oh, you're handling it by yourself. Don't want me to feed you?"

"I can manage," he smiled. "But I like the idea. You did this? Thanks! I'm sorry it's so late. I had a good sleep though."

"I'll bring some coffee."

"No! I'll get up... one last spoonful," he transferred it to his mouth.

"I don't mind. Besides, I'm competing with Jean and Dinah you know. Can't let them out-do the doctor's own daughter."

"There... done. And thanks." He wiped his mouth and stood up finding to do so easier than getting back into bed at dawn. However as he turned to fix the sheets she moved past him.

"What're you doing? Trying to put me out of a job? We have union rules here you know."

He laughed. But there was a tinkling sweetness about the performance he would not easily dismiss. Not so much in the way or excellence of the act but in the very fact that she was doing it. He had made his bed as a matter of course ever since he could remember - first thing upon rising from it, so it would not have mattered to him, even with one hand. But this was personal. She was actually making his bed; tucking in the sheets and fluffing the pillows. Just as though they had been going through the ritual for years.

"There!" she rose and smiled as one proud of a simple act where 'no big deal' was to be made of it. "Incidentally, you made the news."

"Where?"

"On the table outside. Don't hurry."

"I'll have to call home."

"We have a phone."

He glanced back and caught her playful smile. It was then that he realized that not toying with her would not be so easy a promise to keep.

CHAPTER -49 - a meal, a discussion, and making love

GERALD MOHAMMED WAS NOT pleased when he visited the Carringtons and discovered a painter had invaded his prized domain. *'He seems well enough,'* he told Memin and was glad at least that Memin agreed. *'Apart from which,'* his tirade went on, *'how long did it take for a hairline fracture to heal. It wasn't even a break. And ribs. Shouldn't someone tell him that people play cricket with broken ribs? Just a suck. A suck with floppy ears. Maybe that's what Mary saw in him. She liked flicking his floppy ears.*

In the three weeks since the accident, the Carringtons had entertained a flood of visitors many of whom had 'just dropped in', staying for lunch or dinner and at least on one occasion, for breakfast. All such visits were pleasant, the attention well meaning with great fuss made over the guest of honour. He responded well. Flattered to the point of embarrassment he nevertheless handled his celebrity well though he tended to lean heavily on Fauna for direction and etiquette. Family members drifting in from Matura and Sangre Grande, old friends from the school, the clinic and the town in general, and new friends born of the occasion; all managed to maintain a decorum that was appropriate and a dialogue that was at least not overly intrusive.

Mohammed was the exception.

He had met the overstayed visitor six times. He had been to the house seven times. This last time he had not bothered. Mary as a matter of fact did not even come out to meet him. He had to talk instead to Memin who in the past never really talked to him. But it was obvious that Memin did not like 'floppy' either.

They looked the odd couple; one hundred twenty pound Memin in huddled conversation with two hundred and twenty pound, six foot two Mohammed. Their demeanour and appearance too were as different as their size and weight. Memin spoke with enthusiasm and passion on any subject that crossed his path. Mohammed brooded, seldom even voicing an opinion except for the occasional spurious quip that was as far removed from Elwood as himself from Memin.

The Carringtons did not invite him for supper that night, but he came and stayed anyway. He talked too. Just when he should have kept quiet, he managed to bring any discussion to bear on Elwood, ofttimes questioning and hinting and on one occasion challenging Elwood's honesty so that

Doctor Carrington was forced to reassure him that Elwood's injuries were not fabricated.

"Oh, be that as it may," Memin countered, "this is the very area of medicine that we find suspect; diagnosis."

"Memin!" Ansaro chided. "This is bordering on insolence..."

"And bad manners," Fauna added.

"Then forgive me," Memin pretended injury and penitence, "but this is a first. It will be the first time a line is drawn in the sand. At least where discussion is concerned. I mean we've attacked Mom's religious idiosyncrasies and Dad's bedside manner... not to mention my principles and Fauna's naïveté. Is it time to end it?"

"Not at all," Dr. Carrington assured him, "but we must have some consideration for our guest."

"We have two guests," Memin reminded him.

"Touché," Elwood mumbled, the word obstructed by a mouthful of green figs with a flavouring of hot, butter-sauced red fish. "Therefore, please don't spare me."

"Oh!" Fauna exclaimed. "Feeling feisty, are we? Ready to do battle?"

He smiled and shrugged.

"What was the point anyway?" Dr. Carrington asked. "Something about 'diagnosis' I believe. Is it the same argument about cause or treatment of disease? Or have we progressed."

"What's the synopsis," Elwood wanted to know.

"Oh, Memin has suggested..."

"...Said outright!" Memin corrected.

"...That medicine has not progressed beyond the middle ages..."

"Chemotherapy, for instance," Memin explained, "is not only Middle ages, but pre-pre-Middle ages. Think of it. Wendell went through hell..."

"Wendell was his college friend. He had Leukemia..."

"You have no idea... Not even the grossest treatments, even the 19th-century treatment of Gonorrhoea could come close to it."

"And diagnosis?" Elwood wanted to know.

"The great 'Oops'," Memin said dryly.

There were chuckles all around. Even from the doctor. Only Gerald did not smile. It seemed to Elwood that as the humour skirted him he found some comfort in his scowl.

"It's easy to laugh," Gerald pointed out with the surly look of an outsider exercising his disdain for an inside joke. "But I don't see what's so funny about all this. I just drive a taxi and you just paint pretty pictures. So what's so different about us? I work for ten hours a day sometimes. How long it take you to paint a picture?"

"Depends. Depends on the subject. Sometimes no time at all."

"You see."

"But it's not how long you work," Fauna interjected. "You perform the mechanics of everyday life – like cooking and cleaning – but Elwood creates beauty from the very staidness of that life."

"Beauty!" Gerald sneered. "What is beauty? They say is in the eye of the beholder. So your beauty is my pig-shit... oops, sorry."

"Not true!" Elwood said calmly. "And it's not beauty I paint. It's symmetry."

"Symmetry!" Fauna and Memin exclaimed simultaneously.

"Yes. Symmetry. What we call *Beauty.* You see I believe it is to symmetry that we are drawn. What we call *Beauty* is our interpretation of that symmetry as it relates to us. Perhaps a better word might be *Harmony.* But to me *harmony* is just as vague as *Beauty.*"

"Are you talking about the linear aspects of visual life?" Memin asked.

"In a way, perhaps, but geometric shapes and patterns are only one aspect of symmetry. Eventually, perhaps there may be another word coined to describe what I'm talking about, but I think *Symmetry* is the best so far. It means our attraction to things in their proper place. Art, yes, but music, architecture, even our health. When things are in the right place they bring us joy. But why? Because we are ourselves symmetric when we are aligned with our surroundings. We do not always find ourselves so, especially when we are learning these expressions. A child playing a violin is not symmetric. Not yet. But as it moves toward symmetry the child finds joy in each step along the way; the sound the instrument makes, the accomplishment of a tune, a composition. And the child knows, instinctively, when it draws closer. I myself... I'm always seeking balance in my work. This is where I find my beauty. And I do find it. In faces with character, in scenes with alignment, in a piece of wood, a shell, a leaf... just so, standing on its own but against the counterweight of background and perspective."

"Well, you lost me all to hell," Gerald broke in.

"Oh shut up, Gerald," Memin and Fauna chided simultaneously. "Go on, Woody," Memin urged.

"Oh, basically that's it. I'm still reaching."

Despite Gerald's silence at the admonition, he did not keep quiet for long as the discussion continued unabated. His quips added nothing to it and were moreover annoying in terms of timing or point made. Once even Mrs. Carrington told him to shut up. Apparently it was not the first time he had ever been told to shut up and he seemed to take it in stride. Six beers later, he offered his final stab.

"All of them," he referred to artists in general, "don' know about real work.

It was ignored by all but Elwood. He felt it was Gerald's way of flicking his ears. Perhaps had they met as children, the large scowling Mohammed would have been in one of those gangs that pushed until respect was earned. But they were not children. It was therefore funny.

"I tend to agree with you," he said with a smile, which annoyed Gerald. "I sometimes find myself wondering what people pay for. I mean, after all, it's all just an extension of myself. Nobody is paid for combing their hair or brushing their teeth. So why am I? But, yes, it is work. Van Gogh would get up early in the morning and take his tools into the fields and paint till the sun went down and even then his work would not stop. Did he too enjoy it? I'm sure he did. As one enjoys breathing or eating perhaps, but if you can see the love in every stroke of his, feel the mixing of his colours, compose with his eyes and fingers what his mind saw... Yes, I would say he enjoyed it. And perhaps this is what sets us apart as well as what makes us similar – me the painter and you the taxi driver: the joy of doing what we do well."

Elwood paused then as he seemed to come to the end of the discussion. He was now paying greater attention to Siba who had hurriedly finished his meal and, now retired to the family room, peeped in through the beads from time to time, not bothering to hide the reason for his inquisitiveness. He would have his sketch-pad, the one Elwood gave him.

"I'm needed elsewhere," Elwood smiled after that last rambling mumble. "Mrs. Carrington, an excellent meal. Thank you."

The discussion paused.

"I cooked the plantains," Fauna said proudly. "But you had too many. You're going to get fat."

After a week of Mrs. Carrington telling him he was skinnier than Memin, they all laughed. He rose nevertheless and after a brief visit to the washroom where he washed and brushed emerged to stand just inside the curtain and look and listen as the discussions continued, Memin, easily agitated and animated, Mr Carrington always jovial, Mrs Carrington submissive yet perhaps as a root submits to the tree. He then chased Siba (who had followed him) into the living room.

Fauna followed laughing.

Leaving the table had been one of those practices Elwood always regarded as impolite. Yet at the Carringtons, it was not only accepted, it was encouraged. Unless one had a lot to talk about. In such cases discussions at the table would continue till the subject was completely spent. Those not involved would simply get up and leave, often without seeking to be excused. Those with more to say often took it into the family room or outside on the porch. During the course of the week, another pattern had emerged. Siba.

The small boy had talent. More, he had a love for art. Elwood confided this to Fauna (he told her everything) yet never mentioned it to Siba. The only thing he told Siba were the things that upset him, chief of which was that Siba liked remaining indoors to draw instead of going out into the yard or riding his bike with Dharo. They had friends a mile down the road on the way to town and Dharo made use of that friendship. However Siba preferred Elwood's company and although Elwood thought it might be the novelty of his visit, he had begun to fear an overly traumatic separation in the offing.

"You don't want to go out and play?" he asked. "There's still light outside."

"No. I want to show you this."

It was a remarkably good likeness of Elwood, the proportions not quite flattering, but the image easily recognizable.

"Very, very good," Elwood said showing it to Fauna.

"Very good," she echoed.

Behind them Gerald Mohammed had emerged from the dining room. Though the argument still raged from within, the noise of the beads made Fauna turn, but she neither rose nor acknowledged his presence. When he departed through the storm door, banging as it closed, Elwood looked up... but she only smiled. He went back to Siba.

"Here," Elwood demonstrated stripping the leaf and exposing a blank page. "Let me show you something..." he said, making a series of gentle arcs on the page. "These will help you with proportion. This arc (vertical) you use to show the angle at which the face is positioned as well as the size of the head. Now these (three arcs intersecting with the first) show the relationship of the eyes, nose and mouth to that position. Now show me the rest... you draw the eyes, nose and mouth, at those angles." He handed Siba the pad.

"But not now," Fauna interrupted. "Go out with Dharo first."

"Oh..." he whined.

"Yes," Elwood insisted. "Siba, if you don't enjoy the world out there, how can you be an artist."

"Oh, all right," the young boy conceded though obviously reluctant to postpone what he had just learned. He carefully placed the pad and crayons on the table, aligning them symmetrically with the edges of the surface, then walked outside.

"Can I go outside for a walk too, teacher?" Elwood asked playfully though struggling out of the divan.

"Do you need any help?"

"Surely. I'm an invalid. You heard Mr. Mohammed."

"He was being sarcastic."

"Well, he wasn't being it very well."

She laughed but, her hand lightly on his elbow, still helped him outside as far as the porch.

"Like a crash; cymbals and drums going off with one great bang, then the sound drifting away quickly," he said looking up at the line above the trees. The sky was still quite bright though the sun had long descended behind the hill. "Isn't it amazing how daylight continues right up to the point of absolute darkness?"

She squeezed his hand. He glanced sharply, catching her quizzical look. "You have such a wonderful view of life and such a way of expressing it."

"No! Without my brushes I am wordless."

"That's not true. You may be shy and reticent, but when you are on the spot, you can be quite poetic. Did you go away to study?"

He smiled. "No. I did not go away to study. Not the way you mean anyway. My mother, the nag, was my constant educator. She censured my grammar, my choice of words, my every slang. I'm not complaining, mind. Not now at least. For the rest, I suppose I must have acquired something else from all the... speeches I had to make, explaining this work and that. What I did, why I did it, how... Yes! It must be true that I can say what I think. But it's not school or study that has provided me with this. If anything, necessity, or maybe arrogance - not caring what people think, so not letting it matter. They'll think the worst anyway, won't they?"

"Did you have to make many speeches?"

He reflected. "I don't even regard them as speeches. Not the kind of speeches you all find so easy, even at the dinner table. That is wonderful if you wish to make wonderful of anything. That freedom and support you give each other... Your parents must surely have planned it. Not even the language, mind. But the very nature of expression, without deference to position or age or stature. Even your mother. Even she!

She was quiet for a moment then leaning closer asked softly: "Do you want to walk?"

"Sure. But we need shoes?"

"You do?"

"You too." He thought of the snake. "But... perhaps not. Too much trouble."

"I'll tie it for you."

"No. Let's sit on the steps."

He sat on the top step and she sank beside him. Her leg and arm touched him and he immediately felt excited at the warmth of her presence. There was little breeze to counteract the heat, still it was a pleasant heat. She leaned closer. He could feel the warm tremble of her flesh against his. Their silence continued as with a rush the sky deepened and the shadows below the distant trees grew black. The two sheds cut grey lines into this blackness as did the posts supporting the fence. The fence itself disappeared. The ground too slipped into shadow leaving an indistinctness which nevertheless still hinted at substance. Then the shroud descended completely as on the road a single street lamp cast not enough light to pierce the darkness.

"Fauna," he said hesitantly, "I'm starting to be tongue-tied and awkward when we're this close. It's such...," he felt her arm and her fingers sought his, "such an amazing feeling."

Awkwardly he reached out with his splinted arm and gently pulled her shoulder. She turned, uplifting her face to his descending head. Sweet. At the first touch, flesh to flesh, her lips opened. Such a strange, compelling texture; a fruit, yet not, though it was not met in sensation but tasted. Her warm breath and soft, moist lips were as a veil of pleasure enveloping him. She murmured, gently moving her mouth against his. When he could think, drawing back only far enough to still feel her quickened, trembling breath, the first thing that came to his mind was that there was not a single bone in her body. More, that she was not even flesh, but moisture flowing about him in waves of undulating warmth. Compelled to refute it he brought up his artist's hand and caressed her face seeking size and contour in her cheekbones and chin, earlobes and neck all the while drinking in her eyes, deep in shadow though twinkling with some inner light that no darkness could mask. Sure in her reality he again descended to her lips.

This kiss seemed to go on forever for actual time was now myth. Cloaked in darkness there was a certain sense of invisibility that seemed to isolate them from the world. It seemed to grant him too the right to take from her whatever she offered and give to her whatever she asked. The instinctive knowledge carried with it some lingering doubt as to the boundaries of such privilege yet at the same time having any boundaries dependent solely on their own agreement. As he bent to her mouth each time such limits seemed to dissipate and there now appeared to be only a series of exchanges accompanying each kiss; permission to, and permission granted.

Other things too puzzled him. The first was control. There seemed to be none. Yet there must be. Otherwise he would sweep her up in his arms and simply take her. But that urge was indeed stayed; and not completely by him. Therefore she controlled. She called for his lips; he gave them. Nothing more. As yet. But that she could contain the rest, force him to such restraint, was indeed a mystery.

The second was that which railed against such restraint. There were hundreds of words for it, yet not one alone described it. Passion, emotion, feeling, sensation, fondness, tenderness, sentiment, longing, impression, fascination, excitement, desire, need, craving. 'Being', however, seemed to be closest to the mark. He was there in oneness with her. In spite of who controlled, who needed, who allowed - this was the essence of each kiss.

The discovery that he was crushing her with such force that it would otherwise have caused pain prompted another discovery – that she was responding in like manner. Had she lost control? What limit now?

He grunted and mumbled something.

"I know," she somehow managed.

But how could she? Age? Experience? Or simply intuition! But she did nevertheless ride his wave upon his board, guiding him from within himself toward her end.

"Ohhh!" came involuntarily as he moved; his position now too awkward and uncomfortable despite the demand of imminent pleasure. Suddenly he twisted her, her thigh now against his...

"Forgive me..." seemed wrenched from him as he forced her against his body. And yet there was no pity or concern for her in his physical demand. Impossible? As a great boulder rolling down a mountainside he could not ask why or how of it. But that it was so indeed puzzled him. Where, therefore, was the shame? Surely there must exist some form of conscience in this obscenity, some disgust in this rankness he seemed destined to experience. Even without copulation! Yet she too strained; her mouth hungry upon his as a contest of strength. Surely he must be hurting her. His hand lowered, descending from her back to her slim waist and along the ripe, sensuous curve - even forbidden, this too was permitted. He could feel the line of her panties under the thin garment, the soft roundness he now dared squeeze with urgency. Then burst...

Then slowed.

The hunger abated though still she kissed him. Tenderly now and smiling with her eyes, she relaxed against him.

He discovered she had been kneeling, straddling one leg, her own against him infusing him with a sweetness he had never known before. A bag-full of mangoes and balata to be savoured at his heart's content. Not a forbidden fruit that brought after the sense of shame, but one that was his right; a right granted by her.

He put his arm under her leg and defying exhaustion lifted her, seating her in his lap. She curled against him.

"You know..." he began still breathing deeply.

"Shhhh," she whispered. "It's so nice here. I'm not hurting you, am I?"

"Hardly know you're there, except for..."

"Shhhh."

For the next half hour or so as he kissed her forehead and caressed her cheek, not another word was said.

Excited screams approached from the hill. Widely scattering beams from the bicycle headlights flickered through the trees then suddenly brightened as the two boys turned into the driveway. Carelessly throwing their bikes down, the light from each dynamo suddenly going out, they ran to the house and up the steps before realizing it was Elwood and Fauna in the shadows at the top of the steps.

"Can I finish the drawing?" Siba asked gasping out each word.

"Of course," Elwood agreed.

"What're you guys doing?" Dharo asked coming to a breathless halt.

"Just go inside," Fauna ordered shyly.

"Okay... but you're not kissing or anything are you?"

"Will you get inside," she threatened, her dark eyes now flashing. "Mind your own business."

Laughing, Dharo followed his brother, banging the storm door loudly as he disappeared into the darkened interior. A light then came on flooding the porch as well. In the light Elwood caught her profile against the black distance and felt the shame that had eluded him throughout the encounter though, somehow, holding her seemed to excuse that shame. *Lack of practice,* he thought, already composing for his diary those final moments of the day. But there was little satisfaction in that excuse and less comfort in her nearness because of it and he began to blame it, not on external forces or internal desires, but on those aspects of youth that had been denied him during those crucial formative years.

And the reasons why not.

CHAPTER -50 - 'Mrs Carrington among the chickens'

ON THE FIRST MORNING of the fifth week they took a long walk, all the way to Cocoa beach. There Elwood drank from the freezing spring and splashed Fauna who ran shrieking to the water's edge. He chased her but without success. She however waited for him on the embankment in much the same way as he first saw her in profile and wanted to paint her. The tide was high and the surge carried up almost to where she stood awaiting him. When she sank to the loose sand he followed her, cradling her with both arms as he held her against one upright knee. They remained so, wordlessly and with minimal nuzzling for about an hour - or so it seemed. The actual kissing must have lasted longer. Eventually though they rose and wandered back along the road, an hour's walk, yet, two at their pace, holding hands and talking desultorily of school, rainbows and the price of bananas. Surprised that it was eleven o'clock when they returned, they resolved to start earlier the next day.

However, though starting earlier the next morning, they still returned at eleven o'clock. By the end of the week they had begun to walk just as the sky lightened. But always they returned at eleven. No one complained though. However it seemed, at least to Fauna that as the days drew by, Elwood had begun to grow distant. She felt he was preparing to leave and even so accused him. But he denied it.

"I'm here forever," he said sadly as they sat at the long, otherwise empty dining table, "as long as you want me. But there are many things about me you do not know. Things I would not begin to know where to start."

"A girl," she smiled, which smile he examined as his own.

"You are all seeing and all knowing. But not a girl. A woman."

"Oh!"

Himself startled that it had come out so easily he now sought to retreat.

"Older."

"How much older? Ten years?"

"More."

"And what happened?"

"Not today! Someday, perhaps, I'll tell you all about… my whole sordid life."

"Why not today?"

"I'm not ready I guess."

"But you want to tell me?"

"Yes. But when I'm holding you and you can't run away and leave me to suffer in loneliness."

"There is no fear of that," she assured him tenderly. "But, you know I'm going to think all sorts of weird things, don't you."

"Yes. And you'll be right. Every time."

"Then, I don't want to know. Promise me you'll never tell me," she wagged a finger at him.

"Okay! I promise!"

"Unless... Unless you really have to talk about it."

"Okay!"

"Or if I ask again. Promise!"

He laughed and said, "Okay!" But a quiet followed into which his laughter faded and from which a seriousness grew. Both seemed so embroiled in personal thought and the comfort of each other's nearness there was hardly any reason to break the silence. Finally however he glanced at her though her head was turned away and she did not know that he was looking at her.

"I feel like I've known you all my life," he said introspectively. "Like all the things I could have said to you have already been said. You know what I mean?"

She kept her face shyly away. "I fell in love with your bicycle first." A tight little smile punctuated it. "There was something so personal about it. I once saw a picture of the *Yellow Chair* by Van Gogh and it seemed to have the same qualities. It seemed alive...

the bike. I don't know why. I suppose it must have meant something to you."

"It did. Till it was stolen."

"Stolen. Oh, I'm sorry."

"That's ok. But you're right. It did mean a lot to me. Here..." he dug in his pocket and took out his wallet withdrawing from it the scrap of tightly folded paper. Opening it carefully, he said, "This guy seemed to say it best." And he pointed as she read:

Trigger, Champion, Silver; cowboy horses that took their heroes across the plains of the wide west! That's what a bike is too - Companionship, Obedience, Security. With it one can defy the world or challenge injustice, or simply ride into a sunset.

If left to time and complacency one is gently weaned from the relationship as those of us with these testaments to our youth are aware. Somehow they never really leave us; ours forever, even as they lie rusted and forgotten in the back of some overcrowded garage, or perhaps dismantled and confined to boxes in the attic. But circumstances can alter that easy transition. Radical circumstances like an accident or more voluntary incidences like the ultimate betrayal: selling it. And then there is theft where one can never fully accept or reason that kind of loss especially when one is aware of the special worth that goes beyond price, beyond measure for that matter; that singular, most important word that defines the essence of harmony and company: friendship.

As with most childhood treasures, realization of this special value makes loss more keenly felt. Not just knowledge, mind, which has to some degree its own sense of value, but realization - the kind that involves measuring the relationship of worth, placing value where it is seen to be greatest, not running from it, betraying it because the pain is too great. So if the bike meets those personal standards by which friendship is defined, in many ways its loss is a loss of those very qualities upon which personal worth depends - security and trust in particular. Then is such a theft indeed great for it not only impoverishes but attacks the very foundation on which our society is - or should be - built. Moreover if such a loss represents the first, really great traumatic loss in life, one's whole future can hinge on it. And further, if you're sixteen and everyone else still has their bike, such a loss is little short of catastrophic; the effect beyond scope mainly because in memory that special friend grows in use, dependability and affection and the association that might have been taken for granted once, now increases in stature and importance to a degree that defies simple logic.

Now some would argue that, relationships notwithstanding, too much is made of the bicycle per se. It is after all only an extension of the wheel; the conjunction at which the lever and the gear meet at a fulcrum to produce force and motion. But those who dismiss the personality of the bicycle see it only in the multitudinous numbers traveling Beijing streets, not the individually if ridiculously wrapped present under a Christmas tree or the Happy Birthday gift that signals not only a new age, but a new era.

However the undisputed truth of the matter is that with a bike at your side, the world - or at least, the little corner you call your own - is at your feet. Literally. Especially if you had the knowledge to fix it; patch the tubes, change the tires, tune the spokes, adjust the brakes, re and re the chain, grease the bearings and even know where and how to use all the little misunderstood oil holes along the frame as well as the all important ones on the wheel hubs. And the more you know and the greater your competence, the greater your own importance increases. Everyone who has a bike now comes to you with all their little bike problems. True, some of those Tom Sawyers are just lazy and believe they are conning you into doing what is essentially their job, but others have genuine problems, are genuinely ignorant and feel genuinely safe in your company especially on long trips. And you never disappoint. As long as you remember to carry your little tool-kit.

And your sense of humour.

"Oh, who wrote that?" she asked.

"He used to be an editor... or THE editor at the Gleaner's. I used to correspond with him till he stopped writing for the paper. I still send him stuff though he doesn't reply anymore. I suppose everyone has their priorities. But usually when I have something to say, I send it to him. But nothing so important as when my bike was... taken. So, you liked it too."

She nodded. "The first time I saw the painting I asked my Da for it and he pointed you out and told me you had painted it. It shocked me. But not half so as you, the artist of such a sensitive work. You were so tall and awkward. And serious. I felt you didn't want me to have it. And when Da bought it, he looked for you to sign it with your real name but you were gone. I was disappointed - but glad. I didn't want to meet you. I was afraid you would want it back. Then when we came home and I knew it was mine, I wanted to keep it in my bedroom. But everybody wanted to see it so we hung it outside instead. But every time I looked at it I saw you. All these years with a schoolgirl crush. What do you think of me?"

He remembered. "I said you would put it in an attic with your dolls and forget about it." He sighed. "I've been so wrong about everything. Seems I've spent my life being wrong."

"No! Not wrong. Just a little out of step."

That day he donned his poncho and straw hat and painted for the first time since the accident. Setting up his fold-away easel and placing upon it a twenty-four by thirty-six canvas he spread his paints and accouterments on newspapers to protect the floor. He next selected from his sketches the chicken coop behind the house. This he did for the obvious convenience and reference it offered, but more as a challenge wondering how he would replicate mesh-wire. Then sitting on the back step he painted till it grew dark. Though Mrs. Carrington had not been aware of his painting, she not being anywhere in the vicinity, he nevertheless created an image of her (in her favourite flowered skirt and apron) feeding the white leghorn chickens.

He retreated to his bedroom and painted all night and just past dawn of the following day and when he was done he examined it as usual for any mistakes, anything incomplete that needed touching up. There was none. But there was something he had not seen before in any of his works: it was happy. He looked at it closely then from several feet away. It was so. There was nothing dark about it. Mrs Carrington's face was serene and focused, but he had captured her contentment and the pure joy of belonging. Even the chickens seemed to smile.

Satisfied but exhausted, he fell asleep with only his shoes removed. When he arose later that evening he presented the painting to Mrs. Carrington at supper. She gasped, put both hands o her cheeks and, weeping, fled to her bedroom. Startled, Elwood offered an apology.

"No! No! Not at all," Dr. Carrington responded, laughing, but without his accustomed merriment and eventually losing the laugh altogether as he withdrew into reflection. "In truth," he murmured as with a sigh, "in all my life I've never seen her so happy."

Later that evening when they had exhausted all discussions of the painting, he revealing all the little technical details to Siba's queries and allowing himself to bask in Fauna's pride and finally in Memin's awe, Mrs. Carrington stole out of the bedroom and gazed, still sniffling, at the unframed work the doctor had advised they hang in the dining room on the wall opposite his 'Bike'. When Elwood sidled into her presence she shook his hand stiffly with both of hers and uttered a very soft, very meek, "Thanks!" Then both stood for quite some time gazing so, hand in hand, upon 'ten dollars of material that didn't even take a day to paint.'

CHAPTER -51 - clean love

CONFESSION SEEMED INEVITABLE. THE day it happened Elwood had been holding Fauna crooked against his knee and listening to the surf raging against the rocks just outside Cocoa Bay. They had been talking about life's expected course; how different from person to person. He told her about the hunter and the deer.

"How dare I question the method by which he chooses to live? Samuel. I think we do that all the time. We always have a better, more honourable way of doing what others do by fault it seems. Life is indeed powerful and the courses demanded of life too. The things that people do in a moment that last a lifetime! Should it be so? Love, fear, sex? Or what happens to them. Have we the right?"

And then he was quiet. She asked him why he was sad and he told her he was thinking of Frankie Biggs.

"A friend. A good friend. And a good swimmer. He was a boy scout when we only played at scouting. He liked that sort of thing and when we stopped being a band of merry men he just dropped out of sight and, of course, out of mind. I didn't think of him at all. Then one day I heard on the news about an accident on the highway; a rainy day, a car had skidded and slammed into a group of cyclists training for the Olympics. I had so been out of touch I didn't know he even rode a bike anymore. The Olympics! I wish I had known. I wish I had kept up with these faces in my past. They never leave me, and yet... And yet..." He paused to reflect. "There are times I could see his face so plainly."

She kissed him. "You have such terrible memories! Is the other as bad?"

It seemed the right time. All was right with the world. Too right. It needed despoiling. Just a little. He was holding her and kissing her, nuzzling her neck and ear-lobes as the words came matter-of-factly, not explosively nor even with much energy but narratively and without emotion as one reports an event that has little to do with the present or even the future. He was someone else, the friend of the hunter and the friend of the deer and the friend of Frankie Biggs whose tragedy far overshadowed any escapade that could have marred their young lives. He spoke of himself as such; another entity from the distant past who's need to unshackle far outweighed the threat of rejection and when he was over the worst, astounded that there was nothing more he was surprised to find she was still there.

But the kissing had stopped and there had even been a pause in the nuzzling.

"That day..." he continued the long sojourn into the past now with some hesitation and parrying objectivity, "...that day, I should have known how it was with women. And yet, how could I. I never even had a girl... one to teach me when I could be taught. Instead I became the fool, suddenly faced with desire and a willing woman. I knew that she was vulnerable. Something instinctive I suppose, but in retrospect. But she was... at the mercy of her own life, her dreams, but especially of her children, and of her own love for them. Vulnerable! This is something a man should never know about a woman. It does something to him. It makes him great... or feel great. Yes! They're both the same anyway, for a man who feels great, is great. And a man in his greatness always feels it's up to him, no one else but he himself, to protect a vulnerable woman. I know. It's silly. But I wonder how many women enjoy this absurdity. Well, I knew she was vulnerable. Of course I didn't know that I knew it. Not then. Not till long after, when I found myself her... equal, at least, at least as a man is to a woman; where age or position or wealth matter nothing." He looked afar off and seemed to find a new guilt - this time in the telling. "I'll never be clean," he said; his despair abject, his assessment final.

"But why? Surely it was just a mistake, for her as well. Why take all the blame. Should there even be blame. If you were ten years younger and I ten older, could I love you less? As you told me before, 'it happens'."

"But not to me. And not to the mother of my friends. That, I won't forgive. Not easily."

"Have you..." She hesitated. Had she gone too far in peeling away his shame? "Have you not been with another... since?"

He shook his head slowly. "Not in the way you mean. Not in the way it should be. Only in strange, unfulfilled ways, half attempts, more sad than... as it should be. For a long time I wondered if I could be... that other way."

"Gay?"

He nodded; distantly. "I wondered once about Michelangelo. They teased me that I was like him; one of those boomerang compliments meant not to praise but to demean. Not his art, but his sex; even his passion, but in a... how can I put it – a sub passionate way: impotent, effeminate, small."

"Small!"

"Yes! You know, when men belittle men they have this childish way of..."

"You mean your penis..."

He smiled. "To the point as usual, teacher. Anyway they said that about him, and guessed it about me. At times they said it in a way that required me to prove or disprove it. Ah! Ignorance makes a deafening sound at times! Yes, I suppose I would have liked to be like him, no matter the way he was. When I read about him and saw a movie about him and heard all the talk about him I wondered back then if a man had to be... so... gay, to be a great artist. Then I looked at the lives of the others - Van Gough, Degas, Renoir, Gaugin - and I realized that, in spite of what they say or would like us to believe, these great artists were not latent anything. They were simply focused on something far beyond sex. As Michelangelo was; undisputedly. Every moment of their lives they painted or sculpted, creating images that never left them, day or night, till their passions were emblazoned on canvas or, as one put it, 'released from their marble prisons'. And if some did managed to be caught up in that lifestyle, what could it have to do with art? One either craves it or ignores it or works beyond it. As with everything else."

"Are you saying then that you have no need for sex?"

"No! To the contrary. It's with me constantly – but as a battle, or the threat of a battle, just over the hill on the plains of Marathon or the seas of Trafalgar, the Russian Steppes, the Roman gates." He grunted wryly. "Dramatic, I know, but... The thing is, passion will out, will have its say. Isn't that why some engage in that type of sex? To avoid the distractions of real... true human relationships. Because that sex is meaningless, without future, without continuance, without the responsibility of history or the debt to one's own lineage.

Passion, on the other hand is real and human and immediate. There is no hiding it in desire. It cannot be a part of desire. It is what it is; not one wants it to be. If one has no passion, he has no art. I sometimes wonder if, like Michelangelo, my passion is sexless, or subdued at any rate. I wonder if his works were all prolonged sessions in ecstasy. I don't know. I know only that I cannot enjoy sex as ordinary people do. There is no joy in it. It is a hard, cold, person-less, passionless pleasure, without point or satisfaction or end."

"Do you feel that you might be gay?"

"Wish that I were. Wish that I had such a pretence that would take me away, release me from this threat of... coldness."

She held his hand. "Make love to me," she whispered.

He did not move at first and she might have thought he did not hear the strange stark request. But then with a frown more denoting helplessness than pain, he looked up slowly.

"Not till I'm clean," he answered so softly and finally that she only barely caught the word, 'clean'.

CHAPTER -52 - Toth report; of love and lust

Warren Toth's report on Diary entry of June 3rd:

'But what was clean,' he thought later that night, stealing out to sit on the plastic chair and look out at the darkness as he relived those days and nights in Toronto.

Grades of deceit, shades of sin, degrees of pleasure. Statistics? How often, how much, how large, how soft... Was 'clean' the lesser portion of accepted filth? The splash of water on a grimy face! A fallen sandwich brushed off! Anyway it did not matter then. Only one thing mattered; how much time did they have before the inevitable.

There is an aspect to sin, a darkness perhaps that, rather than hide, more overshadows the action and by so doing absolves all guilt. Within its shelter, perpetrators seem to find a freedom of expression not encumbered by the basic rules of etiquette, taste or caution. This atmosphere of secrecy seems hinged on a forgiveness that is total and all encompassing, without limit and without end.

In spite of his resolve to the contrary, they had made passionate, unbridled love at least six times in the two days, much of it, he at first thought, due to his own youth and energy. Yet it was no less reciprocated by her and with an equal passion she herself thought was dead. However, though unspoken, fear of disclosure was paramount although in the heat of passion there seemed little time for such distractions. Yet after each encounter, rather than employ room service, they had dressed completely, electing to go out, lunch or sup as two old friends happening upon each other. Then immediately following each meal they would return sheltered by a notion of pretence, yet faces flushed, talk guarded, stilted and wary, and entering each room separately would come together, each time testing at first the strange familiarity, then exploring in disbelief as they found new triggers, new excitements to the adventure.

Throughout the first night, discovery was accepted as atonement for the great sin, a punishment they would happily, if fearfully regard as a fair price. Even in sleep they jumped fitfully at noises or movement, even against each other. Yet always upon awakening they reached for each other.

The third night was longer. There was no sleep. There was only one long, languid exploration, excruciatingly slow, rising to the point of ecstasy and holding it there with soft kisses and a familiarity that knew no bounds. At one time in the midst of such caresses, Elwood shuddered and went limp. "Oh... you came," she accused against his lips. "Next time, don't waste it..." It was a lesson he learned quickly and an utterance with which he often brought her to frenzy as he impaled her with vicious, demanding strokes.

Yet not once did he call her 'Susan'. He called her 'Dear'; Dear One, Dear Sweet One, My Own sweet Dear, Dear Heart and at least on one occasion, My Dear Sweet Mrs. Metcalf. His words in the throws of love were without curtailment; full of ardour and poetry even as his actions were filled with virility to the point of pain.

She matched him in both tenderness and urgency without fear of adverse reciprocation or injury, quickly dispelling the differences in age, station or sex but acknowledging only their hunger and then their satisfaction.

The exhibition on the other hand was handled with polite distance and aplomb. In a land of strangers, where strangeness itself was a daily fare, they played the part of alien custom and conduct that matched the control he showed in the richness of his art; friendship with dignity, excellence with humility.

All seemed happiness. If there would be pain, it must come later. What was indeed clear, was the action he must take; a rash action.

And perhaps wonderful.

But reality had other plans, and the end, when it came, allowed no room for alternatives.

The wheels touching down.

Elwood remembered the moment as he remembered all those other key, innocuous and totally meaningless events in his life. But somehow this was unlike them all for this was not only a signal that the escapade was over, but the beginning of a new life filled with a whole new set of objectives and priorities he had never even considered, as well as emotions he had not experienced before; shame, confusion, regret!

And a residue only time could wash clean.

CHAPTER -53 - proposal

"MARRY ME."

The words were hardly out before Elwood realized what he had asked.

It was only the next evening but seemed like a year in thought when, after supper he had risen contentedly and ambled out to the porch. He had not long descended to the steps, his back against the railing, when she appeared and like two old people who knew the routines of life with each other, insinuated herself against him, lifting his arm to enfold her like an old, tattered, warm cardigan she would wrap about her shoulders.

Fauna's mouth fell open. For a moment she did not breath.

"What!"

Elwood hovered between repeating it and smiling it away. *Don't toy with her.* The doctor's words seemed directed at that particular moment. It was as though with crystal clear foresight he had seen that pivotal instant in time when past and future were hinged upon the word, the exclamation, perhaps even the brief sentence.

"Marry me," he repeated, his tone somewhere between a plea, a question and an ultimatum. "Please?" decided it.

"Yes!" she answered happily. "Oh yes!" She kissed him quickly then bounding up ran inside... "Mom, mom..."

He smiled but remained seated on the front steps. He smiled even wider as the sound of squealing drifted out faintly from somewhere within. The house, emptied of everyone but Mrs. Carrington, now seemed full. Before the day was done, it would be bursting.

It would soon be noon and the kids should be popping in for lunch. The doctor would be in just after two. He would not stay long; just enough for a light snack and a glance at the morning paper. Memin and Ansaro would come home at around five. Ansaro would change and drift around for someone to talk to. Memin would shower, change into his evening wear and read till seven. By then Hasim and Zora too would take a walk or even ride his bike over. The decibel level of talk and the children playing would increase right up to the appointed time. Then they would all come together in the beaded room and dine at the long table under 'Feeding the Chickens'.

Or not.

No matter what everyone did on any days in the past, that day things would be done differently. Elwood was sure of it.

From the moment he rose quickly as Mrs. Carrington hurried to his embrace and Fauna too hugged him, he felt at home. As though he too would eventually be predicted, following patterns, modes and schedules linked to times and seasons; in what he would wear on particular days, in what he would do and say on occasion, in his laughter, the manner of his eating, would he remember to put on his shoes or forget to take them off. It would all be Home! Loud discussions at table, ill manners with a smile, arguments and chuckles within, confrontations between snakes and frogs outside, chickens in a coop, bikes in a shed, birds at dawn, cicadas at dusk. Home.

"Oh I'm so happy," Mrs. Carrington cried - not so much the sad/happy as with the painting, but more a bubbling happy, in spite of the tears. "Can I call and tell anyone?" She meant the doctor of course, but the 'everyone' now took on universal proportions.

"Sure... if you like."

She hurried inside but Fauna remained in his arms.

"We are together," she said. "Always!"

"Always!"

Yet even as he repeated the word he found in it too much analysis and in the analysis too much foreboding. Leave it alone!

"Always!" he insisted.

"Oh Woody, let's not make it too long!"

"Next week?" he teased.

"Oh, you're crazy," she pushed away and looked at him with matrimonial familiarity suggesting an already established bond which no disagreement could break. "I didn't mean 'next week'. I meant not next year or two years... But 'next week'! Oh, Woody, I'll have so much to do, to prepare, Mom will be... then there's Auntie and Grammy... What about June!"

"But June is next year!"

"Oh... then... soon."

"All right. I'll leave it up to you."

She put her head on his chest and rocked. "Oh, you have no idea how much I love you, do you? So much I could burst. You never..." she looked up, "you never even said you love me, do you know that?"

"Are you sure? I thought I said it too many times."

"Not once. Not once." She began to cry into his shoulder.

"Fauna... Fauna, I do love you," he urged comforting her. "I'm just clumsy with such words. But I'm sure I said them. When you met me on the beach that time, when you turned to drink in the wind and the sea with the sunlight catching your face, the perfect image of a full woman dressed as a fragile little girl in all her shyness asking if she was pretty... and I'll bet knowing that she was. And when I asked to sketch you, that's what I was really saying - 'I love you; marry me.' And every time I looked at you, stared at you, even with my tongue tied and my actions awkward, I was saying, 'I love you; marry me'.

He was quiet after he said that and they just rocked in each other's arms. Then fauna stopped crying but still rocked gently with him.

"Next week will be fine," she murmured.

CHAPTER -54 - the news breaks.

NO ONE COULD DOUBT that Warren Toth was still very much a newspaperman.

Even with an intimate and practical knowledge of every drunk tank and hospital ward on the island the slight, sharp faced, hawkish newsman nevertheless still had access to all aspects of society - the wealthy fools as well as the intelligent poor - and could cite connections all over the island. Most of his connections, though, were women - his other, more delightful weakness. And one not lacking in numbers. Just one big family, he boasted. But it was through this medium that he had first taken notice of Elwood Lucien when the hottest piece of ass in Mayaro was reportedly interested in the 'fag', which, in Toth's mind disqualified Lucien from any degree of fagness, but certainly fit the description of one of his detractors through the word: Haunt. Still, Toth's source, not the only one on the western seaboard, swore he was the 'cutest' thing and had the girls batting their eyelashes at him. But he belonged to Tessa. Tessa said so and nobody crossed Tessa.

Toth therefore had to check out this Tessa. He was not disappointed. But how could she go for anyone less than a God. He checked out the Lucien kid. And was disappointed. Nothing special there. After all, how the hell was he to know that the kid who made such a big deal about a stolen bike was the Obzocky of the Art world?

Toth had not seen a single painting of his. His grading opinion was based on the image of a floppy-eared kid pulling seine; rubbing elbows with the grime of society, and being outclassed by them. But Toth, always the reporter, albeit a very constantly drunk one, digging further did discover something else about this other Elwood Lucien. He dug up some earlier reports and read the rave reviews with not a little disbelief. At first he could not believe his own eyes. Not from this puzzled, unassuming 'haunt' who was more beachcomber than celebrity. Still, it was there. In black and white.

And then the accident. And the aftermath where the 'haunt' one-upped him.

Not since the disaster of his earlier years as Editor of the Gleaner had he been so disgraced. In his most drunken stupor he had never botched a story and did not intend to let such a simple task slip by.

Left with so much egg on his face, Toth slipped into the shadows, eased up on the drinking (though not by much) and did some more digging. Although Lucien seemed to have dropped off the face of the earth, Toth went back to the last place he'd been seen. At the same time he dug up the reason he himself had visited Le Poui in the first place. She did not disappoint. He stayed with her all weekend; not only because her husband had gone to Tobago to visit his own girlfriend, but because she had dropped the one name he found most interesting.

This time, Toth did not call it in. He took the Monday off, then the Tuesday. The husband was back by then, but it didn't matter. Toth had his own room and his own welcome mat was out. One more day. Then another.

The story broke on Friday morning.

Because Toth submitted his piece at ten on Thursday night, 1020-Newsradio was not even aware of it till some sneak in type-set called it in. But by then it was too late. The Gleaner was on the street at five am; News-radio's first full news package was on at seven.

"We're left sucking a hind teat," Bernie LaTouche raged from his home. "What the fuck ever happened to co-operation. This whole organization is hinged on co-operation - not sometimes, not once in a while, not when the story's big enough for everyone or if the story's too small for your consideration. And definitely not because some reporter wants to get back at us. And that little prick... Slimy little fuck... Make us look like assholes a month ago, then turns around and does it again... from the other side. What the fuck is his problem? Not enough bottles under his bed?"

Ari Francis, The Gleaner's present editor, could only listen. Suppressing the little smile (as though LaTouche could see through the phone-lines) he knew more than LaTouche that Toth had gone to great lengths to do just that; screw 1020 News radio. Toth may not have been always sober, but as a reporter he was always clever and at times a vindictive little cock-sucker (standard knowledge around the newsroom).

The rest of the storm broke in the newsroom itself. Fan Cottrell, the Gleaner's society columnist had also been kept out of the loop. She was in at eight - Toth would be in at ten. She stormed for two hours being there when Francis entered the newsroom and immediately berating him throughout the entire walk across the floor to his office. This would continue for two hours (with a coffee break) till Toth was scheduled to relieve him. Understanding her did not matter; she refused to be understood.

The thing that really puzzled Francis though, and that was the reason he took Toth off the accident in the first place and handed it to News radio, was that he couldn't figure why this artist was that important. He was just a painter, for shit's sake! Not even that guy, Louisville who everyone seemed to get their knickers in a knot over, had created such a stir! He didn't play cricket, wasn't an actor, and knew nothing about calypso. This was his argument, almost his exact words when Toth asked why he had to give the piece up to 1020-news then write a little jerk-off for 'society bitch'.

Of course this little soupcon of information would not be made known to 'society bitch'. He would, far from it, handle her gently. He knew that before the day was out she would be harnessing her forces for a major dig. She would even get her husband, the Rt. Honourable Digby Cottrell, to join in, as well as the other formidable force in the industry - Mrs. Susan Metcalf who, he had summarily learned, (from the Louisville episode) actually handled all of the Lucien business. Now that 'biatch' was one 'biatch' Francis did not want to face. Nobody smiled when she was mad.

The moment Toth staggered into the newsroom, everything seemed to come together as the intersecting lines of a concentric circle. His first few greetings were pleasant and loud, congratulations from pats on the back to 'way to go buddy' meeting his every step to Francis' office. He even paused for a chit-chat outside with Laurie Blanchard who had dumped him almost a year ago. Even she had nice things to say, things he would be sure to pick up in the near future.

So it was with a smile that he entered the lion's den where the 'witch' could barely restrain herself and Francis fought valiantly to keep his lips from relaxing. The stench of rum against Cottrell's liberally applied Eau de Espirit also added a certain unreality to the early morning encounter Francis found almost unbearable in its irony.

"Fan," Francis said, "I'd like a few words in private with Warren. We'll talk later." He had moved to the door and opened it (it had closed after Toth entered - it did that).

She pursed her lips at Toth but said nothing as she left; her steps profoundly resolute and victorious.

"Before you say a thing," Francis warned opening his drawer and removing from it a bottle of Limacol, "there are some more people coming down here. Fuck, there they are. Now, listen to me you fucking disgrace. First, slap some of this on; not that it's going to help much."

Toth had stopped smiling, which was just as well, for the visiting troop entering at the far end was not in a smiling mood. Cupping his hand he filled it with the liquid then applied it liberally to his neck and hair which he hurriedly combed to a sick slick.

"You're going to be quiet or you're going to be humble. But you're going to regret that the story did not come together till too late in the day. Also that you could not call it in because the competition was up there as well. Now I'm shaking my finger at you for two reasons. One is for show. The other is to tell you that if you ever do this bullshit again, you're out. Not my say-so, or even from this office, but out of the industry. This is big brother talking. Fuck!" He had ventured too close. "You know what? Don't say anything; you fucking reek! Just let me handle it."

Almost on his last word the door flew open, none of the group believing they had to stand on ceremony for Toth or even Francis.

"You little prick," LaTouche yelled before the door had closed and even with News radio CEO Blaine Magnason and Gleaner president Lance Po still filing in, he strode toward the subdued Toth now leaning against the desk behind Francis.

"Hold it Bernie," Francis said quickly stepping in his path. "You'd better hear the whole story before you do something you'll regret. You wouldn't want to apologize to Warren after, would you?"

That froze LaTouche. The very last thing in the world, including his own death, Bernard LaTouche would have considered possible was apologizing to 'the washed-up, has-been little prick'.

"How are you, Ari," Lance Po said stepping to Francis and offering his hand, which Francis took cordially yet almost suspiciously.

"How are you, Sir?" Francis was a little taken aback at his supreme boss's geniality. The reason could have been LaTouche's immediate placidity, something even Po had probably been unable to achieve. Francis also took the hand of Blaine Magnason, although this was offered with less affability.

"How do you do, Sir," Francis repeated. "May I introduce Warren Toth." Toth leaned forward disengaging himself from the desk and shook the hands offered. LaTouche abstained. Francis went on: "We of course will investigate further this breakdown in communication, but Warren has enlightened me as to two important facts, which you gentlemen have not as yet been privy. First, this is a hot story; that you will all agree. Secondly, both 610 and 730 had men in the field and as you know, they have in the past scooped us on our own stories." All nodded, even LaTouche. "Now while it's true that Warren had some making up to do - you know, sir, the accident story - which though not his fault, I might add, given only bare facts and not enough time to follow up, was blamed for it. I'm sure you all understand that reporters have a certain reputation to uphold. Mr. Toth is no less concerned about his reputation as the greatest in our field."

"We understand Warren's obligation, Ari," Magnason seemed impatient, "but surely he could..."

"I'm sorry sir, but we all know in hindsight what could have been done. But had we been stung again and had both 610 and 730 been broadcasting our story all night, I'm sure your accusations here would be 'incompetence' not 'secrecy'. Gentlemen let's face it. We're on top. The Gleaner first, it's true, but News radio is a very close second. I'm sure you would not trade those stats for a scenario that would have put News radio ahead by one hour, at the most, and the Gleaner nowhere in the running."

They all again nodded in unison.

"Now, Fan has a point - why was she excluded. I understand of course. But, I'm sure you all appreciate that holding on to a story of that impact, giving it over to the social column would not be the first consideration of either Warren or even last night's Gleaner staff. I'll talk some more with Fan and I'm sure Warren will work closely with her on tomorrow's edition, but gentlemen... We're on top on this one. Let's not forget it."

"Is this why we pay you the big bucks," Po joked taking Francis' hand again then the smilingly dazed Toth's. "Congratulations Warren!" he pumped. "You'll be a busy man today I think. Isn't he working as well with Lawry?"

"Yes sir!" Francis answered.

Magnason, still brooding as was LaTouche, nevertheless shook all hands. LaTouche said nothing but left the office with the execs.

"You owe me, big time," Francis said to Toth, not smiling as he saw through the glass Fan Cottrell meet the group and exchange some unsmiling words. However Po did pat her on the back with his final words and then ushered the visitors toward the elevator. Cottrell cast one glare toward the office then walked slowly over to her desk.

Toth, as if to emphasize the statement, hovered between smiling and frowning. "I don't even know what the hell just happened."

"I know," Francis assured him. "If you had thought of it, that's what would have happened. Now that we both know you're full of it, remember what I said before. This is your last chance. Congratulations anyway." Francis moved back to his desk. "Now that's out of the way, remember you're working for the Gleaner," he smiled throwing Toth into more confusion. "From here on in you've got one assignment: Elwood Lucien. Get everything on him;

and I mean everything. Everything you know about yourself, I want you to know about him. Work with Fan. She's got lots of contacts...."

As if on cue Fan Cottrell knocked and entered.

"...And speak of the devil... Fan, I'll talk to you later alone. In the meantime, get a hold of your contacts... that Mrs. Metcalf in particular. She's the one..."

"Susan's not answering. I've been calling her since seven this morning but the phone's just ringing. She was close to Elwood, the whole family as a matter of fact. Maybe she's been told long ago, maybe not. But I agree she's now the key to the rest of the story."

"I don't think she knows," Toth interrupted. "I called the gallery on Thursday morning and she answered. I didn't want to reveal anything, so I just asked her when Elwood Lucien is having another show..."

"...Exhibition!"

"Right, exhibition! Anyway she said in two weeks. She was quite pleasant and wanted to know who was calling. I thanked her and hung up. But the thing is she talked as if Elwood Lucien getting married was no big deal. I mean, look what happened here! If she had known, I don't think she'd be as nonchalant about it."

"Well..." Cottrell mused, "There's more than one way to find out about how much that family knows."

"How?"

"I don't know yet," she narrowed her eyes, "but if there's a way, I'll find it."

CHAPTER -55 - Mrs Metcalf takes the news badly

SUSAN METCALF LAY ON the pillow with a wet face-cloth covering her face from forehead to lips. She had not moved much from that position since three o'clock on Thursday afternoon when Woody had broken the news to her. He had not called. She had. He had merely answered his answering service and returned her call. She had asked him simply for an exact date for his display. Immediately she could tell something was not quite right.

"I wanted to be with you when I told you," he had begun. The rest was a blur. Twenty hours later she was fighting to accept it. She had to prepare herself for the questions. She had to be calm, to reassure everyone, calmly, that, yes, she did know about it, but it was up to Woody to break the news. She of course wished him well and all happiness. The girl... No, she did not know the girl, but she was sure Woody would introduce them. After all, she would now be a part of the great family of art. She had no doubt it was the girl in Woody's last works. That was Woody's way.

She cried again. But this time there were no more tears, just the cold dampness against her forehead and her eyes closed tight against the horrendous thought of him leaving. The feeling drifted in again. Hopelessness. *'Please Dear God, let it not be so.'* She prayed. Turn around and walk the other way. But it was not possible. At least it was over. No more tears; her heart was empty.

Thumping footsteps on the porch heralded the approach of her first test. The front door was flung open.

"Ma!"

It was Joe. She did not want to answer but knew she had to.

"In here Joey." She had raised her voice but did not think it carried to him. But it did.

"Did you hear," Joe said excitedly.

"Yes, yes. About Woody, you mean. Yes, he told me last week!"

"Last week!"

"Yes... and Joey, not so loud. I have a splitting headache. The phone hasn't stopped ringing and I'm afraid sitting on the news has taken its toll. Oh, what a headache. And I'm out of Tylenol. Have you any?"

"Ma! Last week! But we talked! You never even told me!" He dug into his pocket and produced the little capsules; two - extra strength.

"Joey, it's up to Elwood who he wants to tell. You know that. I suppose with the news out you may as well tell Pete the rest of it and, yes, call Adrian and tell him. I tried to call Adrian last Friday - Elwood said it was okay to tell him - but I couldn't get a hold of him."

"Yes... he called, I'm sorry. He said you called him but he had gone down to New York."

Thank heaven for small favours, she thought. She had actually called Adrian to tell him there was another shipment on its way and as well to have a little chit-chat with somebody. Now at least Joey would believe Elwood did call earlier. She was not so sure he would believe the headache though. Her last migraine came on the same day of the accident.

"If you can E-Mail him that would be fine," she suggested. "He may want to call Elwood. The number is on the desk. A little town called Le Poui. Have you ever... oh, oh, I'd better stop talking."

"I'll get you some water!"

"Thanks! You're sweet."

She dared not remove the wet cloth in his presence, now she quickly sat up, almost fainting in the process, and gulped down the capsules. A glance at the mirror revealed red, sobbing eyes and a swollen nose. She lay back quickly.

"Here," Joe said on returning with the brimming glass.

"Just put it on the table. And Joey, get the phone, will you?"

"It's not ringing."

"It will. Trust me."

And as if on cue, the phone rang.

"The one in the living room, please Joey."

Joe ran out leaving the door open so that in spite of the distance his words came clearly. Pete. Joe assured him she knew about Woody since last week. She's fine; just a headache with all the phone-calls. Yes, he would remain and answer for her. Or he would disconnect the whole lot. No, he couldn't very well do that. And no, Pete didn't need to come over. One thing Ma did not need now was a houseful of people trying to take care of her.

More than at any other time in her life since his birth, she truly loved Joey.

CHAPTER -56 - to decide to end it

Report on Diary entry of April 7th:

When Toronto and the honeymoon of frenzied trysts had abated, Elwood found himself aged. Even as it waned he had discovered within himself certain attributes that had puzzled him since childhood. One in particular: passion. It had been a word only, flung carelessly as an expression without understanding fully the dimensions of its meaning. But his energetic almost violent love-making brought this understanding to the fore. Frightened at first by the nature of rage it projected (not just the urgency of the act itself), he had been forced to realize how close to the process of art it came. Often when in a state of relaxation either in body or in thought, eased by some success or other, he had felt this racing, surging force, an inert excitement triggered by the success or the promise of an as yet undisclosed project. His early analysis determined it to be some sort of pent-up power awaiting release.

As he saw it now it was the same release that could take the form of closed fists against a face or gentle fingers around a brush. The action would be there in full force, except that one would be released quickly and without construction or plan, the other slower, more deliberate, and with painstaking structure. As he saw it, sex too fell within that category; though raw and untrained, undisciplined, unskilled and with more subjective analysis than determined focus. But gentle and soft or raging with demand, it was passion. In full understanding of the word.

No matter what New York offered, it would be anti-climatic. The first weeks after their return were spent in such recklessness on both their parts that it was difficult to understand how they were not discovered. In spite of the fact that Pete never called, Joe was at college in Canada and Lucy had gone to her mother there were literally hundreds of opportunities for discovery. From early morning, legitimate meetings which always ended in bed, to late night visits that could never be explained, the occasions became more frequent and careless. At the end he would not bother to knock or even call, but simply open the side door, walk to the bedroom where she would await him in little more than a light chemise ofttimes with nothing under it. Hardly pausing for an exchange of greeting he would strip off his clothes, occasionally having no time to remove his shoes or shirt, and almost leap into her. More often than not he would ejaculate soon upon entry then collapsing in exhaustion would permit her to mount him and submit to her control and her needs. The rest was wonder.

Then that night she met him at the door. 'Lucy's here', she whispered. 'No!' he had begged. 'You must,' she pleaded almost in tears. She conceded a light kiss. Then she was gone. He left; reluctantly.

Lucy had asked who it was. She told her it was he, Elwood, clearing up some things before he left for the summer. But he did not leave immediately. He holed up in his room and sought ways to see her knowing that the tiniest slip would not be forgiven. At times when the promise of passion was so great, he was unreasonably incautious to the point where Mrs. Metcalf had called him a reckless child. He did not allow her petulance for it had cut to his soul and it was then that he first wanted to run away. Some weeks later at Logan's shop, he found a way.

He left early one morning in the rain and did not stop at San Fernando but continued on to the oil spotted beach at Cedros and for the first time visited every one of the island's southern beaches. It drizzled and rained throughout. He had one fall; slipping off the winding Penal Rock Road on the way to Moruga. It was not serious, but enough to force him to spend a week in a small town, the first with a room he could rent. There with the cockroaches and lizards he resolved to end the affair though he found the resolve far simpler and easier than the implementation. Each morning he renewed his resolve and each night he changed it again. Black coffee and sardines could not combat the onslaught of depression nor could it be solved with a quick temper and flying fists. During one particularly one sided brawl he received a bottle to the head and spent two days and one night in a hotel room with a high fever and a possible concussion, though at no time throughout the convalescence did he think of the injury but only of his resolve.

At the end of this marathon of indecision however, he had found some peace. The knot in his stomach would last all summer but at the end he was resolute. It had ended. Moreover, had he any lingering attraction to New York, it too was gone. Even in secret, they still were both paying the price for Toronto. But Elwood was adamant; the hell of returning home would not be revisited. And though it continued by design of nature, by choice of self it was over. His aging was complete. His expression no longer needed coddling, nor his technique, tuition. Moreover, his passion did not need a place to stir him. It would always be with him. It was him. The reckless child had finally grown up.

CHAPTER -57 -
buying a beach

THE SMALL, ALMOST TINY man at the Real Estate office did not have a clue as to what the tall gentleman with the soft voice was talking about. Cocoa beach was not on the map. He had never heard of Cocoa beach. But that never stopped him before. He looked again at the information on the paper: area 317, lot 53. He drew out another map of the area, this one numbers 219, 220 and 221 of the larger maps insets. The coastline seemed all taken up, but there! He followed the finger. Lot 53! Ah now! So that's Cocoa beach. That little splash, no bigger than his fingernail. Well, he would investigate.

"No!" the tall gentleman said firmly with now an edge to the soft voice. "Who owns this area?" he asked indicating an area north of Le Poui. "It's not for sale, but I want to know."

Elwood had already checked out other real estate offices in Le Poui and Matura without success. However the latter had suggested their head office in

Sangre Grande. The term 'head' did not adequately describe the little two room 'shed' in the middle of town with one large desk, a row of filing cabinets and an old air-conditioner noisily struggling against an inadequately sealed front door, six feet from the broiling street. But it was not the badly white-washed facade nor the efficiency of the air-conditioner that concerned him. It was the little weasel faced, nattily dressed agent. Elwood had dealt with other Real Estate salesmen before. They were nice to sellers; not so to buyers. Two years before he had been through hell trying to secure a tract of land south-west of Macqueripe, one that had not been on the listings till his inquiry. Once the seller knew who was asking, the price shot up. Elwood changed his mind. The agent almost died with grief. The seller too. Elwood could have had it for a song then, but on principle he declined. The last time he was up in the area he noticed a 'for sale' sign tacked against a tree. Even that sign, small and inconspicuous as it was, marred and forever disfigured his 'pristine escape'.

The agent went through his books as Elwood waited. Nothing. He made a call.

"Yes, put me on to Neville." Then he had to wait. "This is Hadji. How you doing. Listen, do something for me. Check out lot 317, area 53 and tell me who own it." He waited again. "The Land Registry office... City Hall," he informed Elwood in his loud, secret voice. "They looking." He then covered the mouthpiece but said nothing. His eyes though never left Elwood.

"Yes," he said suddenly startled as though he had expected to be kept on hold much longer. "Yes. Or course man. No, he doesn't... but I'm sure... Yes! Uh huh. Uh huh. Uh huh. But... Yes! Repeat that for me!" He wrote furiously on a pad. "Yes. Yes. Uh huh. Yes. Thanks, man. No! That will be all. See you around." He turned to Elwood. "Like magic. I have a number. Mr. Fred Collins. Would you like me to take care of it?"

"No. Just dial the number for me. I will talk to him first."

"It's long distance."

"I will pay the charges."

The agent was suspicious but nevertheless dialled the number."

Elwood opened his hand. The agent put the receiver into it.

"Hello!" Elwood said, "May I speak to Mr. Collins."

"May I ask who's calling," the woman's voice inquired.

"Mr. Lucien," Elwood replied stiffly then waited.

"Yes," a somewhat gruff voice answered. "Can I help you?"

"Mr. Collins, I'm interested in buying a piece of land at the every western tip of yours. It is listed as under your ownership. It's a little known area just north and west of the town of Le Poui, sometimes referred to as Cocoa Beach."

"Oh yes... Cocoa bay. When the government put the road through my property they cut it off from the main lot. I've never actually seen it. I understand it is at the bottom of the hill. Is that the spot?"

"I believe so. Can I meet you somewhere so we can discuss it... that is, if you want to sell."

"Mr. Lucien did you say? Mr. Lucien, I'm a businessman. Everything I have is for sale. Including my wife," he laughed too loudly. "Are you in the market for a wife? She's not bad looking... turn around honey, ha, ha, ha!"

"Not quite," Elwood interrupted, "I'll soon have my own. Are you far from Le Poui? I could meet you there."

"Well, why don't you just make me an offer? I don't want to come all the way out there for a few thousand dollars. How much are you prepared to spend? I have a nice little cottage about fifteen miles north of that. I don't use it any more. Why don't you make me an offer for that?"

"No! I'm only interested in Cocoa beach."

"Well, I'm sure we could come to some understanding."

"That's up to you, sir. I don't like dickering. If your asking price is reasonable, I'll pay it. If it is not, I'll leave it. I'm sure, as a businessman, you have some idea what it's worth?"

"All right... it's what, about five, ten acres?"

"Actually, ten point five, though most of that is the hill."

"Well, give me, say, five thousand for it, as a start. If I come out there we can go higher, but not lower. It will be a waste of time to come out there for just a couple of thousand. I will be giving it away at that price anyway. No, I would say five... maybe seven thousand. Is that a fair price?"

"Very fair. Seven thousand. Is that agreeable to you?"

"Yes, I think so."

"Sure?

"Yes! Sure?"

"My agent, Mr. – he glanced at the name plate – Ramkisoon will be out to see you with all the papers... so we need not meet. Nice doing business with you, Mr. Collins."

"I could throw in the wife...ha, ha."

"No thanks," Elwood managed a laugh, "but thank you for the offer."

Mr. Ramkisoon had not stopped beaming since his name was mentioned. He beamed even more when Elwood returned the receiver.

"Seven thousand," Elwood said. "Mr. Ramkisoon, you are my agent. You can tack your expenses and commission to that and I will pay it. However if the price suddenly climbs to even one penny above our agreed on price, the deal is off. No negotiating. You understand?"

Ramkisoon's smile waned but did not altogether die. "But sir, this is not the way it's done," he protested though more as an appeal to the same sense of fairness he had heard in the exchange. "I haven't any idea what I'm handling. You're the only one who knows anything."

"Then come with me and bring one of your 'sold' signs. Today I'm going to be a landowner."

Elwood emerged from the small office with the small, bespectacled, dapperly dressed man in his early thirties. Together they walked along the street to a late model Honda. Hasim emerged from it.

"I'll be going back with Mr. Ramkisoon," Elwood said. "We have to check out the boundaries. Afterwards, I'll get him to give me a lift to Le Poui."

"How's it look?"

"I think we've got it. But... well, anything can happen. So, till it does or does not..."

Hasim winked and patted him on the back before entering the car and driving off. Elwood and the agent entered a small Corolla that was parked four cars down from the office door. They entered the car and drove off.

An hour and a half later they pulled up at the side of the road overlooking Cocoa Bay. The smaller man had been an excellent tour guide, describing for Elwood the lands and houses he had sold or at least known about. Many of these he recalled in exceptional detail although not visible from the road. Others, flying past at forty-five miles per hour, he could nevertheless rattle off lot size, number of rooms, views and salient points of interest as well as the families, complete with children's names. It seemed Mr. Ramkisoon <u>was</u> the head office, and whenever he left town it went with him. Impressed,

Elwood had come to believe him a real estate God; a seller's dream as well as a buyer's best friend. However, once exiting from the car he stood craning his neck from the top of the hill.

"Any snakes down there?" he asked. "Is it steep?"

Mr. Ramkisoon had put his deity on hold. He had doubts about descending to the bay, but he needed (he said) to find the marks that bordered the property. Otherwise they would have to conduct another survey.

He balked at the quicker route straight down but agreed to walk to the flatter area north of the beach. There standing on the rocks he craned his neck again and could at least see that part of the beach. At the very edge of the rocks he found what he was looking for; a faded but recognizable orange splash on one of the outer rocks. The first marker.

"Ah," he beamed. "This is very promising. It looks quite new."

Definitely not the right shoes, Elwood thought as Ramkisoon craned his neck again. He was obviously unwilling to seek out the other markers and chance wrecking his Italian cut loafers.

"Tell you what," Elwood suggested. "You do what you need to do and get back to me. This is the spot. I need to know if I can build on it and what services are available."

"Here! By the rocks, yes. I'll do that. You don't have to worry. But I'll need a deposit... for the offer and some expenses." He raised his eyebrows.

"You'll have it."

"You want me to get a lawyer for you?"

"Why?"

"Well, you should have somebody look over the deed."

"Yes? All right! You handle it. I'll see you before the weekend."

The eyebrows fell and the little man resumed smiling as they ascended the hill. Elwood too took up the smile as a few minutes later they drove off leaving one of the 'sold' signs fixed firmly as a sentinel on the ridge. Elwood kept it in sight till they turned the corner leading into the Le Poui. The image though remained well into the night.

CHAPTER -58 - painting Fauna on the beach

"DID YOU SEE SIBA in Town?" Fauna asked as Elwood strolled merrily up the drive. It was getting dark but he seemed unconcerned by the loss of light. He had walked back from Le Poui where the agent had dropped him, a good stretch of the legs in any part of the island, except in that region where Le Poui was considered by anyone within miles of it: *just over there.*

"No. I went with Hasim," he smiled greeting her with a happy hug at the bottom of the steps.

"I think Siba followed you." She smiled at the greeting but her brow was furrowed. "He came back and told me you and Hasim went to an office. Then you went out of town."

"Why did he do that?"

"I think he thought you were leaving. I showed him your paints and I told him you wouldn't leave without them. Where's the bike?"

"Hasim took it into Matura. He has a friend there - a master craftsman, he says, who will make it brand new again."

"Oh. But then..."

"What?"

"I'm sorry. I was a little worried. Silly me. But you're most secretive these days. Is everything all right?"

He hugged her as they walked.

"No! It's not a secret. It's a surprise."

"Oh! My surprise?"

"Uh huh."

But she was still concerned and though trying to mask it with a smile, he caught it.

"Are you still worried?"

"No! Not for me. For Siba. He follows you because he thinks you are going to leave. Would you do me a favour? Please? Could you tell him what the surprise is? Nobody else. He's good at keeping secrets. But..."

"Sure. I didn't know he was so inquisitive, but I like it. But you can't get it out of him, okay? No cheating!"

She laughed. "You don't trust me?" she teased.

"Not till you make the big promise. Love, honour and obey."

"Yes Master! For you, anything, Master."

"Anything?"

"Of course."

"Then I have a special favour to ask. I need to go to Cocoa beach. I want to paint you there."

She drove him over in her car and helped with the paints; helped to carry them down to the beach and helped to set them up. She had taken too, three dresses he had chosen into which she changed for the many poses he would sketch and others he would paint. But one day would not be sufficient. In a frenzy of gluttonous feasting he devoured every scene; every rock, twig, piece of driftwood and heap of seaweed cast up by the sea. Returning home only at night to eat and sleep, they returned each day where he painted five works of the Basin and many more of Fauna only one of which could be considered dark: of her face against the cracked rock, looking out to the sea from which daylight lit her reflective beauty. And then two weeks later, having finished twenty five such works of *Cocoa beach and the little basin,* they remained all night seldom moving from the blankets and towels upon which they made love, till morning engulfed them and sleep ended all their yesterdays.

CHAPTER -59 - Cocoa Beach

SIBA AND DHARO WENT along with Hasim and Elwood to take delivery of the bike.

When Elwood invited Siba to ride with him, Siba could have injured himself with the smile he put on. Seated in front, his feet on the high footrests astride the engine and wedged between Elwood's arms, Siba grinned and hung his tongue out at Dharo, then squealed as the bike moved forward.

Elwood did not go straight home. He took Siba to Cocoa beach and parking the bike on the plateau aside of the rocks, they walked down to the beach.

"This is my surprise," Elwood announced jumping down the last remaining feet to the beach.

"What?" Siba was confused and looked about for the present he had supposed was Fauna's surprise.

"Cocoa beach!"

Siba looked at him as though he had suddenly lost the power to think.

"This... Cocoa beach is the surprise. I'm buying it."

"Oh! Can you do that?"

"Yes!"

"So it will belong to us?"

"Yes. It will belong to Mary and me, and so to you too."

"So... what will we do with it?"

"What do you mean?"

"We can play cricket on it and build a fire?"

"Yes! And I will build a house up there on the rocks where we parked the bike and I'll build a balcony where I can look out on the sea and a studio with a skylight to paint when it's raining, and then I'll not have to run all over the island, for everything is right here. Everything I want. Everything I need."

"Can I come anytime?"

"Of course."

"And will you let me paint too?"

"Of course."

"But what will I paint?"

Elwood guided him by the shoulder and brought him over to the side of the hill where he picked up a stone and washed it off in the stream.

"You see this little rock that just sits upon the ground? The sun beats upon it and the rain washes it and it says nothing but reflects centuries of weather and wear and being. See these little yellow streaks, the blue blotches – different strata, each pressured into the other by the weight of the world. And look, the crack here where the earth split, and the smooth face on this side where once it might have sat in a stream and been moved about among hundreds of other little rocks? Well it has been waiting for you. To capture it as it is now; this age, this moment. This is a sedimentary rock, each colour representing a different deposit – from beach sand to coal swamp – you'll have to learn about them. You'll have to learn about other rocks too – Igneous and Metamorphic."

He held up the rock close to his face and smiling glanced at Siba's puzzled face then dropped it on the ground and clapped his hands ridding them of dirt and sand.

"Don't let it worry you. One day you'll want to learn all about them. All around," he waved his hand, "is life and history; beauty, imprisoned, secreted, waiting to be exposed. That is what you will paint."

"Oh, I will come over every day and bring my paints…"

"It may be too far to ride your bike."

"No! We don't ride our bikes here. We walk over the hill."

"That hill?" Elwood pointed to where the bike was.

"Yes! It's not far. Just over that little hill. Come, let me show you."

He eagerly ran up the rocks as Elwood followed as easily. At the top where the driveway led from the road Siba pointed up.

"Want to walk over to our house?"

"No!" Elwood answered while working out the route; the right hand turns that led all the way back to where both properties met on the other side of the hill. "I don't want to leave the bike here," he explained still thinking of the morning mist and the sounds of awakening. "But that's very interesting. Is it steep?"

"Yes. You can fall down. But not me."

"No! I don't believe you would. Anyway, this is our secret, don't forget."

"I know!"

"Don't tell anybody."

"Nobody. Even if Da wants to know."

"If Da wants to know tell him to talk to me. Now don't lie to him or to Mom. Tell them to talk to me. Got that?"

"Yes! Can we ride again?"

Elwood mounted the bike and Siba almost jumped on.

"Absolutely."

Elwood turned the key.

CHAPTER -60 -
Tessa; finality

Report on alleged love interest from author's notes:

For two days Ms. Tessa Loomat was indisposed. The cause of this unfortunate state had been suggested as a heart murmur, a very sad discourse between that said heart and one, slightly used head - hers. This one-sided dialogue, it was further reported, was brought on by the impending loss of one, Elwood Lucien, a painter of some repute. Few men could claim that they had ever caused Ms. Loomat to be indisposed for even a minute or a second or even the tiniest, minutest fraction of a second. Any man so claiming such an atrocious thing would be deemed a liar and would be banished forever from Ms. Loomat's favour and from Mayaro itself. The entire eastern seaboard for that matter. So, it stood to reason that Ms. Loomat's indisposition was not caused by a man, but by... say, the weather, which had of late been less than perfect - perfection of course being in the eye of the beholder. Or was that beauty. But whatever the cause or the effect, the great beauty was in fact not available for visitation or as her grandmother put it: 'She eh seeing nobody.' Or as the rest of Mayaro secretly thought: Indisposed.

On the third day, the recovery was little short of miraculous.

Ms. Loomat had breakfast at Toby's. Just she and her Gran. At first. She had bubbled in just after eight o'clock, greeted the girls at the counter, taken a booth and prepared herself to hold court. The two, teen waitresses were her first subjects to call. Ignoring the other customers (actually there were only two others at the time - both men!) the girls bubbled along with Ms. Loomat till the diner began filling up and, as they ran to duty, others simultaneously dropped by the table to wish her well and inquire on her condition. However, of the thousand or so questions asked that morning, none were of an artistic nature.

For her meal, Ms. Loomat had one weak coffee and a saltfish pie. She was finished in just under two hours. In that time she had seen over two dozen of her former friends and subjects who filled her in on the two days of her 'indisposition'. One slip was made; that Erin Lee had agreed to marry Jason Arnold. But Ms. Loomat, far from a negative reaction, bubbled her joy at the news even congratulating Ms Lee on her acquisition. The subject quickly changing, several of the 'boys' had confessed to being miserable in her absence and she announced that she would be having a party that very afternoon at her place, a sort of Dutch do, in that the 'boys' would bring the beer and the girls bring the food.

On leaving the diner, Gran going home, Ms. Loomat went to the beach. She helped with the seine and received much attention from the fishermen, especially the two, handsome Barrow brothers, Len and Lester who flanked her age, each by one year. Though both young men had girls of their own, they peacocked for her, jostling each other, splashing and prancing about next to her and flexing smiles and muscles shamelessly. The older man laughed and called them fools. But they would not be deterred. When the haul was in, she invited them to the party. They asked if they could bring their girls. Ms. Loomat unhappily agreed.

That afternoon, with her Gran again in tow, Tessa went to the supermarket on Border street then to several of the stores along the 'Mall', (spelt M A U L, by many of the jostled), a partly enclosed plaza, where she elbowed her way through several purchases for the party. Happily tugging along her grandmother (who wore a constant frown throughout the entire experience) she filled four large bags with frills and frippery so unlike her usually selective sprees that her Gran was forced to protest at many of her choices. (Many of the items would remain in the same bags for weeks after. Some would eventually be given away to the St. Vincent De Paul society.)

Being a work-day, the party would begin at seven. Tessa (who did not work) had ample time to prepare for her guests. With little to plan in terms of food or drinks, she prepared herself. A visit to Sylvia's Beauty salon produced a short cut and a complete manicure. The result was astounding.

"Any beauty contest," Sylvie assured her, "you could whip they ass!"

In the process, Sylvie was herself invited to the party. She was well within the age bracket of Tessa's friends, herself being only three years older than Tessa. She, of course, accepted. She wanted to know however if it was a Carnival party and should she dress up. No, she was told. She brought her famous spinach dip.

Bruno Cobbs heard about the party as he delivered beer to Rico's Grill, so he just ambled in an hour or so late. He was well received. Bruno was an amiable enough sort of fellow when not aroused, but he had a very explosive chip on his shoulder the size of a tree. (The chip, that is, not the tree, although his shoulder was up there with the tree size.) The chip was, coincidentally, Tessa Loomat. He seemed to read into other men's observations, comments or even very clearly expressed statements concerning her, his own interpretations, which were so remotely distant from the intent that the young men so confronted often puzzled over his capacity to think. When he saw Sylvie wrapped in attention, looking at something on the wall of a little shrine Tessa displayed as a collection of special pieces, he ambled over. It was a line drawing of Tessa in the act of joyfully, if awkwardly throwing a sand-ball. The resemblance was uncanny.

"What do you think?" Sylvie asked not sure who stood behind her. "I hear he gave it to her. Just like that. I bet it's worth... thousands now. She looks so happy. Is a pity. When she used to talk about him she was, like, proud. I really thought that was it. I really thought no man could do that to her. I used to tell her about my men and she used to laugh and tell me they all the same. Once she even tell me she never getting married again. But... We can't plan that kind of thing."

She had turned and saw it was Bruno who had his own truck and sometimes delivered boxes of body and hair-care products which she sold as well in the salon. He didn't smile much, except when the other girls teased him and called him big and handsome. Then he would put on that little raised eye smile that was always accompanied by a shuffling walk as he tried to hurry out of their range. But he was always pleasant to her and not so shy in her company. She would sometimes follow him outside and ask him how the driving was and he would tell her about rainstorms in Toco and the heat in Arima. Then they would wave to each other and she would watch his truck disappear. But, apart from the fact that they both had their own businesses, they had nothing in common.

Tessa brought a beer for Bruno. He raised his eyes, nodded and grinned as he accepted the beer.

"You like it?" she asked looking up at the picture, the question directed at both.

"Of course," Sylvie answered immediately, quicker witted and more informed than Bruno. "Where's the oil. Jen tell me he gave you a oil painting too."

"Yes..." Tessa answered distantly, "but that's hidden."

"In your bedroom?"

She nodded not taking her eyes off the drawing.

"You must let me see it."

Tessa shook her head.

"Come on, Tessa, snap out of it. This is you. This is Tessa. If he could see you with that cut and those eyes right now he would be kicking himself."

But it did not comfort her. She turned and joined her other guests. Sylvie looked at Bruno with some distaste.

"Why do you men have to be the way you are? You break our hearts and not even care. You phone and say you are busy and we find that you are busy with other women. Is it the other women's fault? I don't think so. I think it's you men who have no trust and no honour. That's why we play games. Because otherwise life would be too hard. Do you have a woman somewhere, who is waiting for you? Do you tell her you are busy?" He shook his head slowly. "Do you see her only when you can't see anybody else? All men should be ugly. You should be ugly too so even old fools like me wouldn't think about you. Of course," she smiled realizing what she'd said, "you know all women like tall handsome men who have their own truck. Just as all men like beautiful young girls whose hearts are broken. But why is she so appealing when her heart is broken? Is it that men like to fix things that are broken? Do you?" He was puzzled and did not reply. "My heart has been broken so many times it cannot be fixed." She sighed. "Look at her. She is smiling, but not smiling. She is listening to everyone talk about everything else when she's with them. She cannot hear them talk about her when she's not with them, but she knows it. Ah! That is how it was with me when my heart was broken. I knew they talked about me and I wanted to scream. But I did not. I was sure that another man would repair my broken heart. And there was always another. Till he broke it again. Now I think it's dead and I don't want to make it alive again. It is better, don't you think, not to have a heart, than to have a broken one. Your beer is finished. My glass too. Here, let me get you another."

"No. I'll get it." He smiled awkwardly and took her glass.

At around ten thirty there was one fight - taken outside. The combatants, subsequently disfigured nevertheless were allowed to return to the party. They shook hands and drank more beer. The girl in the dispute smiled throughout.

When Tessa looked for Sylvie someone told her she had left with the truck driver. Tessa smiled for Sylvie's hope but she knew she could not be happy with Bruno. Sylvie talked too much and Bruno not at all. They would find out. But she wished Sylvie had not left. All around were now pockets of happy talk, some quiet, some loud. The quiet ones she feared, as one fears being discussed. At least Sylvie had just enough sadness to comfort her. Happy discussions about boyfriends and girlfriends did not. Apart from Lester and his brother, no other men brought their girlfriends, nor were any of the other girls escorted although all had boyfriends. As a policy, no girls ever introduced their boyfriends to Tessa. Whether or not Tessa did anything about it, it was considered an inherently stupid thing to do. In this, Tessa was never pitied. Though she bounced from group to group she never stayed with any one. In spite of her cherry disposition, she seemed to bring a light pall to every discussion. As everyone minded 'P's and 'Q's with diligent care, the evening grew long and weighty.

By midnight, Tessa's bubbly disposition had worn thin. When the guests had all gone, she allowed herself to become sad again. Her Gran cried. Later, as she lay in bed, her Gran bringing her a cup of milky tea, she confessed to her that she was in love, but that it was too late. She had a price to pay for her whimsy. But she had been warned. Not perhaps to the letter of the warning, but in essence, true nevertheless. And now it would take the rest of her life to pay for her folly.

She finally fell asleep with her Gran stroking her forehead.

CHAPTER -61 - the letter

Report on Lucien letter - taken verbatim:
August 29th.

My Dear Mrs. Metcalf, the world has not stopped spinning nor are even the Heavens still. Life surprises the complacent in so many ways it is difficult to fathom how anyone can expect things to remain as they were. A shroud has been lifted from my soul. I am at peace, not only with the surrounding earth, but with myself. The fondness with the past remains however. That will never change. It is the basis of all that is or ever will be. Yet it is only memory and memories too pass on.

I would like you all to be my living memory. I would like it if you could be that joy that must be revisited with gratitude and great frequency, a joy I could pass on to those who can share in it as they share in me.

I have sent a letter to Adrian outlining many of my plans, chief of which is the house I am planning to build on a small tract of land called Cocoa Beach. I spend so much time there now I wonder why I need a house. When I see you I will tell you more about it. Let me assure you though that in this area, (the beach, the valley, the town) I have found an infinity of subjects for the canvas. As well as some twenty five works which I call 'Cocoa beach and the little basin', I have completed six major and several minor works (one of a Coral snake you may find though small (8 by 10), is most arresting.) I find though that I am constantly out of stock on paints and now of prepared canvas. The supplier in Sangre Grande is quite limited. (You know how difficult it is for me to accept what is only available and not precisely what I need.) Range of colour has become crucial. You have no idea the impossible clashes and riches demanded of simple things like the red dot on a bird or the yellow line on a snake, without which the work falls into mediocrity. I could paint for instance the stones on the beach or daily sunsets and never repeat. Nor could I settle for only one. (Sunflowers!) But here, were distractions offer greatness and interruptions increase dimension, I am unsatisfied with each work – and happy in my discontent.

I had not intended this note to run on like this, but I have much more to say and need time to say it. Mitchell's (the paint store) has agreed to supply me and I am to be in your area on Tuesday to meet him and take delivery of some items. (Have you ever heard of black canvas?) I would like to see you then. Before I am married. It is important.

Elwood.

Mrs. Metcalf read the 'note' calmly and as calmly dropped it on the dining table next to the envelope.

It was over.

CHAPTER -62 - the fight. Clean

WHEN ELWOOD AWOKE ON Wednesday morning his face hurt and his nose was swollen. It was so comical that when Fauna saw him she burst out laughing. He laughed too after he had looked in the mirror, but his laughter was not as painless. She made him coffee and fried bakes and took them out to the porch where she insisted he tell her what had caused his face to be so.

"At least it's over," he had said, itself not enough information to satisfy the young teacher. Nor did "I've paid for my sins" fulfill her request. He in fact spent the entire breakfast mumbling through mouthfuls and the discomfort of chewing, without saying anything. However when the bakes were eaten and the coffee almost done, he asked: "sure you want to hear all of it?"

"Only enough to satisfy my curiosity," she cautioned.

He then leaned against the banister and looking into the trees began.

From the moment he kissed her and watched her drive away with Ansaro and Memin he felt a sense of trepidation not easily dismissed. He had known fear in the past of course, but this kind of fear that brings its own baggage was new to him. Usually fear relates to bodily harm; even the consequences of actions newly accomplished have that presence of pain one can easily associate with a fresh memory. However in revisiting the past, in this case a place more than a time, he felt he was doing something that he did not have to do. The only encouragement to facing it was the thought that it was a threat, and he did not avoid threats.

The ride was pleasant and without worry as far as riding was concerned. He had no thought of bringing back too much to carry since all that he would order would be delivered in two weeks. Nor would he have to pick it up then. The following week would be his honeymoon. Europe! The duration of the trip was left entirely to Fauna. They could remain for a whole year. It would not be wasted. He would paint. There would be no avoiding it.

At that point he could only think of scenes from books and movies of the Eiffel Tower and Pisa's leaning tower and certain Renoir and Van Gogh places that could not possibly compare with the places he had seen, even those he passed over for better, yet still longed to paint. He wondered at Gaugin's resolve, that he would narrate on canvas what mere words would fail to convey. Did not he, Elwood feel the same; a boastful pride of ownership, that he possessed what others by distance and dictate were denied. No tower nor bridge nor chair could match his crashing surf or weathered rock or the grand eternity of a distant horizon under a descending sun. But he would visit the vineyards of Asti, even the rice paddies of Nanking because it was necessary to touch them if only to make grander the imposing majesty of his own little niche. And when he returned he would never again have to leave. He ever would. Why should he? He would never be able to exhaust all the scenes his mind created: driftwood, stones, trees, the thousands of varieties of birds and their geometric quantities of positions and settings, waves lapping, breezes blowing, reeds waving – and the Basin. It would be his office, an office just around the corner and down the street, an office from which he need never leave except to visit his pleasure and his belonging.

And then he was in Port of Spain and the throaty roar of his metallic blue machine joined with the urban noises that gave the city a presence and discomfort neither word nor art could reproduce. The heat hung thick in clouds of blue/black smoke and dust plumes swirling from all pavements whether concrete or asphalt. The aromas too, of diesel and gas engines, market smells of fish, rotting vegetables and raw meats, the sun's relentless effect on cedar and pine, and above all the street mixture of cooked paint, baked brick and the hot pitch of the softened street.

When he parked the bike at Mitchell's (he did not mention the gallery as he had intended leaving it for last) he was surprised to find Pete there. (He also did not mention Pete by name; only calling him someone he once knew.) Spat Lester was with him. Spat though stayed with the car at the very end of the parking lot. Pete's brow was black and the rage in his eyes overshadowed any greeting Elwood might have considered. Still he did offer his hand. Pete did not take it. He crossed with his right; not a roundhouse that Elwood might have avoided, but one straight and without the warning of shoulder or position.

The blow glanced, Elwood turning slightly, but Pete's following left caught him full on the nose. Elwood remembered clutching then pummelling blindly at his aggressor. He must have caught Pete with a good one because Spat was suddenly on him and his fist caught Elwood on the top of his head. He could hear Spat scream and though he felt dazed could see Pete plainly standing before him. Elwood did not wait this time. He threw his left and felt the bone in Pete's face crunch. Pete gave a yelp. Spat groaned. Pete swore. He had not heard Pete swear since they were nineteen. And then there was a blow to the back of his head that sent Elwood to the pavement.

At first, as he groggily looked up, he thought it might have been Joe. But it was not. There were two other faces he had never seen before, one kicking at his ribs, the other trying to lift him. Elwood tried to protect his face but there was another blow to the side of his jaw; Spat, probably for he could still hear Pete swearing in the background and directing much of the action. But Elwood also heard Pete calling on the others to stop which might have been directly related to the one still kicking Elwood for he stopped and allowed Elwood to roll over and prop himself against a wall where he could see the four retreating to the car and Spat, getting into the driver's seat.

Seconds later, they drove off.

"My tooth was loose," Elwood concluded. "I hoped I would not lose it. Funny how things come to mind. Once in Rio Claro I wrestled this guy and the only thing I could think about was that I didn't want to fall and get my shirt dirty because then I'd have to wash it and I didn't know of any Laundromats in the area. Anyhow I could hardly touch my nose without it hurting and I'd thought it could be broken. Probably is still. Anyhow I went and ordered my paints and brushes and Conn Mitchell must have thought something was the matter because I kept rubbing my chin. Anyway, he didn't ask and I didn't tell him. But I got my licks and..."

"And so now you're clean."

"Well, I don't know about clean," he laughed, "but let's just say, I've been chastised."

She kissed him then and said: "I'm glad," and didn't ask any more.

CHAPTER -63 -
prophetic words

THE FIRST DAY OF the regional cricket finals between Matelot and Fyzabad took place on the playing grounds of Saint Mark's College in Fyzabad. The second day of the match would be held on the outskirts of Le Poui where a clay pitch had been carefully groomed, and the field mowed and tended and all obstructions removed.

Ansaro played for Matelot.

The rest of the family attended the match and sat on the grounds just beyond the boundary line where most of the people were gathered in a thin line defining the oval field. Some ate tomato and lettuce sandwiches and drank lemonade and pop and some brought beer and others flasks of rum which they mixed with coke and the talk was loud and enthusiastic.

Elwood sketched throughout and his scenes caught the bubbly faces of the winners and the consternation of the losers, the lines of the pitch and wickets, the action of the bowlers and the flair of the batsmen and every few moments when he was not looking at Fauna in happy conversation with one of her siblings or her parents, he would catch Siba trying to copy his work and he would experience a sense of belonging which as he confessed to Fauna, he had never experienced before.

When they returned home it was to a feast of blue-backed crabs and callaloo with okra over a black-eyed peas and rice pelau made all the more appetizing through an excitement-postponed hunger. When Elwood could eat no more, that is to say well past the point of discomfort, in order to avoid the embarrassing spectacle that demanded he loosen his belt and the top button of his jeans, he retired to the front steps where he could discretely perform this necessary function while enjoying the now customary ritual of nature's nocturnal course. When Fauna was done with her own post supper chores she joined him on the steps fitting herself into a just-so position: shoes off, legs along the step, shoulders lounged against his chest, his arms linked in hers and placed along her belly – just so.

The frogs and crickets seemed to be either in harmony or competition with each other. Other sounds – the creaks and groans of the night and the yard, the rustle of trees and the occasional slap of the unlocked gate – could not compete, and Elwood had to listen carefully for any other noise above the cacophony produced by the two species.

"Why are you so quiet," he asked once he had assured himself she had not fallen asleep.

"Thinking."

"Anything you'd like to share?"

"No! Just stupid things. Stupid girl things. I love you, you know."

He was silent. His was a contentment not easily expressed.

She continued: "My Gran once told me never to tell a boy you loved him. If you do, you give him too much power over you and once he has power over you, he can break your heart like a piece of cocoyea[11]. Are you going to break my heart?"

"I'd die first," he murmured above the sound of the crickets and the frogs.

11 The spine of coconut leaves when dried.

CHAPTER -64 - Woody goes to town

IT WAS SATURDAY; THE second day of the match.

Since Ansaro would not be batting that day, having batted the day before, and since the doctor would be at the clinic with Fauna, Elwood decided to remain home with Mrs Carrington and put some of his sketches to canvas.

Before leaving for the game, Dharo reported that the rear wheel of his bike had 'dished'. He had caught a stone as he and Siba raced home the night before and had fallen on the turn into the driveway. It was not a bad fall, but the bike could not be ridden in that condition. Fauna therefore dropped Dharo to the cricket match while Siba, armed with his sketchpad, rode his own bike.

When they had gone, Elwood set about fixing the dished wheel. The one key element, a spoke wrench, was missing from their tool-box so he could not fix the wheel till he acquired it. In the meantime using the available tools he stripped down the bike, corrected all its little misalignments, greased the hubs, oiled the chain and generally cleaned it up. Then he went into the house and washing up told Mrs. Carrington he was going into Le Poui to check on the cricket match and buy the little tool. She told him not to bother. That when the others returned they would get it for him. But he seemed impatient to leave the job half done and assured her it would be no trouble for him. She asked him if he could pick up a bag of hops bread on his way back. He promised he would but told her he would be jogging so it would take a little longer. She asked if there was something the matter with his motorbike. He assured her it was fine but it was a beautiful day and he loved jogging. Anyway he wanted to see the road. When she was puzzled - he traveled the road almost every day - he told her that in motorized travel people overlook too much.

For weeks, he explained, he had passed a clearing on the top of the hill before descending to the valley, and on the top he noticed a flare of yellow which might be a Poui tree, but although he had thought of stopping, he was often far past it before he could make up his mind. She informed him that indeed there were Poui trees all over the hills but they were not in full bloom. When they did, she promised him a spectacle. With this happy thought Elwood donned his running shoes (a gift from Ansaro), blue jeans and T-shirt, stuck his wallet in his pocket, and set out. Mrs. Carrington saw him last turning into the street from the driveway.

Dharo and Siba came home at lunch-time (Dharo riding with Siba on the bar). Dharo was disappointed that the wheel was still dished but happy that the bike was so clean. He tested the brakes and spun the good wheel and talked about getting Elwood to show them how to fix the bikes on their own. They tarried longer than they should have, waiting for Elwood, then had to race back to school. He never showed. The doctor came home at two. He and Mrs. Carrington talked about the Poui trees that were starting to bloom. She was quite excited that Elwood would paint one and they speculated that he might be so lost in the venture as to be completely unaware of the time. She asked the doctor to bring a bag of bread when he returned at six - that is, if Elwood had forgotten about it or did not return by then.

By five, when Fauna, Memin and Ansaro returned home, Elwood still had not shown up.

After Ansaro had talked a little of the game, receiving little encouragement, the house grew quiet. When the doctor returned at six he found within such apprehension he was at first annoyed with Elwood for his inconsideration, then realizing he could be in some trouble, called the police station in Le Poui and talked to Sergeant Fontain. The sergeant assured him he would do everything he could but was sure Elwood would turn up by sundown. He had heard, though never himself seen it, that the painter often turned up in the oddest places, sketching or painting, and sometimes with a little group following. He would ask around to see if anyone had spotted him around town or on the road.

At dusk the doctor went out on the porch and hugged his daughter who had been looking out toward the darkening road.

"I can't wait any longer," she told him. "Maybe he fell again and re-injured his ribs. I'll take Ansaro with me."

"I'm sure he just wandered too far off," the doctor suggested softly. "He's probably coming home by a different route."

But she did not heed him. She had already told Ansaro who had gone inside to inform his mother. When he returned they took her car and drove slowly toward the town.

Ansaro drove. He used high beams all the way. In every dip they hoped, on every rise they despaired. They stopped several times, giving a flashlight check to ditches and dark spots at the side of the road. Without success. The tall trees seemed to mock them, yet had there been one place of entry that offered hope, they would have dared enter the foreboding forest. It was a night to do foolish things like that. Even considering it was several steps beyond common sense. Before they lost all inhibition however, the town appeared.

The police station, a red-brick structure off the main road was the undiscussed first stop. Fauna was first in. Pushing through the front door she immediately accosted the desk sergeant. He sat on an elevated platform in a small open cell the so-called desk in front of him filled with papers and stacks of files. He was not pleased at being startled but recognizing Miss Mary, the teacher whose father was Doc Carrington, the same one who made that call minutes ago, the sergeant smiled.

"You make me jump," he began with an embarrassed smile. "Ah just talk with yer father again..."

"Any news," she interrupted, her tone demanding an answer - and quickly.

"No! Sorry. Ah have a officer comin' in, in a lil while. Ah tell him about it already... before he go out to eat someting'. You want to talk to him?"

"No. He obviously doesn't know anything. Have you asked around yourself?"

"No. Ah really cyah move from here till my relief come. In about a half hour."

"What about a search?"

"No man. Tha's crazy. Not tonight. I eh want nobody else to get loss. 'Sides, they have a lot of Ma-pa-pee (Mapepire - Fer-de-lance) up there man. Tomorrow mornin'. Ah sure if he eh come by then, the officer go organize some kind a search for him."

Ansaro had come in and stood at her side. "Lets ask around," he suggested.

She nodded and turning left the room.

"Thanks," Ansaro said politely as he hurried out.

The town was not well lit. Tall street-lamps offered much of the illumination. Then there were the occasional stores kept open till eight or nine o'clock, a small, two pump gas station, a rumshop and the plaza (three stores set in tandem sharing one parking lot). Apart from the major road on the way to Matura, few of the side streets were lit. Each house had front lights though and these would be kept burning till very late or until the residents went to sleep. The one advantage was that the police knew what everyone did in town. In cases of missing persons the police would call on everyone and so trace the previous whereabouts of the victim. (One child completely disappeared two years before. She was never found.)

The two stood outside the police station and looked around. There was no one else on the street. Music came from somewhere distant - the rumshop perhaps. Other than that there didn't seem to be any life around. Cars were all parked. Nothing moved.

"There's no way he's here, Mare," Ansaro said shaking his head. "I don't even know where to start."

"I know... I know. What's the time?"

"Eight thirty."

She sighed. "Let's go home."

CHAPTER -65 - missing

AS THEY TURNED INTO the driveway the porch filled; the doctor and Hasim leading the others out.

"He there with you?" Hasim called out shielding his eyes.

"No!" Ansaro answered swiftly exiting the car behind Fauna. "We went to the police station but no word yet."

"Come and eat something," Mrs. Carrington called out. She greeted Fauna tenderly and led her inside past the two wide eyed boys. "You two go to sleep," she chided as she passed them but did not stop to insist.

"What did the sergeant say?" Memin asked from his chair.

"Nothing," Ansaro answered walking over and sitting heavily. "They have someone working on it." He shook his head. "It's such a puzzle. Like the ground just opened up and swallowed him. I don't know. The last time we talked he was telling me how fantastic our family was. How fortunate he was."

"Goat mouth?"

"I don't know. I don't want to think. I just hope I get to yell at him. Just once." He had sat on the divan and Siba had edged up to him and was now leaning on his leg. "Maybe you should get some sleep, what do you think," he told Siba gently while rubbing his head.

"Go to sleep, Siba," Memin ordered a little more sternly.

"It's okay!" Ansaro put in, "in a little while I'll take him up."

"Who was on the desk? That fat officer?"

"Yes! The same. Do you know his name?"

"Fontain, I think. I heard Da talk to him."

"I hope he's not the one on the case."

"Me too."

Fauna picked at the rice and managed one spoonful but when her mother encouraged her to eat more, she shook her head and stopped playing with the fork.

"I couldn't get it down mom. Later maybe."

After this she excused herself and went to the porch joining Ansaro who was seated on the top step. She sat in the white plastic chair and looked over the banister. There was nothing to see but the dim road and the two cars sitting in shadow just beyond the shed. At around nine forty-five her mother brought some tea and a large army blanket she herself used when the nights got too cold. At ten her father came out for a few minutes. He stood with his legs wide, unsupported by either post or banister and folding his arms watched the road. He did not remain but before going back he squeezed her arm reassuringly and took the cup inside. Ansaro's leg fell off the step and awakened him. He rubbed his arms against his face and stood up. Quietly he entered the front door and headed for the divan. The door closed.

The heat and humidity grew more oppressive to Fauna. Now even the Cicadas and frogs' songs were mournful. Only a few nights before those same noises had serenaded the lovers. Now there was more mockery than playful tease to it. The taunting melodies were more a reminder of mortality than the eternity they had been promised. The stars began disappearing at around eleven. A cloud had come up from the south east and swiftly covered the sky. It threatened rain, but she was sure it would not come. According to the an old adage, *when the Poui blooms, then the rains will come.* Had the Poui bloomed? At midnight there was indeed a sprinkle but it went unnoticed.

With the drizzle, a quick breeze fanned the valley. Fauna wrapped the blanket more tightly around her but did not retreat to the shelter within. She curled upon the chair bringing her feet under her. But as swiftly as it began the breeze and the rain stopped. Then the stars came out again. It was as a hand passing over, soothing and comforting that which refused to be soothed or comforted. It was as though something was expected of her, yet she did not know what.

She wanted to call out to her mother. The urge was strong yet she fought against it. What could her mother do? Pray perhaps. But to what end? Was the end already determined as a book already written? Was she perhaps only the reader seeking discovery. How then could God, if indeed he could answer prayers, how could He change what already was. And if not already determined, why would He need to change it?

She remembered the fascinating story taught in one of her Religious Studies classes, of an Old Testament prophet who wrestled with an angel all night. This in a nutshell was the conflict that waged within her. Argument and conjecture! But Doubt was a formidable foe. With every reason to hope, Doubt suggested a fatal outcome. Perhaps it was not entirely her fault for the void that had replaced Faith. Yet, hadn't her mother continued to cross herself every day in spite of all sound, logical arguments deriding the sign? Was it strength in Faith? Or fear of the void? And now, on her part, to what did she cling. The reverse? Did she fear Faith enough to cling to the Void? She needed something... Yet still she refused to call out to her mother. Superstition! Perhaps if she called out, the direction toward a happy conclusion would indeed be changed. Goat mouth!

The door opened. It was Memin; not her mother. He looked out. Their eyes met briefly as directed by his glasses and the glimmer of light in hers. But neither spoke. He backed inside, closing the door softly.

Call Mom! Her mind pleaded. But no words came. Still, what could Mom do? Call Da! But what could logic say? Who could offer comfort? The night? The stars? Perhaps the ghosts that prowl between dusk and dawn seeking wounded hearts to help them mourn. Even they would be comfort. Even in their presence. Or in their sound.

Should she cross herself? She squeezed her fist instead. She could not concede hypocrisy. But just a sign... A sign of what?

She hated him! No! The moment passed. Another void. This wherein love sat only hours before. The great chasm into which she must place something now retched at the offering of hate. Rather fill it with hope. More than hope; delusion.

Perhaps he had fallen asleep and now lounged against a log he opened his eyes briefly and thought it would be foolish to return home. Rather wait till morning, when at first light he could safely begin the journey home.

Then she would scream at him and hold him so tightly that she would hurt his still rather tender ribs.

Or perhaps he had been curious and wandered off into the forest somewhere between Le Poui and home. It was quite thick beyond the fence of tall trees and intertwining bushes surrounding this wilderness. Perhaps he had seen and followed a deer, one of the many families that ofttimes strayed down the slopes and upon a start, would hurry back into cover that was as protective for them as it was deadly for man. One was easily lost within. Even hunters with their dogs have been known to wander for days, for once past that mile-long bottleneck separating the Le Poui Woods from the vast Matura forest reserve, luck was the only provider of success.

Or did he think he could short-cut along that same bottleneck?

But of course Woody was smarter than that. With only jogging attire he would not stray beyond the road. Though perhaps he did go too far along the road. Perhaps he was now on his way back from a long, long jog along the coastal road. Then again he could have looked into another small cove along the coast. As he did with Cocoa Beach. Some of these though were no more than a dozen yards wide and at the bottom of steep inclines, clay walls or cliffs of crumbling rock. It would be so easy to slide down. Not so easy to scramble up again.

But they would find him. And when they did the result would be the same; she would scream at him and hurt him against her.

The door opened. This time she did not look. The blanket now drawn up to her cheek felt softer now.

The door closed.

CHAPTER -66 -
searching for Woody

DR. CARRINGTON AWOKE WITH a start. He had thought only to close his eyes for a few minutes but it was now light outside. He changed and hurried through the quiet house. The boys were asleep in the living room. Out on the porch Fauna too was slumped, the blanket wrapped around her body up to her neck. The doctor stood over her for a few minutes. She did not awaken. He softly descended the steps and made his way to his car. It started quietly as it always did and he backed it into the street.

He drove to town.

At the police station he talked with the desk Sergeant on duty. The sergeant had been awake but started as the front door opened suddenly. He was doubly surprised to see the doctor. Yes, he had been told of the missing painter. He offered a cup of coffee which the doctor gladly accepted and sipped greedily. It was black but not very hot. The doctor did not comment on it. The sergeant looked up the reports from the night before. He told the doctor that a constable Avtar Minhas is looking after the case. The constable, he further informed the doctor, had not gone home but was asleep on a cot in a back room. The doctor asked to talk to him.

"Yeah..." officer Minhas responded sleepily rubbing his face as he entered from a room behind the front desk. "Just had to catch some sleep," he apologized. "Ah leff de report over here..." he indicated one of the folders and opening it read the last entry.

Eleven thirty five. No news yet.

"Ah talk to some people over by Matura too. But nuttin'. An it was cold las' night. So... I don' know. It don' look too good. They tell me he does do dis kind a' ting regular."

"No!" the doctor stated. "Not at night. And he always says when he is going to be late, or even if there's a chance he could be."

The constable looked again at the report. "Jus' a T-shirt and some jeans. Mama yo! He go be cold, oui. Lookin' to get some serious Bronchitis."

"Did you check the road?"

"No! Was too dark las' night for any kinda search. Is now... six o'clock. Man! Da's still too early."

"You people don't seem to be too concerned," the doctor said testily.

"No! It eh dat. Look, we eh supposed to even take it serious... not for forty eight hours, or if is a lil chile what missin'."

"Sorry!

"Nah, is all right. Ah know yer worry. Which way you come? From de 'highway'? You see anyting on de way... like birds or animals actin' kinda funny?"

"No!"

"Well, y'know, if you could wait a lil longer, ah'll come out to de house an see if ah could pick up his trail from de start. Lemme jus trow some cold water on mae face an' change mae shirt."

"Yes! All right. Can I read the report in the meantime?"

"Sure! If you could read m'writing," he laughed. "But you's a doctor..." He let it hang as he returned to the back room.

The report was quite comprehensive, even more so for the limited elapsed time between eight and eleven thirty the night before. One entry stated that he had been seen in town just before noon. The owner of the cycle store definitely remembered him. He itemized his purchases and remembered that Elwood joked that he had come only for the spoke wrench. That, along with the rest of the stuff - 3 in 1 oil, Vise Grips and a box of spanners - he asked to wrap in a strong cloth bag because he would be jogging home. The bread vendor in the market too remembered him. She had asked him about Fauna and he had told her she was at school. She asked when the big day was and he laughed and told her it was up to the bride. She also double bagged the bread because he told her he was jogging home. Other people saw him; some talked to him, others saw him talking to other people. One man thought he saw him get into a car with another man but he wasn't sure it was Elwood and didn't recognize the young man he was talking to. Then again if he was out for a jog, why would he accept a lift? Unless...

Immediately the doctor thought Elwood might have gone to Sangre Grande or Matura where his Cocoa Beach 'surprise' was being prepared. Elwood had to tell him about it to get Siba off the hook. The doctor had no problem lying to everyone else.

But no matter the importance of the surprise, the doctor could not see Elwood going away without saying something. To anyone. Just walking over to the clinic would be enough. Then the bread and the tools! No! Something was wrong.

The constable did not have a car; only a bike. The doctor offered to take him and bring him back. He agreed.

"Well, he was in town at least," the doctor said as they drove off.

"Yeah... it seem so. Ah have to fine out who is dis fella he was talkin' to, but everyting else check out. Ancil... Ancil Mayo, the fella who say he see him talkin' to de other fella... Ancil say he was laughin' with him. An' nobody see him leave. Y'know he's a tall fella, an' joggin' wit two bags... Ah feel somebody musta see him."

"I agree. There's just a chance he could have gone over to Matura I feel, but that is too slim. He would have called."

"Still, when ah get back ah'll call up de station dey. But..."

"Very slim. Very slim. Then there's Cocoa beach. He's always there and there's no phone there. Let's go there first. Maybe he was sketching.... No! I don't think he had his stuff. And the bread and tools. Let's just check anyway. You never know. Maybe something did happen and he lit a fire and stayed the night. I don't know. Maybe."

It took only five minutes from the decision to check out the beach to their arriving at the rocks above. Both the doctor and the policeman descended the path to the beach. The doctor prayed silently; that he be there, that he be uninjured and that he had a good excuse. The policeman's face revealed nothing.

"He not here," the policeman said even before stepping onto the sand.

"How do you know?" the doctor asked impatiently.

"No tracks. We had a lil drizzle las' night. See how the sand puckerin'? Is clean. Look, a lil lizard track over dere."

Looking down the doctor understood.

"Could we take a look anyway?" It was what Fauna would request.

"Sure!"

They walked to the beach and to the opposite side with the little basin flowing down the rocks. They called too. But there was no returning sound save the distant sea and the birds. Now, far from no news being good news, the doctor feared the worst. He followed the policeman in silence to the car and still quiet, drove off.

On the way back as they traveled slowly, the mist having risen to well above the trees and rapidly leaving the distant valley, a splash of colour caught the doctor's eye. He crossed the street and pulled over.

"You see something?" the constable asked.

"Just some yellow. A Poui tree I think. My wife told me he wanted to paint it. I think he may have come here, either on the way to town or on the way back."

He opened his door and leaving it open crossed the small ditch. Mounting the small incline he walked over the top of the hill toward the Poui. Though rooted on the other side of the hill, the crown stuck out above it. Not quite in bloom, it presented enough colour to promise a fantastic display when it did. The policemen followed.

At the top of the ridge they looked at the tree and the valley that extended down and beyond to a thick canopy of green and the thin coastal road snaking through it. Beyond was the sea upon which white dots danced all the way to its hazy blue horizon. The doctor breathed deeply. This was a scene he felt Elwood would have given his life for. He had been so excited over the little brook at the very bottom of the valley, bubbling over his find, making endless sketches and talking happily about it for two days. And that was just the brook. This was the universe. The Poui was the sun... or would be in a few days. Perhaps on the very day of the wedding...

"There!"

The word itself was startling. It was the very word and the very way in which it was used that would have brought intense distress to a cardiac patient. Even so, even the strong, robust doctor whose heart was fit and ready for anything the clinic could throw at him, paled and now seemed unsteady on his feet.

"There!" the constable repeated.

The doctor flinched at the word. His lips moved as one in prayer, yet he seemed afraid to utter a single syllable. As though Hope would have to be enough. Straining, reaching, hope with thew and tissue screaming with promises and regrets should be more than enough.

But it was not.

Below the embankment a blue covered leg and a white running shoe stuck out, hardly discernible yet once seen and identified would leave no doubt in any mind.

The doctor almost leapt down the few feet to his right where access was easier. Reaching the spot he immediately discerned that the inert form had not moved for some time. Twigs, leaves, stones and some dirt was sprinkled over him. Still, in spite of the disfigured face, the clotted blood and the insects that swarmed over, there was no mistaking Elwood.

The doctor put his hands to his head and screamed in agony, the word 'No' repeated, wrenched from deep within as the prayer he had been afraid to utter.

The pitiful wail touched even the policeman who coming up behind put his hand on the older man's shoulder and squeezed it. With the other hand he wiped a tear from his own face. His lips trembling, his throat tight, he was silent while the doctor sobbed. But when he eventually could he turned the doctor away and led him back up the hill. Weeping all the way the doctor returned to the trunk of his car where he removed a blanket.

"Ah'll do it," the constable said his words uttered with some difficulty. "Wait here. Ah don' want nobody dere till ah get de ambulance."

He covered the body then returned to the car. The doctor handed him his cell-phone as he entered.

"I called the station. They'll be sending a squad over. The sergeant wants to talk to you. I also called Dr. Mah. I don't think I should be the one to exhume. We'd better wait here for them." The doctor's voice was only a whisper.

"You all right? You want me to take you home?"

"No! Not now. I need time. I don't know how I'm going to face..." He put his head into his sleeve as his body shook.

CHAPTER -67 - death

AS THEY PULLED INTO the driveway Fauna, still wrapped in the blanket stood up from the steps where she had been seated. Both the doctor and the constable emerged from the car at the same time. Neither spoke.

"Da..." Fauna called out hopefully.

"Da!" she repeated reading into his silence a terror beyond words. She walked unsteadily toward him.

"Da?" Her voice was louder. Appealing.

He shook his head and bowed, standing as his body shook.

"Nooo... God... Da, nooo," she screamed as she came to a stop a foot or so from him. "Woody.... O God, no... Nooo," she shrieked. Her body now arching in pain, he reached for her. But she sank to the ground and though he knelt and held her, covering her with his embrace her screams were not subdued.

From the house another scream resounded. Ansaro held his mother adding his own sound to the tragedy. Hasim and Memin along with the two young boys who had appeared on the porch now ran down the walk. Hasim fell wailing as a child as he sank to the ground and held his father and Fauna. Memin turned away and walked to the shed where he remained quietly weeping. The two boys began to cry. Their cries were confused and empathetic at first, yet as the truth took hold, as Siba asked "where's Woody", repeating the inquiry, his voice louder with each silent answer, he finally broke down completely forming no distinct words but instead adding a thin, childlike wail to the overall sound of deep and profound lamenting.

CHAPTER -68 - Warren Toth reports

DETECTIVES FROM THE CID (Criminal Investigation Department) arrived from Port of Spain before noon. Detective Inspector Burdett led the squad of four - three detective sergeants and himself. By that time the little town was swarming with attention.

The media was fully represented - press, radio and television. In the immediacy of television program interruptions, the press and radio sank into the distant background. In the course of new developments directly attributable to the event, news that former newspaperman Warren Toth and his immediate superior Ari Francis were hired by stations TTV and ITV respectively seemed hardly pertinent to the tragedy, yet it was a clear indication of the degree of importance given to the story. BBC exposure was likely. The American and Canadian networks too would vie for some of the 'action'. And Toth would be the face they saw.

It was discovered that Toth with his still boyish features and smooth style had a certain appeal to women. (The demographic study of the time had women viewers leading their male counterparts by a healthy fifteen percent.) His contract was undisclosed but it was rumoured that termination would immediately follow his first appearance as a drunk. There seemed much credence to it. He dove into the new position with a zeal that virtually put the other side of his life on hold. Yet, though cool in front of the lens he spent much of the time off camera in a state of agitation, one he seemed to address only with this newly acquired frenzy of work.

Toth spent much of that first day broadcasting from a satellite remote directly out of Le Poui. Surrounded by a staff of ten, including field producers, a director and production assistant and two reporters, none of whom had Toth ever met, the well organized bustle was set up just south of the one major road through the town. It provided easy access to the key figures in the drama. There was some reluctance on the part of some of the townspeople to take part, but once interviews from certain merchants and local figures were aired, there was no shortage of comments. Toth and other personalities as well as local police and CID officers found themselves in a spotlight that at times interfered with the performance of duty. Still, this same spotlight nevertheless opened some doors. However the one door closed to them, was the main door - the Carringtons.

At first the police kept their initial reports to themselves. But in their thoroughness they progressed too slowly and by the end of the first day they were taking directions from television broadcasts emanating from a source five hundred yards from their own command post. This, coupled with a reluctance to use much input from the local constabulary, made them aware of their shortcomings. By nightfall, under direct instructions from their superiors in Port of Spain, they changed tactics.

Although promises of cooperation were made to all the media and local administrators, it became clear that the main figures with whom they should deal were Constable Avtar Minhas and TTV's Warren Toth.

Toth supplied them with a list of very willing informants and interviews already aired, as well as helicopter video of the area including the murder scene. One piece of speculation gleaned from an interview with Constable Minhas suggested the assailant was a very strong woman or small man. It hinted that a stout branch from the hardy Poui, already deemed to be the weapon by virtue of traces of hair and blood found on it, was wielded from a position below and behind the victim. The police countered that in fact the blade of a kitchen knife was found in his back. The blade had been broken off at the hilt and so imbedded between shoulder blades and neck as to concur with the policeman's view of the assailant. Both the detectives and Constable

Minhas agreed however that Woody must have put up a fight after the knife broke. However no traces of human skin were found under his nails nor was the handle of the knife found. As well they concluded that it was the branch that delivered the death blow or blows. All such information, the police demanded, should not be aired until sanctioned by them. This was agreed upon. For their part, the police allowed the reporter access to the victim's personal effects, in particular, his diary and notebook. He was denied any access to the family. In this the CID was adamant.

Using the diary information, Toth was allowed to transcribe; using his own words to describe the artist's feelings and accounts of his life. This as well was under an embargo. He would not be allowed to use it until the case was solved.

Toth agreed.

By the morning of the second day the police had their profile of the killer - but nothing more. Suspects ranged from Mayaro to Sangre Grande and included homosexuals, bikers, vagrants and spurned women. By nightfall, it was apparent; the investigation had hit a brick wall. The main door would have to be opened.

CHAPTER -69 -
Siba's drawing

AT THE HOUSE THE CID took statements from everyone, leaving Fauna for last or until she was able to compose herself. The session took place in the living room with the Inspector sitting on one of the chairs while the family members and the interviewing sergeant huddled over the living-room table.

On the other side of the large room, other members of the family sat and waited. Constable Minhas stood at ease in that area his leg just leaning against the desk. Although he had already submitted his report and given his own statement, Doctor Carrington had insisted Minhas remain to remind him of anything he himself may have missed or forgotten on the day the body was discovered. The doctor also felt it necessary to have his statement corroborated by the policeman with whom he had developed a certain bond.

The two boys sat in the other divan next to the policeman. Both were quiet, seldom looking at each other but staring off into distance. Ansaro was being questioned as to what he might have observed at anytime during the day. Asked if he had seen anyone strange hanging around the school area or around the house, he thought long before answering that he had not.

Siba on the other side of the room looked up sharply. "I saw a car on the hill," he said meekly.

Constable Minhas looked down. He too had been listening to the interrogation though had been paying only absent attention. "When was dat," the policeman asked softly not wishing to interrupt other questions being asked by the detectives. He stooped to Siba's level.

"Yesterday at lunch-time!"

"What you was doin' there?"

"I was riding home with Tommy."

Dharo looked at the policeman.

"Yer see a car too?" Minhas asked.

"I don't know. I don't remember."

"Yes," Siba appealed, "don't you remember, just on the hill top by the Poui tree."

Dharo shook his head. Then nodded. "Oh yes. I think so."

"What kinda car?"

"I don't know."

The constable turned to Siba again.

"You know what kinda car it was?"

Siba shrugged his shoulders.

"What colour? Light or dark?"

"Light. It was a white car and it had a red inside and the man came down after we pass and then he get inside."

"What man"

"I don't know him."

Constable Minhas stood up. "Excuse me, Suh," he said loudly but politely.

"Just a moment, officer," Inspector Burdett held up his hand. "Go ahead," he directed the Sergeant who had been interrupted.

"And when you left school," the Sergeant asked Ansaro, "you did not go anywhere else."

"That's correct," Ansaro repeated wiping his cheek again. "I went to the deli just for a coffee because I had some papers to correct..."

"Suh!" The constable again interrupted.

The sergeant looked up and the inspector turned.

"Constable..." the Inspector began.

"This little boy have someting," Constable Minhas continued not so politely. "He see a white car and a man in de same area... aroung lunch-time too."

The Inspector turned to Siba. "Is that so?"

Siba nodded shyly.

"Could you come over here... constable, would you?"

Minhas took Siba's hand and led him over to the table.

"Now," Inspector Burdett asked leaning toward the small boy, "did you recognize him?"

Siba nodded.

"Who is he?"

Siba shrugged.

"Answer him, Siba," Ansaro said trying to be gentle as he said it.

"I don't know him."

"Did you see his face, then," the Inspector asked.

Siba nodded. "Yes!" he said as an afterthought looking quickly at Ansaro. "But I don't know him."

"Could you describe him?"

Siba shrugged.

"Get Leslie in here," the Inspector ordered. "Maybe he could draw him a picture."

"Siba can draw," Ansaro said quickly. "He's very good. Get the pad," he ordered without waiting for Burdett's approval.

Siba hurried away and returned with the pad and crayons. He knelt between Ansaro's knees and placed the pad on the table. He thought for a second then made one vertical arc then three horizontal intersecting arcs.

"What's he doing?" the sergeant asked.

Ansaro looked up. "Woody taught him...." He could not finish but stifled his quivering mouth and was silent as tears gently slipped down his cheek.

The image came slowly. After every stroke it seemed, Siba looked off in the distance before making another. He took painstaking care to tilt the face at just the right angle, trace the hair-line and one ear then carefully position the eyes.

That alone took the better part of an hour. Siba erased and redrew the ear once and the eyes several times. No one spoke. At one time the doctor emerged from the interior but only looked around then turning, re-entered the dining room. Hasim brought coffee for the detectives and the policeman. They all thanked him softly. No one else drank coffee. No one else spoke. Siba proceeded to the nose.

After some time at the nose, erasing and re-drawing it he drew some lines that indistinctly covered his chin and mouth. It seemed at first that he was scribbling as one would scratch off a mistake, but with the eraser lying on the table it became obvious that he was not correcting an error but shading the area.

"Shit..." Constable Minhas said involuntarily then quickly added, "Sorry suh."

"What is it," the Inspector demanded impatiently.

"He have a beard."

"What!"

"Ancil say de man who was talkin' to Mr. Lucien, have a beard. Dat look like a beard."

To a man everyone in the room rose and approached the table. The beads to the dining room opened and Fauna with her father also entered. Her face was puffed beyond recognition; the skin reddened around her cheeks and nose, her eyes slits within the swollen membrane surrounding them, her hair dishevelled and lacklustre. One of the detectives in her way moved aside. She passed through and stood a few feet from the table looking down intently at the drawing. Siba continued scribbling then stopped. Using the eraser he now made a clear line along the cheek and edged the lower face. Then he stopped altogether and laid down the crayon and the eraser.

"You know him?" the Inspector asked looking at Fauna.

She shook her head slowly. Siba looked up. With a deep rending moan, Fauna sank onto his frail shoulders, hugged him hard and sobbed pitifully.

No one was unaffected.

EPILOGUE

FINAL NOTES ON THE TRAGEDY:
SPECIAL TO THE DAILY Gleaner.
BY-LINE - WARREN TOTH.

It is one of life's supreme ironies that among youth's friends of similar age the one who dares stand out to be counted, becomes the one most envied, despised and often hated. This is not so true of friends acquired later in life. Here friendship is more calculated and tempered as in an exchange where too much is seen as weakness and too little, perfidy. Young friends give all. All they demand in return is perfection – the same perfection they will eventually grow to hate.

Within minutes of the breakthrough, Siba's drawing was televised to the nation. Joe Metcalf however had disappeared. The following day his little white Chevelle was found at the parking lot below the Blue Basin. A pair of shoes, size seven, were found neatly placed on the shore.

Six weeks later, on the morning of a cold, rainy day that would never see the sun, Joseph Metcalf's body was found. It had floated up from the depths of the Basin and remained in the shallow end where the stream continued its journey to the sea. Tied around his wrists was an onion bag with the bottom ripped open as though finally freeing itself from the contents of the bag.

Upon hearing the news, Mrs. Susan Metcalf screamed for the better part of an hour after which she crumpled to the floor of her study and whimpered like a beaten puppy. A day later she was institutionalized. (Adrian would eventually bring her to Ottawa, Canada.) Pete would take over the Gallery, but understanding little of art, he would eventually sell it to Joe's wife's family. It is now a hair-dressers' salon.

Mr. Jonas Metcalf would lose his job and his prestige and all political affiliations and connections, retreating to his house on the corner and eventually dying in loneliness and befuddlement, having had, he always protested, nothing to do with anything that transpired there.

Some days following the funeral service for the artist Elwood Lucien, a small dirge of mourners descended to a little beach on the western edge of the island. Access was difficult but negotiated in spite of the large wooden box that had to be slid down the hill past the little stream at the bottom and carried to a grove of coconut palms. After the ceremony and for many years after, a beautiful, raven haired girl was seen sitting on the ridge above the beach. She would remain there for hours, just looking out to sea.

Just after nightfall on the twenty third of August a large Green turtle lumbered up the beach where the beautiful girl and her oldest brother sat in silence. They remained with the turtle as she scooped out a nest above the high-tide mark and deposited her eggs. When she laboriously returned to the sea they returned home to tell of the event. The girl returned every night for two months. On the last night she and her youngest brother witnessed the miracle run as scores of baby turtles struggled toward the surf. Strangely, there were no predators that night. Afterwards, they both returned home. She would never again visit Cocoa beach and the little basin.

For several weeks after the grave-site was revealed, artists from Canada, the United States and Europe made pilgrimages to the Little Basin, as it became known. There followed next a surge of the curious as well as the entrepreneurial. Not unexpectedly the artist's works soared in price and inaccessibility. A cache of undisclosed works many intimately private and not ever meant for the market, created another frenzy such that his name became the most understated of finds and hence the most sought after works of any young artist of the era. The feeding frenzy in New York was owed in no small part to the entrepreneur Peter Lombardi who started a scholarship for young artists in the name of Elwood Lucien. Both the Blue Basin and the Little Basin became in vogue as places to be and to paint. A small shrine was erected at the Little Basin by the Belmont Art Society and for the better part of that year various art organizations leant their approval in diverse ways either through direct or indirect action. This interference seemed nevertheless to render a certain order and decorum to the site. Tours were conducted to the area with schools and church groups chief among the organizations favouring that venue. A tourist information centre was built where Elwood had visualized his house; three tiered against the hillside the top floor overlooking the trees to a panorama of sky and sea. Several shows were organized there though they lacked the centralization or proximity to a large industrial centre to make them profitable. But the vendors came too and within a short time the scene progressed from coconut carts to the trafficking in drugs. The party atmosphere grew, encouraging the curious as well as the opportunistic. Motorcycle gangs soon discovered it and deemed it a meeting place which carried with it a certain stigma not appealing to the general populace. Attraction shifted accordingly. Disorder set in. Before long the little shrine was vandalized and after several fights and one fatal shooting, the police made their presence felt. They began a constant vigil posting armed personnel and squad cars, which put the stamp of anathema on the area and a damper on spontaneous visits by a more wholesome clientele.

Finally, "No Trespassing" signs were placed along the road and all traffic stopped. The beach and the grave site were cleaned up and no one visited for almost a year. Then one day police discovered an old bike leaning against the headstone. It was a small bike with a long saddle-pole and 24" wheels; a ten-speed Raleigh that once might have been painted a dark metallic green.

The police removed the bike.

It was never seen again.

The end